THE
COMPLETE BOOK OF
GOLF
TECHNIQUES

CLB 4935

This material previously appeared in
Improve Your Golf.

Compiled by Paul Foston and Philip Clucas

This edition published in 1996 by
Colour Library Direct, Godalming, Surrey

Printed in Hong Kong

ISBN 1-85833-564-7

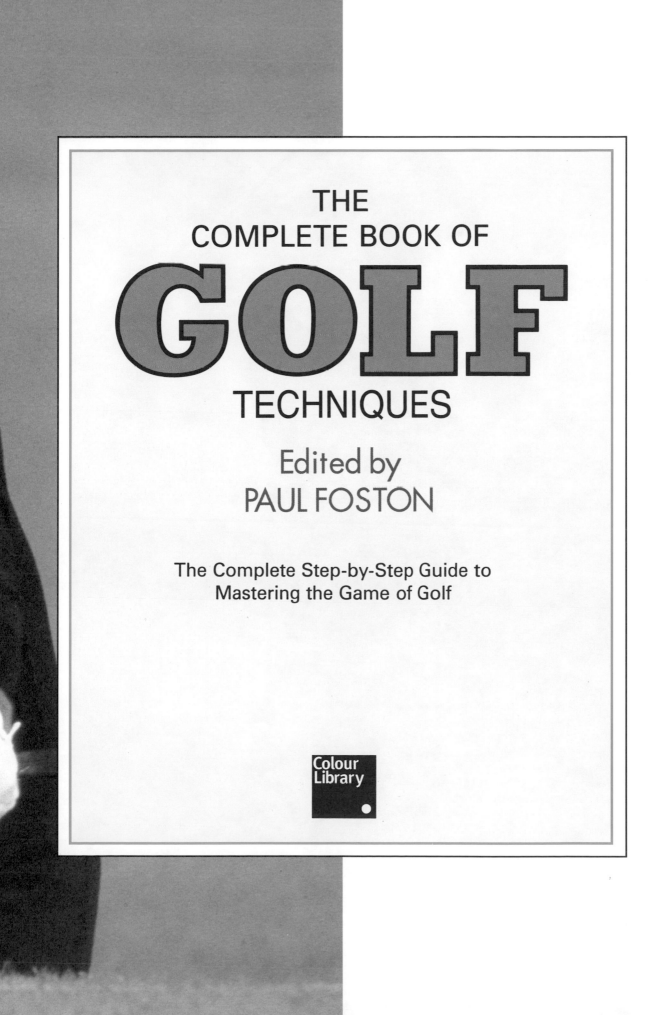

THE
COMPLETE BOOK OF
GOLF
TECHNIQUES

Edited by
PAUL FOSTON

The Complete Step-by-Step Guide to
Mastering the Game of Golf

Colour
Library

CONTENTS

INTRODUCTION

Golf has been around for a very long time indeed. And for almost as long as the game has existed, players and would-be players alike have sought advice on how to play it well. As with any other game or sport, the equipment used has steadily been developed and improved, but the basic requirement – the golf swing – how to deliver the club head to the ball with accuracy and consistency – has changed very little. Everyone who plays golf knows that this is the key to playing the game well; and playing the game well brings not only success in competition but provides maximum enjoyment in the game for its own sake.

Whether we compete against others or simply seek to improve our skills for our own satisfaction, most of us enjoy a challenge – particularly in sports and games. Too great a challenge, however, and we may lose heart and tire of the activity – even give it up altogether. The purpose of this book is to reduce the challenges in golf – and they are many – to manageable proportions; to place each of the challenges in perspective and to show how they may best be overcome. Doing this will not, of course, make us all great golfers, but it will certainly increase the pleasure we achieve from this fascinating game.

Repeatability is a word we often hear in golf. Few things are more frustrating than hitting a good shot and then being unable to repeat it when we think we are doing everything exactly the same. The reason, of course, is that we are not doing everything the same: we haven't achieved that consistency, that repeatability, that we sought.

This book sets out to remedy matters. It shows, clearly and graphically, taking into account ability, age, stature and other factors, how to develop a sound and repeatable swing. It repeats the advice and instruction from various angles, seeking to drive it home in such a way that, once absorbed, it will not be forgotten. This method is used here in teaching all aspects of the game: wood play, how to achieve power and accuracy, maneuvering the ball, iron play from the fairways and from the various types of rough encountered, all aspects of play around the greens – and in the sand – and, of course, that game within a game: putting. The same thoroughness is employed in showing you how to deal with the elements, particularly the wind and rain, which can totally change a game within minutes. And not least it discusses and helps you understand your own emotions: the pressures and nerves that can totally destroy the game of even the very best players. No book can prevent such things, but pointing out the pitfalls, showing you how important a part your mental attitude can play, helping you to recognize the signs and learn to deal with them can be half the battle.

The Complete Book of Golf Techniques contains nine chapters. Don't read them all at one sitting and expect to absorb all the information they contain; this will only lead to confusion. By all means browse through the book, and enjoy it for the good read it is, but then choose an aspect of your game, read that section thoroughly, go out on the practice green and try to put the advice into effect. Note the problem areas and then reread the chapter to try to sort them out. Your success will, of course, depend on your ambition and the time you can devote to the game and to practice; nothing can make you into a good golfer overnight. Try not to expect too much of yourself too quickly. Some of us are blessed with natural ability, and success comes relatively easily; most of us are not and we have to work very hard to achieve our maximum potential, but there is an enormous feeling of elation when we manage to do it. Use this book to help you with all aspects of your play – it works! – but make sure that above all you go out and enjoy the game.

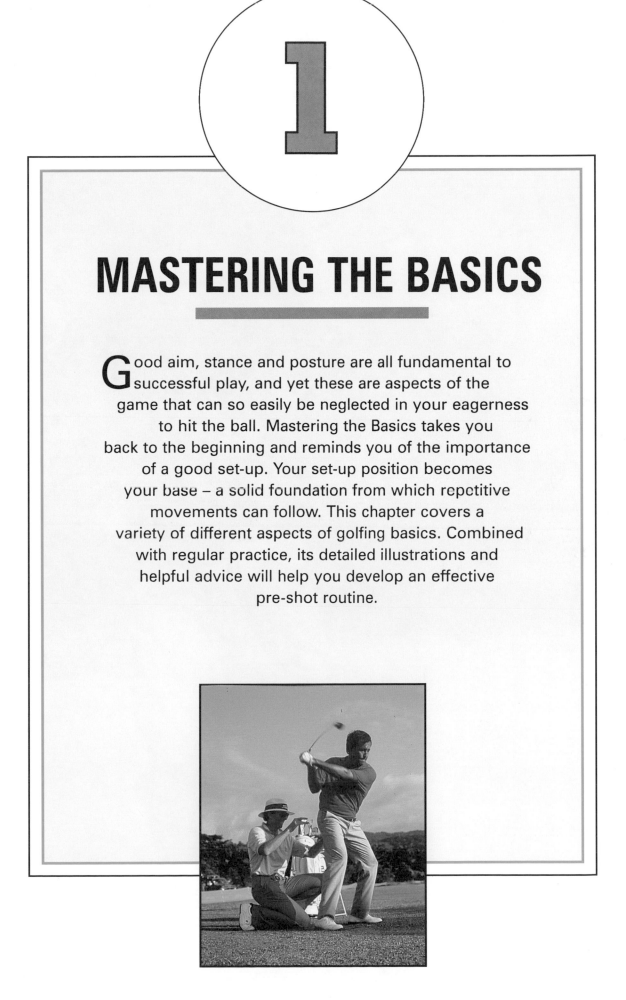

MASTERING THE BASICS

Good aim, stance and posture are all fundamental to successful play, and yet these are aspects of the game that can so easily be neglected in your eagerness to hit the ball. Mastering the Basics takes you back to the beginning and reminds you of the importance of a good set-up. Your set-up position becomes your base – a solid foundation from which repetitive movements can follow. This chapter covers a variety of different aspects of golfing basics. Combined with regular practice, its detailed illustrations and helpful advice will help you develop an effective pre-shot routine.

Alignment faults

Aligning your body correctly is one of the most vital basics in golf. You swing around your body, so if you're facing in the wrong direction you're unlikely to swing along the proper path.

DEVELOPING A FAULT

To make up for misalignment, your body devises a compensating movement – a fault – to bring the club along the path you want. Although this may work to begin with, your consistency is bound to suffer eventually. By then, the fault has become ingrained in your swing and is much harder to erase.

Make sure you're aligned correctly, so that you can build an orthodox swing. The body – your feet, hips and shoulders – is properly aligned when parallel to the

ARE YOU PARALLEL?
Correct alignment is vital for a proper swing path and smooth body rotation. Use clubs on the practice tee to check your shoulder, hip and feet alignment at address.

Shoulder out of sight
When you're on the course, a simple way of checking alignment is to look at the target and make sure you can't see your left shoulder.

Correctly aligned, your left shoulder should be only just out of sight of your left eye. If you can see it, you're almost certainly aligned right of target.

HOW POOR ALIGNMENT CAUSES BAD SHOTS

WRONG – ALIGNING LEFT
A slice can result from aligning yourself too far to the left. You're no longer parallel to the ball-to-target line – your backswing becomes severely restricted because you can't make a full shoulder turn at 90° to your ball-to-target line. This causes you to tilt rather than turn your shoulders. An out-to-in swing path results, making a slice very likely if the clubface is open at impact. Should you close the clubface at impact you pull the ball – it flies immediately left.

It's worth remembering that slicing and pulling are the most common bad shots in golf. At least half the time the root cause is poor alignment.

WRONG – ALIGNING RIGHT
If you align too far to the right of the ball-to-target line, you swing from in to out. This creates too much spin as the club swings across – rather than through – the ball. When the clubface is closed a hook results, while an open clubface causes a push – the ball flies straight to the right.

A slice can also occur, especially with less experienced players. You subconsciously realize at the top of the backswing that you're wrongly aligned and try to adjust. This last minute change causes you to swing from out to in, as you try to pull the club around your body. With a closed clubface in this situation you pull the ball – if it stays open you slice.

ball-to-target line.

The body should face slightly left of target (right of target for left handers). This lets you swing the club easily towards the target without obstruction by your body. Never make the mistake of trying to align your body directly at the target – golf is not like rifle shooting and the clubhead is not as close to your body as a rifle is.

SHOULDERS, HIPS AND FEET

The order of importance in your alignment is shoulders, hips and feet. Your shoulder alignment is crucial because the shoulders begin your body turn. Many players neglect the shoulders in favor of the feet because they can clearly gauge feet position but can't see their shoulders.

Remember that your whole body – for which your shoulder, hips and feet are the check – must be properly aligned, after you've aimed the clubface. You can't swing well if one part is correct and another is wrong. Poor alignment ruins good body turn.

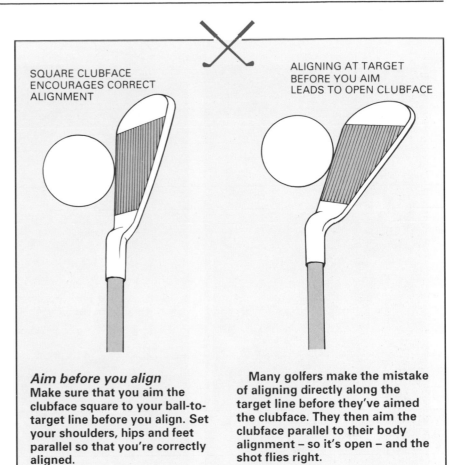

SQUARE CLUBFACE ENCOURAGES CORRECT ALIGNMENT

ALIGNING AT TARGET BEFORE YOU AIM LEADS TO OPEN CLUBFACE

Aim before you align
Make sure that you aim the clubface square to your ball-to-target line before you align. Set your shoulders, hips and feet parallel so that you're correctly aligned.

Many golfers make the mistake of aligning directly along the target line before they've aimed the clubface. They then aim the clubface parallel to their body alignment – so it's open – and the shot flies right.

GOOD ALIGNMENT

CORRECT – ALIGNING SQUARE
Your body is correctly aligned when your shoulders, feet and hips are parallel to the ball-to-target line.
Only then can you swing along the correct path and let your body complete its proper turn.

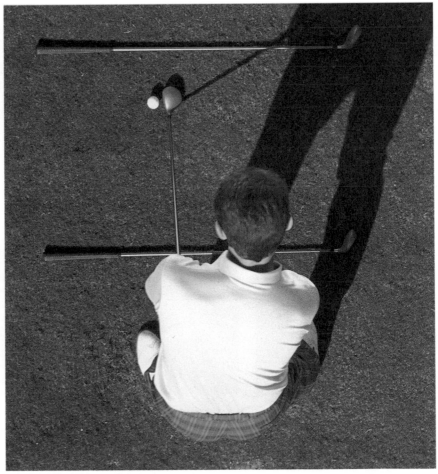

pro tip

Check your alignment
When you're on the practice tee, always pick a target at which to aim. Many players simply whack balls without considering where they want them to fly.

Once you've chosen a target, picture a line running from it through the middle of the ball.

Check the alignment of your upper body to that line by holding your club lengthwise across your shoulders and chest. Then lower the club and lay it along the ground just in front of your feet. Does it run parallel to your ball-to-target line? If it does, your alignment must be correct.

Although you can't carry out this procedure on the course, it's an effective practice tee routine. Many top pros use it, as you'll see if you spend some time watching on the practice tee at a tournament.

HOOKING AND PUSHING

ADDRESS
From a closed stance – when your body is aligned right – you're likely to hook or push the shot.

BACKSWING
You tend to swing the club inside the line early in the backswing causing an in-to-out path.

IMPACT ZONE
The in-to-out path causes a hook if the clubface is closed at impact or a push if the face is open.

Grip problems

One of the most common faults in golf is a bad grip. Even with a perfect set-up and swing, the ball won't travel absolutely straight if your grip is wrong.

The function of the grip is to return the clubface square to the ball-to-target line at impact. Anything other than a perfect grip results in the ball traveling right or left of the target.

However experienced you are, you should frequently check the position of your hands on the club.

It's easy for a tiny error to creep into your grip without you realizing the change.

CHECK GRIP FIRST

Because most bad grips feel comfortable, many players attribute poor shots to a swing fault. They end up changing their set-up to try and cure the problem but this only makes matters worse – two wrongs don't make a right.

Whenever your game goes sour, start by checking your grip because most faults are caused by a basic error. Only if your grip is correct should you start checking other parts of your game, such as body alignment, stance and ball position. Remember that gripping the club correctly is the most important part of your game.

With the correct grip you see one and a half knuckles on your left hand, while the V between your right thumb and right forefinger points directly at your chin.

Keep them clean
Give your golf the best start by cleaning your grips regularly. Dirt gets trapped in the ridges of a grip, making it slippery and reducing your hold. Remove all the grime with a brush and soapy water and towel the grips dry. It's very difficult to return the clubface square to the ball if your hands slip.

HANDS SQUARE AT IMPACT
To feel the perfect impact position, take up an imaginary set-up, with your hands stretched out and square to the ball-to-target line. Your hands dictate the position of the clubface. At impact, the back of your left hand, the palm of your right hand and the clubface should be square to the ball-to-target line.

GOOD AND BAD GRIPS

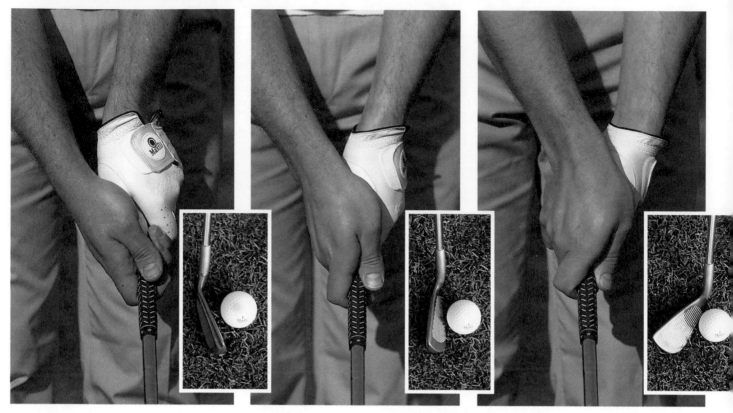

STRONG GRIP
At address you see more than one and a half knuckles on your left hand and the V on your right hand points right of your chin. The clubface is closed at impact, making the ball go left.

CORRECT GRIP
With a perfect grip you see one and a half knuckles on your left hand and the V on your right hand points at your chin. At impact the clubface is square and the ball flies straight.

WEAK GRIP
At address you see one or no knuckles on your left hand and the V on your right hand points left of your chin. The clubface is open at impact and so the ball flies right of the target.

STRONG GRIP

CLOSED CLUBFACE

WEAK GRIP

OPEN CLUBFACE

HOOK OR PULL
With a strong grip your hands close the clubface at impact. The ball is hooked or pulled to the left. It's an easier fault than a weak grip to remedy.

SLICE OR PUSH
With a weak grip, your hands fail to square the clubface through impact. It remains open on the downswing and the ball is sliced or pushed to the right.

GETTING TO THE CORRECT GRIP

(2) GRIP CLUB
Rest the club against the palm of your left hand. Place your left thumb down the shaft and wrap your fingers around it. Add your right hand to the grip – your thumb points down the shaft. The little finger of your right hand overlaps the forefinger of your left hand.

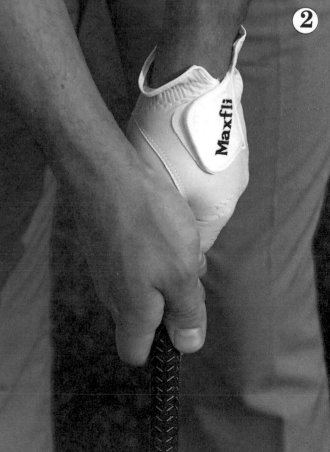

(1) GET HANDS SQUARE
To get your hands square, adopt a set-up with arms stretched and hands open, your left slightly ahead of your right. At address the back of your left hand and the right palm should be square to a ball-to-target line.

pro tip

Strengthen your fingers
Squeeze a squash ball in the palm of each hand in turn. Repeat the exercise several times a day – strong fingers are an advantage in golf. They help you keep a firm grip of the club and prevent it slipping in your hands.

If your fingers are weak it's difficult to square the clubhead through impact. The clubface stays open and the ball goes right.

With a bad grip your hands are too much to one side – how far varies. If your hands are too far right your grip is called strong; too far left is known as a weak grip. Strong or weak in this sense doesn't refer to how tightly you hold the club, but describes where your hands are placed on the grip.

THE STRONG GRIP

If you have a strong grip you see more than one and a half knuckles on your left hand and your right hand V points right of your chin.

With a strong grip, your hands automatically close the clubface at impact and the ball swerves to the left. The stronger your grip, the further right your hands – and the ball flies further left.

THE WEAK GRIP

When both your hands are left of the correct position, the V on your right hand points left of your chin and you see less than one knuckle on your left hand.

This prevents your hands naturally squaring the clubhead through impact. The clubface stays open, hitting the ball right of the target. The further left your hands are, the weaker your grip and the further right the ball goes.

A weak grip causes more prob-lems than a strong grip. Squaring the clubhead through impact is difficult at the best of times – even with the correct grip. A weak grip exaggerates the problem, result-ing in a massive slice.

GRIP IT RIGHT

Spend time setting up the basics of a good standard overlap grip. Adopt a normal relaxed stance with your arms and hands stretched out. Set the back of your left hand and the palm of your right hand square to the ball-to-target line.

Keeping your left hand open, take the club firmly in your right hand and place the grip against the palm of your left hand.

Close the fingers of your left hand around the club, with your thumb pointing down the front of the shaft. Make sure there is about a 2in (5cm) gap between the butt (end of the shaft) and your left hand. You should see one and a half knuckles.

Add your right hand to the grip, so that your right thumb covers most of your left thumb and points left of center down the shaft. Let your fingers wrap around the grip with the little finger of your right hand resting on the cleft between forefinger and middle finger of your left hand. Don't grip the club too tightly. This is the standard overlap grip.

OLD HABITS DIE HARD

Curing a grip fault is harder than you think – particularly if how you hold the club differs greatly from the correct grip. Old habits die hard. It isn't easy to discard a bad grip that feels comfortable, even when you've identified it as the reason your shots travel off line.

The correct grip may feel un-natural at first. But don't be tempted to go back to your old one. Unless you persevere your problems remain.

You'll need lots of practice be-fore you see an improvement. Don't expect your shots to get dra-matically better overnight. And don't expect your grip to feel com-fortable right away.

Only through constant practice with a correct grip that seems strange to begin with does your new hand position start to feel natural and your shots improve.

The practice grip
This is molded to place your hands and fingers exactly on the grip. If your grip is strong or weak, it helps you become accustomed to the correct grip. Fix a practice grip to an old club and use it regularly until the correct grip feels comfortable and you automatically take it up. But note that it's against the rules to use this aid in competition.

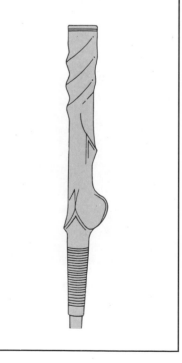

Check your ball position

Placing the ball correctly is one of the most neglected fundamentals in golf. When they play a wayward shot, many players analyze their swings in search of the cause – but faulty ball position could be the culprit.

Being out of place by as little as a ball's width can make all the difference between striking off the heel, toe or sweet spot of the club.

It's all too easy to take your stance so that the ball is too far back or forward – so quickly check where the ball is every time.

STANCE WIDTH

You must strive to use the same swing for all 13 lofted clubs – apart from helping your tempo, it's much easier than having 13 different swings.

To repeat your swing throughout the bag, adjust your ball position and stance width as the club length changes. Your purpose is to hit the ball on the lowest part of your swing with every club – except the woods, which you need to hit on the upswing.

For example, with the long clubs – such as your driver – the ball should be opposite your left heel. It moves nearer your feet and toward the middle of your stance as club length lessens. With the medium irons, the ball is between the center of your stance and your left heel. With the short irons the ball is centered.

Change your stance so that it's widest with the driver and narrowest with the heavily lofted clubs.

PATH AND PLANE

To understand completely the importance of correct ball position it's vital to recognize the part played by swing path and swing plane.

The plane is the angle of your swing path in relation to the ground. It's judged by two things – your height and the distance you

PERFECT PLACING
The ball should always be between two points – opposite your left heel and the center of your stance. This position differs from driver to short iron. Because the face of each club is square to the ball-to-target line only for a split second, it's vital that you set up with the ball in the correct spot.

BALL POSITION – DRIVER

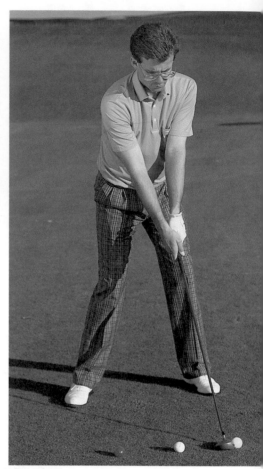

BALL TOO FAR FORWARD
You're likely to hit the ball left, because at impact the clubface is closed and your upper body is open. You may also hit the ball thin (halfway up) because the clubhead makes contact too high on the upswing. The ball probably scuttles along the ground with little power or distance.

▶The white ball is correctly placed opposite the left heel.

WHERE DO YOU PLACE THE BALL?

With the longest clubs – for which you take your widest stance and place the ball furthest away from you – the ideal position for the ball is opposite your left heel. Move the ball nearer the center of your stance – bringing your feet closer together – as club length shortens. The ball should be in the middle of your narrowest stance with the short irons. A normal stance must be square on to the ball-to-target line.

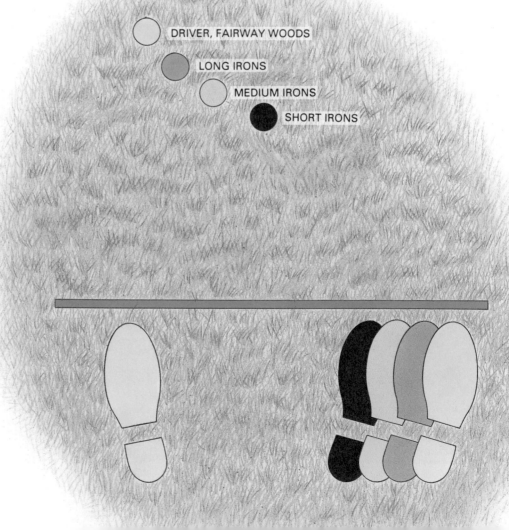

DRIVER, FAIRWAY WOODS

LONG IRONS

MEDIUM IRONS

SHORT IRONS

BALL TOO FAR BACK
You hit immediately right because the clubface is open at impact and your upper body is closed. You may strike the ball fat (behind), because the clubhead has not yet reached its lowest point in the swing, and meets the ball too soon. **X**

CORRECT – OPPOSITE LEFT HEEL
The proper ball position for a driver is opposite your left heel. You make contact the moment the clubhead begins to rise – which helps the ball gain height – and during the split second when the clubface is square to the target line. **✓**

SET YOUR POSITION: SHORT IRONS

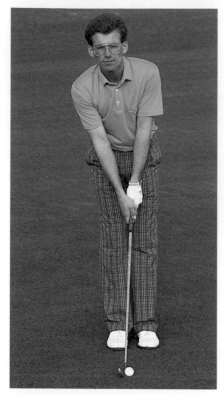

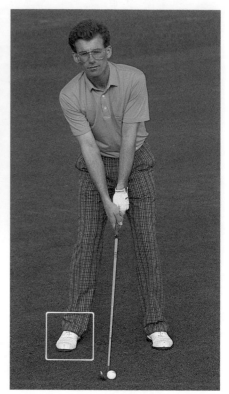

1 FEET TOGETHER
Stand with your feet fairly close together and the ball placed exactly in the middle of your stance. Carefully position the clubface square to your ball-to-target line.

2 LEFT FOOT POINTS OUT
Keeping your right foot in place, plant your left foot comfortably to one side. The left foot should point slightly outward throughout your swing action to promote an effective and balanced body turn.

3 BALL DEAD CENTER
Move your right foot the same distance from the ball as your left so that the ball is in the center of your stance. Shifting one foot at a time keeps the clubface square and helps you maintain good balance from the outset.

pro tip

Try the hand span test
To make sure that you're standing the correct distance away from the ball, check how far your body is from the top of the club.

After setting up as normal, take your right hand off the club. Place your little finger on your left thigh and your thumb on the butt of the club. A comfortable hand span – neither stretched nor compressed – confirms the correct distance.

When the ball is too far from your body you're likely to hit off the toe of the club, losing power and control. A hook is also probable.

With the ball too near your body the heel of the club strikes the ball, so you may shank. A slice is also a strong possibility.

stand from the ball at address.

When you swing the longer shafted clubs, you stand more upright and slightly further away from the ball than you do with – for instance – an 8 iron. This leads to a flatter swing plane than with the shorter clubs, when you're more bent over.

SPLIT SECOND TIMING

Whatever the club, and whatever the shot, the clubface is square for only a fraction of a second during the swing. That's why ball position is so vital – it must be perfect to receive the clubhead in that split second.

Spend time practicing these changes in stance width and ball position. They must become automatic so that you know you can always swing from a solid base. This skill does not emerge overnight – it may take an entire season before your set-up becomes second nature and your ball position reliable.

Ball placement changes

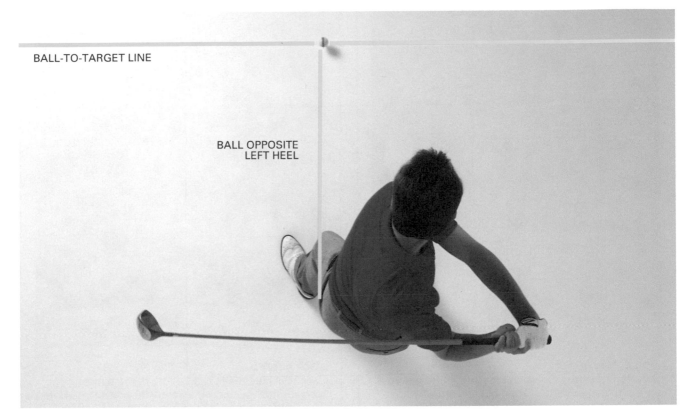

BALL-TO-TARGET LINE

BALL OPPOSITE
LEFT HEEL

T hough a constant routine and set-up position are vital for consistent striking and shotmaking, your ball positioning within your stance can differ slightly from standard to achieve these goals.

Ball positioning can't be viewed in isolation – just as swing styles vary from player to player, so must the placing of the ball. Most top golfers have their own placement systems, which are based on sound fundamentals but adapted for their own personal swing.

You needn't stick to the accepted system of placing the ball centrally for the short irons, between

TIME FOR A CHANGE
Correct ball position helps you get the whole swing on plane so that the top of the backswing is parallel to the target line. Experiment with ball placement if you're struggling after consistency – a fraction of an inch can make all the difference. The standard position for the driver is opposite the left heel (above), but placement can range from just inside your left heel (right) to the middle of the left foot. Stray outside this zone and the clubface is unlikely to return square.

SYSTEMS ANALYSIS

Hogan's footwork

Ben Hogan swung so consistently that he needed only one ball position for all clubs – about 1inch (2.5cm) inside his left heel – although naturally he stood closer to the ball the shorter the iron he used.

The only variable in Hogan's set-up was his right foot – this moved depending on what club he hit. For short irons Ben stood slightly open. Even though the ball was in its usual position, moving the right foot forward had the effect of pushing the ball back in the stance. This helped Ben produce his legendary crisp striking.

For the medium irons Hogan stood square, but for the longer irons and woods he set up slightly closed. This meant he could play with a touch of draw for extra length.

BALL PLACED FURTHER AWAY
FOR LONGER CLUBS

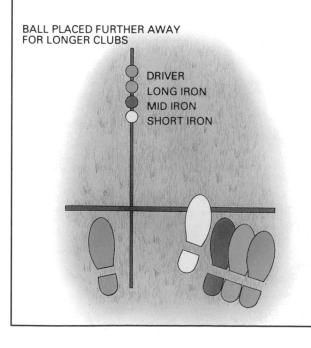

DRIVER
LONG IRON
MID IRON
SHORT IRON

Jack's left heel

Jack Nicklaus plays the ball from the same position for every club, except for specialist shots. The Golden Bear places the ball opposite his left heel – from this position the clubhead returns square at impact, as his style is to drive through the stroke with his legs.

Jack looks for simplicity in his golf, and finds positioning the ball in the same place each time leads to consistency. Placing the ball forward in his stance also helps him to play his stock shot – a slight fade.

Apart from standing slightly open for the short irons, Nicklaus sets up square. The open address for short irons moves the ball back in his stance – this ensures a good strike and avoids the thin. It also means Jack hits the ball high with lots of backspin.

ALL CLUBS PLAYED FROM
OPPOSITE THE LEFT HEEL

Standard lines

The system taught to most beginners recommends a variable ball position. If you understand the fundamentals you're better able to experiment to suit specific needs.

Because the swing arc of a short iron is narrower than a long iron, you place the ball in the middle of your stance to make sure you strike the ball with a downward blow.

With medium irons, pushing the ball forward – to between the center of your stance and your left heel – means you sweep the ball away but still take the ball before the turf. Playing a mid iron from too far back leads you down into the ball from too steep an angle and with the blade slightly open – the result, a squirt out to the right.

For long irons and woods the ball position should be between the middle of your left foot and a point just inside the left heel.

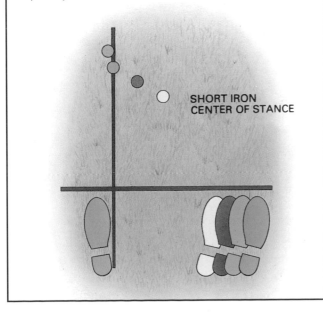

SHORT IRON
CENTER OF STANCE

Seve's natural system

On his ball placement Seve Ballesteros is the odd man out among the world's great golfers. The Spaniard has no set system – instead, he relies on feel to find the position he wants. Though he sticks to the basic principles of placement, the position of the ball varies fractionally every time he sets up – even if he hits the same club.

Seve thinks that feeling comfortable over the ball is more important than sticking rigidly to a set ball position. As he sets up, he places the blade squarely behind the ball and then shuffles around until he's at ease. This gives him confidence for the stroke.

Ballesteros believes that golfers are likely to become negative about a shot if they don't feel perfectly at ease over the ball. And by sticking stubbornly to one particular system you're bound to feel uncomfortable over some shots. The Spaniard recommends flexibility – vary your ball placement to suit the way you feel and your degree of fitness.

the left heel and center for medium irons and opposite the left heel for the long irons and woods.

MOVING EXPERIMENT

If you use the standard method you can't go far wrong, but however correct your placement is, it may not be *perfectly* suited to your swing. Experiment with your ball placement – it often reaps rewards.

But you must follow the basic guidelines. It's no good moving the ball back in the stance for your long irons and woods – unless you're playing a specialist shot like a punched 5 iron – as your shots become badly struck and wayward.

If you're consistently hitting poor shots with certain clubs – perhaps letting your medium irons leak to the right a little – a change in ball position can rid you of the problem. Go to the practice tee and move the ball around in your stance to find the best position.

You may have the ball too far back in your stance so the blade doesn't return to square before impact. Just pushing the ball forward a fraction could lead to a dramatic improvement in striking and direction.

FOLLOW THE PROS

The range of ball placement systems the world's best players use is extensive. Some pros have a different ball position for each club, moving it slightly further back as the irons become shorter. Others don't vary the position at all.

But the top pros practice so often that whatever their system – perhaps playing the ball from just inside the left heel for every club – they know it works in harmony with their swing. Each position is calculated so that the clubface always returns square at impact.

It doesn't matter what system or which pro you follow, as long as it works well with your swing and you are able to reproduce good shots consistently.

Taking turf into account

However well your system works for a standard shot, it still must be flexible to cope with varying ground conditions. And to keep your striking crisp it's sometimes best to change your normal ball position when you play on different styles of course.

On a lush course, for example, you can afford to push the ball fractionally further forward – without fear of thinning the ball – to help you hit the high, soft fade. The turf gives easily so you can hit down on the ball without the club jarring.

On bone dry ground – as on a parched links – it's safest to play the ball from further back in the stance to ensure a good strike with your irons. If you play with the ball too far forward you increase the risk of a thin.

Make sure that the clubface strikes the ball before hitting the ground.

pro tip

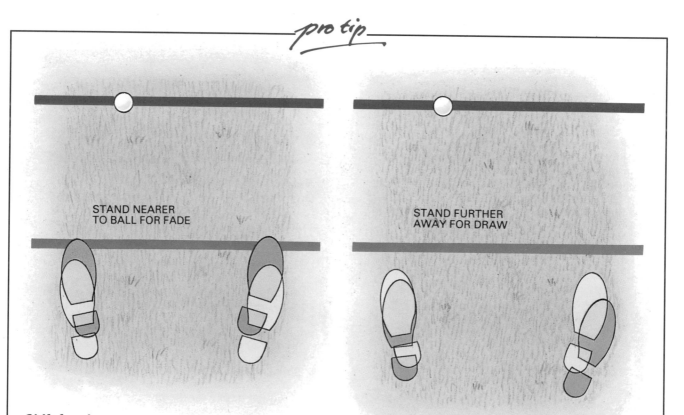

STAND NEARER TO BALL FOR FADE

STAND FURTHER AWAY FOR DRAW

Shift for shape
A change in ball position is usually just a slight shift along the target line between your left foot and the center of your stance. But to hit a shaped shot you can also alter how far from the ball you stand.

If you struggle to hit a fade try standing closer than normal. This leads to a more upright out-to-in swing plane. Combine this set-up and swing with a slightly open stance when you want to hit a fade.

Try the opposite if you find hitting a draw difficult – stand further away than normal from the ball. This promotes an attack from the inside on a flatter swing plane. Combined with a closed stance a draw comes naturally.

Curing posture problems

Before you start your swing, you must position your body properly as you address the ball. Correct posture is vital because it is the basis of an effective golf swing. Although you may feel happy with how you stand, faults can creep in easily and cause problems with your game.

Begin by making sure that you're playing with suitable clubs. Their length and lie must suit your height and arm length.

STAND POISED AND READY
Whatever your build and height you should be able to keep faults from creeping into your posture. Stand comfortably at address in almost a semi-sitting position, feeling poised and ready for action. Your back should stay reasonably straight – make sure you don't stoop.

See a qualified PGA pro to check these essentials – without them you have no chance of swinging to your potential. More importantly, you also risk back pain and injury if you strain too many of the wrong muscles.

BE COMFORTABLE

Treat your posture as a way of moving your body into a relaxed, comfortable position, so that you're poised and ready for action. When you get it right, you are perfectly balanced throughout your swing, because your arms, legs and body can move freely and without strain.

If your knees are locked your spine leans over too much, re-

stricting your muscle movement. Bending your knees a lot forces you to crouch over the ball, so that making a full shoulder turn is very hard.

YOUR STANCE

Stance is an important ingredient of the correct posture. It promotes balance and helps control. Take your stance by setting the insides of your feet the same distance apart as your shoulders.

Narrow your stance for the shorter clubs and widen it for the longer clubs and woods. Too narrow a stance makes you badly balanced and restricts upper body

SHORT

AVERAGE

TALL

HOW GOOD IS YOUR POSTURE?

GOOD: KEEP MOVING
Correct posture is vital as it is the foundation of a good golf swing. Relax and keep your body moving so that you don't adopt faults. Feel live tension in your arms and legs. Keep your back fairly straight.

GOOD: AT THE TARGET
With a correct posture and a good swing, the club points directly at the target at the top of the backswing. Your lower body must stay flexed and fluid, letting your weight transfer smoothly.

movement.

Point your left foot (right foot if you strike left handed) slightly outwards – it must point in the direction that your body is turning as you strike the ball. Pointing your left foot inwards badly hampers your movement and causes physical strain.

POSTURE EXERCISE

When your stance is sound, you can prepare your posture. The point of changing your body position from its normal upright bearing is to create a sturdy yet balanced starting block for the golf swing.

To practice proper posture, think of being almost in a semi-sitting position. Hold a club lengthways across the back of your shoulders. Lean forward from your upper body only, then flex your knees, making sure that you're still comfortable for the swing.

Your upper body should be still

OVERBENDING YOUR KNEES
Bending your knees too much makes you crouch over the ball. Your back is severely bent and you feel extremely uncomfortable.

NO SHOULDER TURN
As you've bent over so far, you lift rather than swing the club, pointing it left of target. You make very little shoulder turn, giving you no chance of a complete backswing.

reasonably upright and straight – be careful not to stoop as it gives you no chance of swinging to your potential.

Your weight should be spread evenly and your lower legs should feel lively – as if they have springs in them.

When you lower your head to look at the ground, bend your neck – not your shoulders. If your shoulders are too far forward, you're in danger of crouching, which ruins your chances of making a full turn.

ARM POSITION

Once you feel happy in the correct position, take the club from behind your shoulders and grip normally.

Your arms form a V shape, with the left arm hanging straight while the right is a little bent at the elbow – which helps keep away pre-swing stiffness and tension.

Check that your elbows are in a good position by making sure that they point at their respective hipbones. Try to let your arms and the club form one unit throughout the swing.

STAY RELAXED

Now that you're in position and ready to swing it's vital to remain calm and comfortable so you maintain good posture.

Every moving part of your body must be poised and ready for action – otherwise your swing becomes labored and stilted.

Keep your feet, knees and shoulders lively by making little movements and waggling the club a few times.

This process tunes you up for your swing – as well as keeping you relaxed in the correct, comfortable posture you need to make a full swing.

Check the span
Make sure you are holding the club the proper distance from your body by spanning your right hand from the top of the shaft to your left thigh. If it reaches comfortably – so that you don't have to stretch or bunch your fingers – you're spot on.

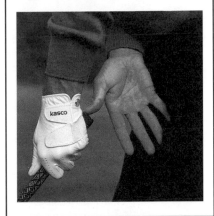

LOCKED KNEES
Straight and stiff legs at address make you lean forward too much as you address the ball. Your body has no chance of fluid movement.

BAD BALANCE AND TURN
It proves impossible to rotate your hips and shoulders to their full extent. Adequate weight transfer and balance become very difficult.

Watch your feet position
Locked knees and toes pointing inwards (left) restrict leg movement. Too much tension in your lower body stops you

making a positive swing. Stand with your feet the same distance apart as your shoulders and point your toes out (right) to promote strong hip turn.

pro tip

Sit on a shooting stick
Imagine you're sitting on a shooting stick. This encourages you to bend your knees from the thighs down. As your knees bend, your back should stay quite straight with your body still upright. Don't use your hips when flexing your knees.

PRACTICE YOUR POSTURE

KEEP A STRAIGHT BACK
To practice the almost semi-sitting position – and reasonably straight back – you need for perfect posture, hold a club lengthways across the back of your shoulders. Lean forward with your upper body only and then flex your knees from the thighs down.

SPREAD YOUR WEIGHT
Make sure your neck – not your shoulders – is bent over and that your weight is evenly spread. Then turn a full 90° – there will be tension in your legs. Turn back and through, so your body twists as far left as it can go.

Seeing the shot

Everyone makes mental pictures in day-to-day life. Whether you are driving a car, eating or walking, the process of seeing in your mind what needs to be done and activating the required muscles in the body becomes automatic. Achieving the same process in golf lowers your tension – and your score.

One of the advantages of golf is that you have time to prepare for playing the shot. Learn to profit from this by seeing and feeling every shot in your mind and body before you play it. Clear vision beforehand promotes confidence in your ability to play from difficult, as well as easy, lies.

POSITIVE APPROACH

Seeing and feeling your shot brings mind and body together. First you imagine how the ball will fly through the air to the target, including any roll when the ball lands. Then you transfer that picture in your mind into a feeling the body can understand – and produce the correct movement to hit the desired shot.

All great players visualize before hitting a shot. They carefully negotiate every situation within mind and body before making any attempt to play the ball. They know that the concentration needed for golf is different from many other sports.

As golf is a stationary ball game, one of your problems is to stay relaxed and composed at address. This is essential if you are to produce the desired flowing movement in your swing.

Golf requires a relaxed yet positive approach. By making your muscle movement automatic you can stay in an absorbed frame of

mind and concentrate on making a successful shot.

MUSCLE MEMORY

Before you take your stance, create in your mind a clear picture of

precisely how you want the ball to travel through the air and roll on landing. Remember that factors such as wind, ground conditions and how you feel on the day affect every stroke.

Rub out negative factors such

Concentrate on where you want your shot to pitch, and where you want it to finish.

Steer clear of the ditch, tree and bunker by erasing them from your mind.

Before you step up to the ball, think positively about your shot.

PAINT A MENTAL PICTURE
Preparing correctly to play a shot means painting a picture of the ball's path in your mind. Simply imagine the flight of the ball through the air and its roll on landing, allowing for wind and terrain. Leave out of your picture any hazards such as bunkers that are positioned between you and your intended target.

MAKE IT PHYSICAL
With the image of the ball's flight in your mind, transfer the picture into the physical movement required to make your swing. Take a few practice swings as if you are playing the shot itself. Try to achieve muscle memory even when on the practice tee until it becomes an automatic and positive aspect of your game.

as hazards between you and the target. They cause nervousness and uncertainty, which destroy an otherwise good swing.

When you have a crystal-clear mental image, you need to transfer it to a feeling within your body. Do it by taking two or three practice swings that imitate the action you'll use to hit the desired shot.

This routine teaches your body muscle memory. You give it a thorough rehearsal of the shot so that the muscles are not taken by surprise when it matters. You swing smoothly and naturally – your mind is free to concentrate on positive thoughts while your swing takes care of itself.

REGULAR PRACTICE

Now you can address the ball and play the shot by repeating the feeling of your practice swings.

Most of the top players go through this routine on the practice tee as well as on the course. Regular practice is the best way to improve mental pictures of your golf shots. In time, positive thought and feeling become as automatic as other activities of everyday life.

Shut your eyes
Next time you're on the practice tee, try this exercise to develop your skill at seeing the shot, feeling the swing and hitting the ball.
    Align yourself to a short target. Close your eyes and imagine the flight of the ball and the swing you need to produce the given shot. After a few practice swings, hit the ball – keeping your eyes shut.
Repeat this several times to increase your feeling for the type of shot required. Once you have mastered the shorter shot, go through the same exercise with longer shots.

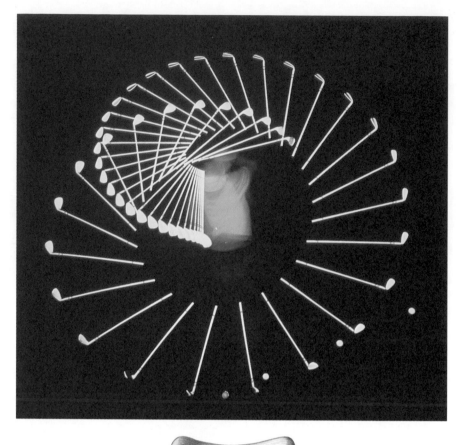

masterclass

Seve's second sight
The greatest visualizer in the modern game is Severiano Ballesteros. As a youngster he had only a 3 iron to practice with. He was forced to use his imagination to create shots not meant for that club, so it required a fine ability to see and feel the shot.

Before playing any stroke, the Spaniard pictures exactly how the ball will travel, sometimes miming the swing without a club. If he is playing from just off the green, he picks the exact spot where the ball should land.

Even today, Ballesteros sometimes plays an entire practice round with one club. It shows the importance he attaches to seeing the shot.

Curing tension with Nicklaus

Mental tension on the golf course leads to physical tension – and tense muscles mean that you feel clumsy and awkward and your score suffers.

Tension at address can be avoided if you learn a simple pre-shot routine which keeps all parts of your body relaxed, on the move and ready to go. Then you can start your swing smoothly and comfortably by keeping your body moving as you prepare for the shot.

Jack Nicklaus, one of the greatest golfers, has built such a system into his game. He is famous for his precise and methodical approach to every shot. Nicklaus' pre-shot routine has helped him to stay that little bit cooler than his rivals under pressure.

THE TWO C'S

As he stands on the tee, Nicklaus remembers two c's: confidence

NICKLAUS' PRE-SWING
The way to cure mental and physical tension as you stand to the ball is to develop a repeatable pre-shot routine for every stroke. Jack Nicklaus stays absorbed by going through the same movements every time and keeping all the important parts of his body moving.

Soft forearms mean a relaxed grip. Slightly firming up his grip, while making sure it stays soft, is Jack's swing trigger.

The waggle reduces tension because it keeps your body moving. It also boosts muscle memory and helps you to see the shot.

Alternatively moving your feet lightly up and down relaxes your legs. This helps to keep you mobile and ready to swing smoothly.

and concentration.

Confidence comes from being able to repeat successful shots in tough situations – and for that you need experience and practice.

Use self-discipline to make yourself concentrate by going through the same movements before you play each shot.

REPEAT YOUR ROUTINE

Always run through your pre-shot checkpoints: set-up, correct club-

INTERLOCKING GRIP

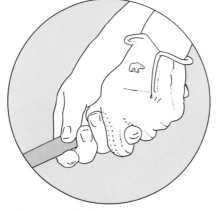

Jack uses the interlocking grip, which is helpful if you have small hands. It is rare among the top players, who use the standard grip.

face aim and body alignment. Jack always checks aim by selecting a marker (a leaf or patch of grass) a few paces in front of his ball directly along the ball-to-target line.

Aim and alignment take time. Jack releases tension by keeping his body moving all the time in the address position. His feet move lightly up and down, in time with gentle swinging back and forth of the club.

This swinging of the club – known as the "waggle" – serves as the preparation for the shot. Nicklaus waggles the club along the line he intends to start the backswing. His waggle is different for every shot: it varies for a fade, a draw or a conventional straight shot.

STAY SOFT

Tension before starting your backswing leads to one particular path of destruction – gripping too tightly. It's impossible to swing smoothly with too firm a grip – it causes a jerky takeaway.

As you stand at address, check that your forearms are "soft" – if your forearms feel supple, you have the correct relaxed grip pressure. Rigid forearms always mean

your grip is too tight.

All that remains in this simple, repeatable procedure is to trigger the swing. Jack uses the "stationary press" – firming up his grip by pressing his hands together a couple of times and relaxing them. It puts his muscles on "action stations," without making them tense. Copy it to give you an effective ignition for a smooth swing.

Clubhead off the ground
Jack Nicklaus does not ground the club at address. He says the habit started at Scioto, the club where he learned to play. The ball used to sit up in the fescue grass rough on the course, and grounding the club sometimes made the ball roll. Young Jack was always concerned about getting a stroke penalty for moving the ball – so he started to hold the club off the ground.

It has other advantages, too. First, lifting the clubhead and waggling it lessens tension. Second, nothing can impede a smooth takeaway. Third, there is no danger of rule-breaking by grounding the club in a bunker.

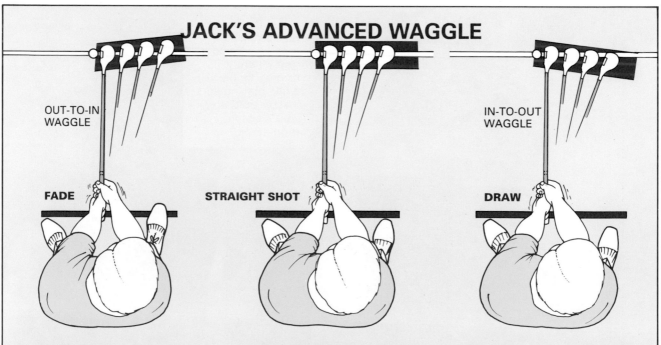

JACK'S ADVANCED WAGGLE

OUT-TO-IN WAGGLE

FADE

STRAIGHT SHOT

IN-TO-OUT WAGGLE

DRAW

Giving his club a waggle two or three times keeps Jack loose before he starts his backswing.

To waggle effectively, include the "moving parts" of your body that you use in the backswing. Moving your feet lightly up and down sends a feeling of mobility to

your legs. The waggle also helps your arms to stay loose and comfortable.

Nicklaus is always careful to waggle along the line he wants to start the backswing. On a normal straight shot, he waggles back and through along the ball-to-

target line. For a fade, he waggles the club on an out-to-in path. If he wants to draw the shot, the path of the waggle is in to out.

This process enhances his confidence, muscle memory and visualization.

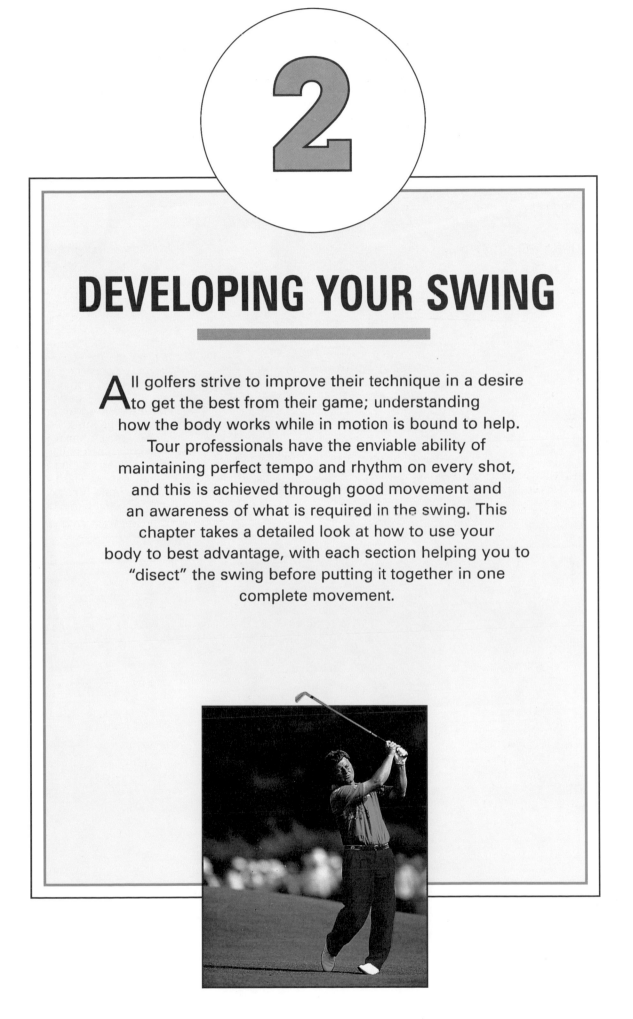

DEVELOPING YOUR SWING

All golfers strive to improve their technique in a desire to get the best from their game; understanding how the body works while in motion is bound to help. Tour professionals have the enviable ability of maintaining perfect tempo and rhythm on every shot, and this is achieved through good movement and an awareness of what is required in the swing. This chapter takes a detailed look at how to use your body to best advantage, with each section helping you to "disect" the swing before putting it together in one complete movement.

Swing with your body

A complete body action brings together the relevant parts of the golf swing to give you greater consistency. Your shoulders, arms and body move in one piece to help you groove a repeatable swing into your game.

When different parts of your body move independently there's a risk of faults creeping in. A loose, wristy action may give you the occasional good result in a relaxed game. But without precision timing you're bound to lack consistency. A loose swing can desert you completely when the pressure is on.

Nick Faldo is the greatest exponent of the swing with the body. Next time you have a chance to watch him – perhaps when a tournament is televised – notice how

ENHANCE CONTROL
Playing within yourself is one of the keys to consistent golf – most poor shots result from trying to do too much. The swing with your body builds in control. A towel under the arms keeps the swing compact and prevents you from overswinging or trying to hit the ball too hard. With the towel in place, shoot practice balls to a precise spot about 140yd (128m) away.

SWING WITH BODY PRACTICE DRILL

(1) NORMAL AT ADDRESS
Hit shots with a towel held securely under your arms to help you swing with the body – your objective is to keep the towel in place throughout. Adopt your normal address position using no more than a 7 iron.

(2) SLOWLY BACK
Swing smoothly away from the ball keeping your arms close to your body. Let the left arm dominate to encourage a full shoulder turn. Keep the right elbow close to your side to stop the arms moving on an upright plane.

(3) THREE-QUARTER BACKSWING
Stop the backswing well short of horizontal – remember the emphasis is on control and accuracy. Make sure you complete a full shoulder turn to place the club on the correct plane. The body is nicely coiled behind the ball.

(4) WEIGHT SHIFT
Start transferring your weight on to the left side as you begin the downswing. Keep your arms close to your body to lead the clubhead down to the ball from inside the line. This arm action also prevents the towel from slipping.

FOLLOWTHROUGH PRACTICE

⑤ HANDS RELEASE
The left side provides support as the clubhead travels from in to in through impact. The hands release and your arms pull your body around to face the target – the movement through the ball is effortless.

⑥ COMPACT FOLLOWTHROUGH
The followthrough position is compact and tidy, with perfect control from start to finish. Vary your practice routine to gain maximum benefit – hit five shots holding the towel in place and five without the towel.

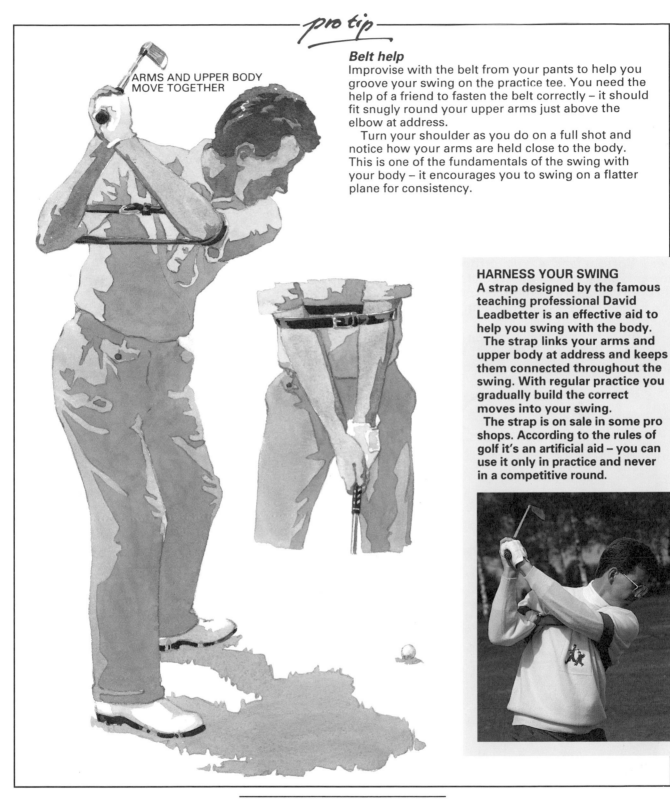

ARMS AND UPPER BODY
MOVE TOGETHER

pro tip

Belt help
Improvise with the belt from your pants to help you groove your swing on the practice tee. You need the help of a friend to fasten the belt correctly – it should fit snugly round your upper arms just above the elbow at address.

Turn your shoulder as you do on a full shot and notice how your arms are held close to the body. This is one of the fundamentals of the swing with your body – it encourages you to swing on a flatter plane for consistency.

HARNESS YOUR SWING
A strap designed by the famous teaching professional David Leadbetter is an effective aid to help you swing with the body.

The strap links your arms and upper body at address and keeps them connected throughout the swing. With regular practice you gradually build the correct moves into your swing.

The strap is on sale in some pro shops. According to the rules of golf it's an artificial aid – you can use it only in practice and never in a competitive round.

rhythmical and compact the swing is, and how fluent his action – no single part of the body moves out of time with another.

Remember, control is the essence of a swing with your body. Never sacrifice accuracy to strive for distance – always swing the club at a tempo that allows you to feel in charge of the clubhead throughout the stroke. Think minimum effort and maximum control.

ONE PIECE TAKEAWAY

The first part of the swing is with your shoulders, arms and club moving smoothly as one away from the ball. Everything moves together to increase your chances of starting the swing on the correct plane.

The coiling of your upper body naturally pulls the left knee in toward the ball – this allows your hips to turn along with the rest of your body. Your backswing should feel compact but not tense – your right elbow remains close to your side.

If you pick the club up too quickly on the backswing and don't turn properly, the clubhead is thrown in all directions. This excessive wrist movement involves a great deal of guesswork – you trust luck more than judgement to place the club in the correct position.

FULL SHOULDER TURN

A one piece takeaway helps you to swing the club on a wide arc and so achieve a full shoulder turn. These moves place the club on the correct plane at the top of your backswing.

A good swing with your body pulls you into a coiled position behind the ball. Your weight is supported on the right side and your upper back faces the target at the top of the backswing.

If you don't turn properly on the backswing all sorts of problems arise. Your swing plane becomes very upright and easily drifts towards an out-to-in path. You suffer the frustration of cutting across the ball and lose distance on your shots.

It's important to maintain control of the clubhead at the top of the backswing – you don't want to ruin the good work achieved earlier in the swing by making a poor downswing.

SMOOTHLY DOWN

The movement down towards the ball is in one piece, with your shoulders, arms and lower body working in harmony. Shift your weight smoothly to the left.

As the body unwinds on the downswing your hands release the clubhead through impact with tremendous speed. The wide arc of your swing generates the power – no longer should you feel the need for a huge lunge at the ball, which upsets your rhythm and timing.

Almost immediately your striking of the ball benefits from an improvement in consistency. Your poor shots are less wild and far less frequent.

✗ FLYING ELBOW
If a towel falls from under your right elbow before you complete the backswing, look carefully at the movement of your arms away from the ball.

A flying right elbow is caused by picking the club up too quickly and moving outside the line on the backswing. Your swing then lacks the necessary width and power – this fault usually results in a sliced shot.

✓ KEEP IT COMPACT
Swing the club smoothly away from the ball, moving your arms and upper body in one piece – concentrate on making a full shoulder turn.

Your right arm folds during the backswing and the elbow points straight down. This solid, compact position puts you on the correct plane at the top of the backswing.

ONE PIECE PUTT
Improve your putting stroke by practicing a shorter version of the swing with your body. Place a club under your arms and adopt your normal putting stance.

Swing the putter smoothly back and through keeping the wrists firm. The triangle shape formed by your arms and shoulders should remain constant. The club under your arms points parallel to the ball-to-target line throughout the stroke.

Swing checklist
○ Remember, a good backswing places the club on the correct plane at the top and makes it easier to swing down towards the ball correctly. Think of your arms and the club swinging together away from the ball – if you keep the parts moving in one piece you can concentrate on one thought alone.

○ The practice tee is the best place to attempt the swing with your body, so make constructive use of your time there. Swing smoothly and always work on your rhythm. If you swing quickly there's very little time to think what you're doing and it's hard to identify faults.

○ When you practice the swing with your body try to stay relaxed, both at address and during the swing. Often when you introduce new moves into your game the tendency is to tense up. But a rigid swing prevents you gaining benefit from the change.

Improve your backswing

Astrong backswing makes a great difference to a player's game. The aim is to get the club-head and your hands, arms and body positioned so that you easily and powerfully return the club-face square to the ball.

It's vital to set up the backswing properly – errors at this first stage of the swing are difficult to put right later on.

Before you make a swing, check the basics. Make sure that grip and ball position are correct. With a relaxed posture, align your feet, knees, hips, chest and shoulders parallel to the ball-to-target line.

Although the swing plane and swing path differ from club to club, the technique remains the same. Your posture varies depending on the length of the shaft, but in all cases your knees must be flexed and your back slightly bent. If your back is either too upright or too hunched, or your legs are locked

THE TOP POINT
At the top of the backswing the clubface must be positioned so you can easily return it square to the ball. To achieve this, from address your upper body rotates halfway – about 90° – and your hips, thighs and knees make a quarter turn of 45°. With a full swing, using a wood or long iron, the shaft of the club points at the target – and is parallel to the ball-to-target line.

PERFECT YOUR BACKSWING

1 BE RELAXED
At address you should feel relaxed. Your posture must be correct for your body to rotate fully. Your knees are flexed and your back is slightly bent. Your feet should be about the same distance apart as your shoulders.

2 KEEP CLUBHEAD LOW
With your hands and arms, take the clubhead away, keeping it low to the ground for the first 1ft (30cm). From here allow your body to rotate to the right. This moves the clubhead inside the ball-to-target line. The clubhead feels closed.

straight, it is impossible to make a full body turn.

Get these basics right and you should make a perfect backswing.

SMOOTH AND SLOW TAKEAWAY

It's vital that you set the right tone for the swing by staying smooth and relaxed

The backswing starts with a unified takeaway, as your hands, arms, shoulders, chest and hips move together.

For the first 1ft (30cm) the clubhead stays close to the ground. From here, the backswing is shaped by your left side – the left shoulder and hip start to rotate to the right (vice versa if you're left handed). This pulls your arms and hands in the same direction and the clubhead moves back and inside the ball-to-target line.

Your left knee moves to the right to allow your hips and shoulders to rotate further. Let your upper body move as one.

From an even distribution at address, your weight then moves on to the inside of your right foot.

MID POINT

Your body continues to rotate to the left and by the mid point on the backswing your right arm starts to fold.

Let your left arm remain comfortably straight but not locked. If you've rotated correctly, by the mid point your left hand, left wrist, left arm and left shoulder should

be joined by an imaginary straight line.

As you rotate further your weight continues to move on to your right side and your right hip feels most of the pressure. But don't let your weight transfer to the outside of your right foot or you'll lose balance.

The more supple you are, the

Mini-club check
Use a mini-club about 2ft (60cm) long to check your position at the top of the backswing. When you look over your right shoulder you can easily see the clubhead of a short-shafted club – which you can't with a normal club. If you have an old club ask your local pro to cut it down for you.

Holding the mini-club with the standard grip, take up the posture and address position for a medium iron. Make a backswing; hold your position at the top.

Your position is correct if the shaft points at the target and the back of your left hand is set at the same angle as the clubface.

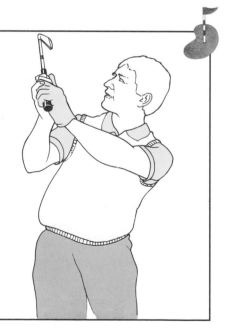

③ MID POINT
By mid point on the backswing your right arm
starts to bend. This opens the clubface. Your rotating
left shoulder has pulled your left hip to the right. Your
weight moves on to your right foot and the toe of the
clubhead points at the sky.

④ MOVE SMOOTHLY
As your upper body continues to rotate, your
wrists set – they remain in this position to the top of
the backswing. Your left knee moves towards the ball
and your weight is now on the inside of your right foot.
Let your head move with your body.

⑤ CLUBHEAD SWINGS HIGH
At the three-quarter point in the backswing, your
rotating shoulders, arms and hands have lifted the
clubhead well above your head. Your left arm is still
reasonably straight while your right arm is bent. Your
legs stay flexed.

⑥ COILED BODY AT TOP
At the top of the backswing your upper body is
fully coiled ready to unleash a powerful downswing.
Your left arm provides the leverage for pulling the
clubhead through the ball. Your upper body has turned
about 90° and your hips and knees about 45°.

BE STRAIGHT AT THE TOP

INCORRECT CUPPED POSITION
If your shoulders fail to rotate correctly, and your arms, wrists and hands do not extend fully, the imaginary line is cupped and you slice the shot.

INCORRECT ARCHED POSITION
If the clubhead moves too far inside the ball-to-target line on the backswing, the imaginary line is arched and you produce a hook.

STRAIGHT LINE POSITION (CORRECT)
At the top of the backswing your left arm, left wrist and left hand are joined by an imaginary straight line.

more your head moves naturally as your body rotates. This is fine as long as you keep your eye on the ball.

Your right knee is flexed but not locked, and your lower body supports your upper body as it rotates to the top of the backswing.

TOP OF BACKSWING

By the top of the backswing your upper body has rotated halfway around – about 90° – while your hips, thighs and knees have made a quarter turn – about 45°. Your right arm is considerably bent while your left arm remains reasonably straight.

This is important. If your left arm is either crooked or limp you lose power on the downswing. A straight left arm provides a powerful lever for pulling the clubhead through the ball.

At the top of a good backswing your body feels coiled and ready to unwind, unleashing power on the downswing.

The exact positioning varies depending on the length of the shaft. Although your upper body must always rotate about 90°, the length of your swing alters. You should make a full swing with a wood and a long iron, but only a three-quarter swing with a medium and short iron.

The back of your left wrist and left hand and the clubface are set at the same angle. With a medium iron you make a three-quarter swing – though your upper body still turns 90°.

Allow for a very slight pause at the top of the backswing before starting the downswing. Although this pause shouldn't be long enough to be visible, it lets your body change direction smoothly. A pause also prevents you from rushing the start of the downswing.

RELAX AT ADDRESS

You can't rotate correctly if you're tense at address. Tension can affect most parts of your body. It makes your muscles tighten, which restricts body movement and stops your chest, shoulders and arms from rotating fully.

There are a number of ways to relieve tension. One is to do a few warm-up or stretching exercises before picking up a club. Another is to lift the clubhead just off the ground and waggle your feet at address. This keeps your muscles ticking over and stops them from becoming stiff.

If you still find it difficult to make a full swing, even after a warm-up session, don't try to force one. Not only can this cause injury, it also affects your tempo. Providing your body rotates correctly and you keep your rhythm, a three-quarter backswing is enough until you are able to develop a full swing.

pro tip

Your flat right hand
Using a driver, the palm of your right hand should be flat enough at the top of the backswing to support a few books. Check this by holding your position at the top. Remove the club with your left hand. Is the right palm flat?

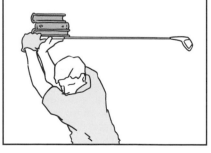

Create good body turn

Full body rotation is vital to a powerful and accurate golf swing. If you want to increase the distance you hit your shots and use the clubs to their potential, you must turn smoothly and competently on both your backswing and throughswing.

You achieve good body turn by starting your backswing with your whole left side. Make sure that you don't fall into the most common trap – swinging with your hands and arms only.

TURN YOUR SHOULDERS

The takeaway begins with your left side rotating towards the right. This continues until the top of the

THE NEED FOR A FULL TURN
Proper body turn is the key to a powerful swing along the correct plane. Rotating your shoulders fully means that you use all your strength to gain maximum distance and helps to ensure an accurate, clean strike. Less supple players can lift their left heel slightly to help them turn on the backswing.

TRAIN YOURSELF TO TURN FULLY

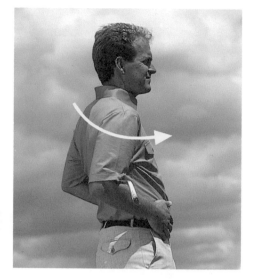

1 Practice making a full turn – both back and through. Begin by holding an iron club halfway up your back and flexing your knees.

2 Slide your left side smoothly around to the right so that your shoulders are at right angles to your starting position.

3 Swivel back fully to the left. Your shoulders are again 90° to your starting point – though facing in the opposite direction.

USING YOUR WHOLE LEFT SIDE

1 PLACE AN EXTRA BALL
With one ball in its normal position, place another about 18in (45cm) behind it, a couple of ball widths closer to your feet. The balls are not level because you want to encourage a correct plane. Set up parallel, as normal – use a spare club for correct alignment.

2 SWEEP THE SECOND BALL
As your left side starts to slide right on the takeaway, the back of the clubhead sweeps away the second ball. If the clubhead passes above, inside or outside the second ball, you're swinging too much with your hands and arms.

backswing, when your left side begins its journey back. It pulls your arms and hands down – they're now loaded with power – and you release the clubhead at impact with force and accuracy.

Body turn does not end at impact. As your hands and arms swing the club through, your upper body keeps turning. Only at the top of the followthrough should your shoulders finally catch up with your hips.

All these movements must work together to form a complete, slick swing. Your body must find the key positions if you're to become consistent.

ELASTIC TENSION

As you start the backswing, your arms and hands – the only part of your body in contact with the club – move because your shoulders do. Your left knee and right hip respond.

Your back must face the target at the top of the backswing and your left arm should be straight.

You need to create lively tension in your leg and back muscles to store maximum power at the top of the backswing – as if you're stretching a rubber band. The only way to achieve elastic tension is by turning your shoulders 90° and your hips 45°.

STRAIGHT LEFT ARM

Many players fail to complete their shoulder turn because they don't feel they can return the club smoothly to impact. They stop their shoulder turn halfway and complete the backswing by breaking the left arm. When this happens you lose all control and power.

Turning your hips as far as your shoulders also causes problems. You lose all tension – and store no power.

The positive tension at the top of the backswing unwinds during the downswing. Your upper body pulls your arms and hands to the downswing's mid point. They're loaded with power and about to release at exactly the right time – impact.

CLUBHEAD SPEED

The more tension you create between your hips and shoulders the more clubhead speed you produce – which increases distance.

Let clubhead speed help bring your right shoulder around to the left after impact. The shoulder in turn forces your head up to watch the ball as you swivel around to a full finish.

3 FULL SHOULDER TURN
At the top of the backswing your shoulders have correctly turned 90° and your hips 45°. To hit the second ball, you had to start your takeaway by moving your hips, shoulders, hands and arms together.

pro tip

LEFT SHOULDER OVER RIGHT INSTEP

Look at your left shoulder
As you hold the club at the top, look down at your left shoulder, which should be directly in your field of view. You've turned well if it fills the space just inside your right foot.

USE A BALL TO MIMIC THE SWING

① Gripping a golf ball lightly between the forefinger and thumb of your right hand, set up with your left hand on your left thigh and your right hand in front of your body as if gripping a club. Your knees are flexed – if they lock, your turn is impeded.

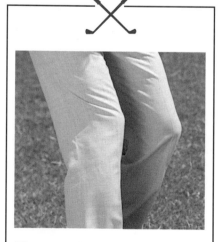

Flex your knees
Throughout the swing your legs must be gently flexed (above) to help your balance and promote the springy tension you need to store power. Locked knees make you tilt – rather than turn – your shoulders. Sagging the knees too much leads to a collapse of your right side.

② Starting from your left hip and shoulder, turn your upper body to the right. Your right arm and hand remain passive as you swing to the top. Your shoulders are at 90° to your address position and your hips 45°, which creates the lively tension in leg and back muscles needed for full power. The fingers now point at the sky.

③ Your upper body slides back to the left and this movement returns your hand and arm to impact, when you release the ball. Power has been provided by uncoiling the springy tension created in your upper body at the top – not by your arm and hand, which were always passive.

Improve the downswing

The aim of the downswing is to return the clubface square to the ball with as much power as you can deliver – you need good tempo and rhythm to maintain the flow.

The downswing is the most complex movement to learn and perfect. You are usually taught the backswing and downswing as two separate parts, but in fact the downswing begins before the backswing has ended. They must now be put together to form one fluent movement.

Your backswing prepares you to strike the ball. In completing it,

the upper body coils 90° while the lower body turns only 45°. The lower body becomes the trigger for your downswing. Your weight has shifted to your right hip pocket area and you should be in a relaxed and powerful position.

THE TRIGGER

The key to making a good downswing is to link your legs to your arms correctly. Your chest, arms, wrists and hands must move together.

If you raise your left heel during the backswing, the downswing

begins by you firmly planting it back on the ground. This action triggers the left hip and starts a weight shift back to the left side.

If you are young and supple you don't need to lift your left heel to complete the backswing. The left hip now starts the downswing, pulling the hands, arms and club down to the mid point position.

POWER AND ACCURACY

This movement automatically drops the club on a path slightly inside that of your backswing. Any sudden or awkward move at this

STARTING THE DOWNSWING

The downswing begins before the backswing has ended – your hips start to move back to the ball before you reach the top point.

YOUR HEAD
Although your left eye should be looking down on the back of the ball, your head has turned slightly to the right.

UPPER BODY
Turn your chest so that your back faces the target. Your upper body rotates 90° from the address position.

LEGS AND LOWER BODY
Your legs are flexed and ready to provide power through the ball. They turn only 45°.

PERFECTING THE DOWNSWING

pro tip

Turn into impact

To imitate the position your body should be in at impact, adopt your normal address position with your hands and arms stretched out. Concentrate on turning your left hip to the left which twists your middle body towards the target. Do this slowly four or five times so you can see how correct hip rotation returns the arms to impact.

① **THE TOP**
At the top point you should feel poised and ready for action. Your upper body coils 90° while your hips turn 45° and provide stability for your swing. Feel your weight transfer to your right hip pocket. The right knee remains flexed to let the legs support the upper body. The shaft of the club should point parallel to your ball-to-target line.

② **FIRST MOVEMENT**
Turn your left hip smoothly to the left. This triggers the weight shift back to your left side. Feel your left hip linked to your left hand and arm – they all move together and must not separate. As the left hip starts the downswing, the hands and arms automatically drop inside the path of the backswing. This natural movement starts before you've completed the backswing.

3 **MID POINT**
The hands and arms respond to the movement of your lower body. The hips continue to lower the hands and arms toward the ball. This is where you should feel immensely powerful. But don't attempt to hit the ball at this stage – your power is stored in your wrists, which must not unhinge too early in the swing.

4 **READY FOR IMPACT**
As you continue to turn the left hip to the left, the clubhead returns back to the ball and is naturally square at impact. Using your hips and legs correctly means no conscious hand action is necessary.

point is disastrous. At the mid point, your left arm acts as a powerful lever, pulling the clubhead into the ball and storing power.

Your hands and arms are responding to the movement of your lower body. As the left hip continues turning to the left the hands and arms deliver the clubhead back to the ball with power and accuracy.

WEIGHT TRANSFER

During the downswing your weight transfers from your right side to your left – by impact slightly more than half your weight is on the inside of your left foot. Your head stays still until you strike the ball.

You must feel the downswing with your feet. They help generate power and coordinate the entire swing. If the hip and leg action is incorrect you lose all smoothness. Correct hip rotation allows your arms, wrists and hands to remain passive.

If your lower body doesn't rotate correctly on the downswing, your hands, wrists and arms shape the swing path. The clubhead moves outside the ball-to-target line at the start of the downswing before being pulled across your body from out to in. At impact the clubface isn't square and you slice the ball.

CORRECT YOUR STARTING POSITION

If the club is in the wrong position at the start of the downswing it is difficult to return the clubface square to the ball. The shaft of the club should point at the target. If the shaft points left of the target (above left) you swing through impact from out to in, producing a slice. If it points right of the flag (above right) you swing from in to out, creating a hook. Most poor positions are caused by incorrect upper body rotation.

pro tip

Better body turn

To develop correct body rotation on the downswing, practice the following routine. Holding the club normally in your left hand, place your right hand mid way down the shaft so that it rests against your open fingers. Reverse the hands if you're left handed. Turn your shoulders and let your arms swing to the top of your backswing. From here feel the left hip pulling the arms down. Do this a few times to understand how your hands, wrists, arms, chest and club are dropped into a position to deliver the clubhead at impact.

Impact

T he impact position is the point during the swing when you're about to strike the ball. It's the moment when – if you swing correctly – the clubhead finally catches up with your hands.

To hit a golf ball both long and straight down the fairway, you must return the clubhead to the ball with two qualities – power and accuracy.

Your body position at impact differs for irons and woods, but ball position and shaft length combine to alter the strike. With woods, no divot is taken as you sweep the ball – which is opposite your left heel – off the fairway or tee.

To gain top benefit from an iron club, it's vital to strike the ball first, before taking a small divot. Move the ball towards the center of your stance as the shaft length shortens.

SQUARE CLUBFACE

There are many different types of correct golf swing – but only one correct impact position. This means returning the clubface squarely to the ball, which leads to straight hitting. Building power is more complicated.

You coil power in the backswing – this power is stored at the top. As your downswing begins, your lower body starts a weight shift to the left and your shoulders, arms and hands follow, before finally releasing the clubhead at impact.

Being in the proper impact

ONE IMPACT POSITION
Although there are many types of golf swing, there is only one impact position. It's similar to the set-up – the clubface is square to the ball, but the lower body is shifting left.

INCORRECT: NO LOWER BODY MOVEMENT

CLUB STAYS AHEAD
Starting your swing with your shoulders and failing to move your lower body left means that most of your weight stays firmly fixed on the right. You swing the clubface across the line, which closes the clubface and causes a slice.

WRONG: WEIGHT STAYS ON RIGHT

INCORRECT: MOVING AHEAD

EARLY WEIGHT TRANSFER
As you start the downswing, you shift your weight too quickly to the left, and you move ahead of the clubhead. At impact the club has no chance of catching up, usually causing an open clubface – and a push.

WRONG: WEIGHT SHIFTS TOO EARLY

PRACTICE YOUR HAND POSITION

1 ADDRESS
Stand with knees flexed in your normal address position. Hold out both arms in front of you, as if about to take grip.

2 TOP OF BACKSWING
Leave your left arm straight and swing your right arm to the top of the backswing position. Slowly move your hips back to the left, keeping your knees bent.

3 IMPACT
Look at your hand positions. They should have returned to impact solely through lower body movement. No conscious hand action should be needed.

CORRECT WEIGHT SHIFT THROUGH IMPACT

CLUBHEAD CATCHES UP WITH HANDS
As you start your downswing, your left hip turns to the left – enough to transfer your weight to your left foot. This movement lowers your hands and arms to the mid point position. You should feel very powerful, with both arms loaded with energy. The muscles in your left hip and thigh keep turning smoothly to the left snd your right leg and knee follow. Your lower body is taut but springy. The shot does not finish with the strike – your weight continues to your left side, letting your upper body turn and face the target. This movement brings your head up to watch the ball's flight.

pro tip

USE AN UMBRELLA

Drive an umbrella into the ground and set up as normal with the outside of your left foot (right foot for left-handers) touching the umbrella. Make your usual swing.

You're in the correct position at impact if your left knee touches the umbrella, but the space remains between your hip and the umbrella.

position ensures that you achieve maximum distance and the correct trajectory. If you're out of position, you're likely to hit fat (behind the ball) or thin (halfway up).

HIP ACTION

To hit squarely at impact, you must start the downswing with the correct hip action by turning your hips smoothly left.

Feel as if your hips pull the arms and hands down until the mid point of the downswing, when your arms should be loaded with power. Your shoulders send power to your arms, the arms to the hands and your hands pass it on to the clubhead.

If everything else is as it should be, the clubface is square on contact. Don't try to control the clubface at this point – it's moving far too quickly.

At impact, the clubhead, arms and hands form a straight line, although your position is not identical to the one you adopt at set-up. This is because your lower body carries on turning to the left, so that your weight shifts fully from your right side. Keep your head steady.

Remember that you haven't finished playing the shot when you strike the ball – it's important to make a full followthrough.

Improve your followthrough

Your followthrough – sometimes called the through-swing – is vital to your swing. You must swing through to a good finish on all your shots – this promotes accuracy and power and helps you keep smooth rhythm and tempo.

Unfortunately many golfers concentrate so hard on hitting the ball that they forget about achiev-ing a correct followthrough. They quit on the ball and lose power and distance. Your swing does not finish when you hit the ball – the golf swing is complete when your body turns around to a balanced finish after impact.

The finish provides a good guide to the rest of your swing as it confirms the movements you have made before. Look for clues

pro tip

Hold your finish
To help you create a positive, firm followthrough, stay in your finished position until the ball either reaches the top of its flight or lands. This encourages you to make a complete swing. Don't feel that you've done all the work when you hit the ball.

COMPLETE YOUR SWING

A solid followthrough is an essential part of the complete golf swing. A repeatable swing is your goal so to perfect your movements you must assume the key positions consistently.

HEAD FORCED UP
Your head is forced up as your right shoulder comes around. This lets your arms swing the club around your body to the finish.

WEIGHT TRANSFER
After impact your body must keep turning – and your weight should transfer – to the left. As this happens your right shoulder swivels In the same direction.

CLUBHEAD SPEED
At a point just after impact the clubhead reaches top speed. It is this speed – with proper weight transfer – that carries you through to the followthrough position.

BALANCE
You finish steady on your feet – most of the weight is on the outside of your left foot, with your right foot almost vertical.

Trouble both sides

When you're playing a tough hole with trouble on both sides, your confidence is likely to waver – just when you need it most.

Lack of confidence in the throughswing causes you to quit on the shot after impact. Without a proper throughswing your strike is stifled and balance impaired. You need to know that you can rely on repeating your finish position, so that you play a powerful – and straight – stroke, even under pressure.

Concentrate on your followthrough – that's when the shot finishes, not when you hit the ball. Thinking about your finish helps take your mind off any pressure – and off impact – so that you focus on rhythm throughout your swing.

in your followthrough to diagnose swing faults.

REVERSE THE BACKSWING

Most players realize that good body turn is vital during the backswing – but forget that they need to repeat this on the followthrough.

To help build your throughswing, you can reverse an exercise you tried when you were developing the backswing.

Set yourself into your final followthrough position and rewind your body, arms and club until you come back to the impact position. This helps you to find the correct throughswing plane – it should feel like your backswing reversed.

It's unlikely that you'll achieve a valid followthrough unless your top of the backswing position is good.

Tempo is vital – it gives each part of your body the time to respond correctly and evenly during the swing. Smooth rhythm leads to a regular, clean strike as the moving parts of your body slot into the proper places. You must have fluid movement from the top of the backswing to the end of the throughswing to promote this tempo either side of impact.

WEIGHT TRANSFER

A good followthrough needs sound weight transfer. From the top of the backswing – when most of your weight is on the right foot – you shift your weight to the left. In your finish position you should be balanced with most of your weight on the outside of your left foot.

If you don't shift your weight properly you're likely to stay flat footed as you swing through, and

MAKING A CLASSIC FOLLOWTHROUGH

① INTO IMPACT Your hips lead your shoulders all the way on the downswing as you make a smooth strike through the ball. At impact you're just beginning to lift your right heel up.

② FLUID MOVEMENT Keep your movements smooth after you strike – just because you've hit the ball, it doesn't mean that you've finished playing the shot. Your head remains still.

A MATTER OF BALANCE

✓ A sound throughswing means that you're steady, with most weight on the outside of your left foot. The ball gains good distance.

✗ If your weight fails to shift from right to left on the downswing, you're left flat footed. In most cases this leads to a slice.

✗ Throwing your lower body weight too much right to left on the downswing leaves you likely to overbalance forward. It usually causes a push.

3 HEAD COMES AROUND
Your upper body continues to clear to the left, so that your turning right shoulder begins to force your head round and up to watch the ball's flight. Most of your weight has shifted to the left side.

4 SHOULDERS CATCH UP
Because your head has come around, your upper body clearance is not obstructed, helping you apply maximum power. Your shoulders catch up with your hips at the end of the swing. Your right foot is vertical, resting lightly on the ground.

WHERE ARE YOU FACING?

①BACKSWING
Use a club to check your position. A good backswing leads to an effective throughswing. At the top of your backswing, your followthrough is reversed – your shoulders are 90° to the ball-to-target line. Your back faces the target and the club is almost horizontal.

②DOWNSWING
The smooth tempo on your downswing should be the same as on your throughswing – the club must not slow down. By impact, your rotating upper body should be parallel to the ball-to-target line.

③FOLLOWTHROUGH
Your finish is like the top of the backswing reversed. Your shoulders are 90° to the ball-to-target line, and your chest faces the target.

Complete your lower body turn

✗ The lower body must be correct if the upper body is to follow suit. Bringing your legs and hips only part of the way around reduces your chances of making a full, powerful strike.

✓ Your throughswing is fully effective only if your lower body completes its turn, and you end in a balanced position with your weight mainly on the outside of your left foot.

you lose distance. This usually happens because you start the downswing with your hands and arms instead of working from your hips. You don't have time to transfer weight before impact.

Pushing too hard with your lower body also causes erratic weight transfer. You fail to swing around your body, making a balanced finish impossible.

HEAD MOVEMENT

Keeping your head down too long after impact destroys any chance you had of achieving a correct followthrough.

Watch the clubhead strike the ball but then let your right shoulder – which should be turning smoothly left – gently force your head around to face the target. If your head stays down too long it gets in the way of your body's clearing action and prevents a full followthrough.

Lively leg action

All golfers know that a good shoulder turn and upper body coil are vital to the golf swing. You cannot achieve this if your legs aren't working correctly for you.

Your legs must feel lively and active because they provide leverage throughout the swing. This is one of the keys to generating power without effort.

At address your legs should be comfortably flexed – ready to spring into action so that when your swing starts, the lower half of your body is ready to react.

TURN OF EVENTS

Think of the ideal backswing. Your left arm and shoulder are the first parts to move – they in turn pull the upper body and hips into a coiled position.

Your physique dictates that the legs must also react, so at the top of the backswing your left knee points directly at the ball and the right leg is flexed and supporting body weight.

Now consider what happens if your legs are rigid at address. They're unable to respond to the moves going on above the waist. This has a restricting effect on the entire swing.

Wider leads to shorter
When you're playing in the wind, try shortening your backswing to give you added control over the ball. An effective way to achieve a shorter backswing is to widen your stance a fraction.

This change is effective because your backswing shortens automatically as a result of the change at address – you don't have to think about it during the swing. It has the added benefit of providing a more stable base in the wind, making it easier to keep your balance.

The only danger in widening your stance is failing to make a full shoulder turn – a wider stance does have a tendency to restrict you slightly. Therefore, making a good shoulder and hip turn should be one of your main swing thoughts.

ALTERED IMAGES
A look at the changing positions of the legs from the top of backswing through to the finish shows clearly the vital role they play. On the backswing the left knee points inward and your weight rocks on to the right foot. Through impact the legs drive forward. And on the followthrough your right knee catches up with the left. This action from the waist down allows the upper body to move into the correct positions.

✗ RIGID LEG ACTION

① **STARTING PROBLEMS**
Stiff legs immediately introduce tension at address. The position looks very static and you can't imagine a smooth swing taking place from here.

② **POOR TURN**
Rigid legs restrict you because it's impossible to make a proper turn away from the ball. Note the positions of the hips and shoulders in comparison to the good top of backswing – there's not nearly enough rotation.

③ **STUCK ON THE RIGHT SIDE**
If your legs don't work, the right foot is anchored to the ground and the left side fails to clear. This produces a chopping action where the hands can't release – you almost get in the way of yourself.

④ **STILL STIFF**
Those rigid legs continue to cause problems. Your right foot has almost taken root and remains firmly planted on the ground – this makes it physically impossible for your hips to turn into the correct followthrough position.

✓ GOOD LEG ACTION

1 POISED AT ADDRESS
All good address positions look relaxed. Your knees should be comfortably flexed and supporting your body weight equally on both feet.

2 TOP OF BACKSWING
Lively legs pay dividends at the top of backswing. The right leg acts as a brace supporting your bodyweight and the left knee points in toward the ball – a product of making a powerful turn.

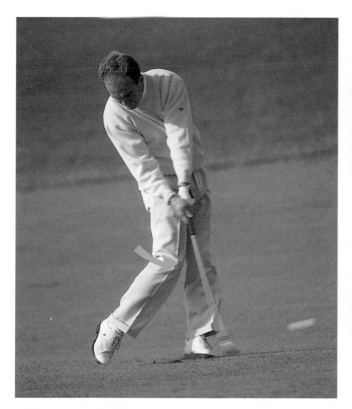

3 NEAT FOOTWORK
An excellent impact position shows clearly how the weight transfers on to the left foot. This all stems from driving the legs, particularly the right knee, toward the target at the start of the downswing.

4 THROUGH TO FINISH
Good use of your legs allows you to roll on to the outside of your left foot. By now, virtually none of your weight is supported by the right foot and the upper body faces the target.

Foot faults
How you position your feet at address has a big influence on the shape of your swing. There are a couple of serious foot faults you should avoid:
○ Turning your left foot outward restricts hip and shoulder turn.
○ Too wide a stance has the same effect – you can't turn properly.
○ If your right foot is splayed outward too much, you may turn more than is good for you. This makes it difficult to transfer your weight on to the left side through impact.
○ A very narrow stance is equally damaging. It's easy to turn but it's hard to keep your balance. This is also true if your feet are pointing straight out away from your body. Remember, your toes should be only slightly wider apart than your heels.

Bend your knees
Sloping lies are difficult because they force you to alter your stance. When the ball sits below the level of your feet, flex your knees to bring you down nearer to the level of the ball. Bend from the waist more than usual – this lowers the angle of your spine and allows your arms to hang down freely, rather than forcing you to stretch.

Make sure you keep your head at the same level on the backswing and into impact. All of these adjustments combine to make your swing more upright, so taking into account the slope as well, allow for the ball to fly to the right of where you're aiming.

However, if you try to stand normally, you have to reach for the ball at address and then dip down again into impact – this is an unreliable method and likely to make you miss-hit.

pro tip

Rock steady
Putting is the only area of golf where moving your legs can be damaging. Try to minimize any movement from the waist down throughout the stroke.

Flex your knees at address and make sure you feel comfortable over the ball (1). From the moment you start the backswing until the ball is on its way (2 and 3), your legs should remain steady. Remember, steady is not the same as rigid. Even though movement is almost non-existent, you should still feel relaxed.

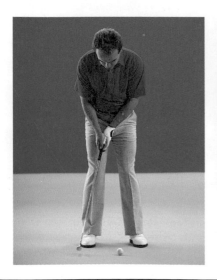

Your hips can't turn and neither can your shoulders – your legs simply don't allow it because they've almost turned to concrete.

Unless you're remarkably supple – or too wristy, which is also damaging – there's no possible way you can swing the club back to horizontal. Stiff legs at address condemn you to a poor top of backswing position.

CHANGE DIRECTION

Your legs play a vital role from the top. You should drive your knees towards the target to start the change of direction from the backswing into the downswing. Your hands and arms then follow – they should not move before your knees.

This sequence of events triggers off the power generating process common to all good golfers. Importantly, your weight moves in the correct direction as you roll on to the outside of your left foot and up on to your right toe. Your legs generate this weight shift.

Once again, if your legs are too rigid you cannot transfer your weight and therefore cannot strike the ball correctly. No matter how strong you are, arms alone cannot generate power – the ideal golf swing is a combined effort.

Weight transfer

There's more than one way to strike a golf ball well, but if you want to hit good shots on a regular basis you must transfer your weight correctly during the swing. With a good weight shift power flows smoothly from your body through to the club and the ball.

For a full shot, a little more than half your weight should be on your right foot at the top of the backswing. As you start the downswing your weight gradually shifts towards the target. And when you complete your followthrough, you must have almost all of your weight on your left foot.

You may get away with a less than classical action. Many great players in the past have prospered with an unorthodox swing – Arnold Palmer and Lee Trevino are two perfect examples. But correct weight transfer is an essential ingredient of every successful golf swing – once you've got it right, don't tamper with it.

ADDRESSING THE PROBLEM

Take the first steps to correct weight transfer before you swing the club. At address make sure your weight is equally distributed on both feet. It's much easier to build a good swing if the foundations are solid.

Any fault is likely to cause you misery. If too much of your weight is on the left side it's extremely difficult to make a wide backswing. This is likely to restrict your weight transfer – and perhaps even cause a destructive reverse pivot where you lean towards the target on the backswing.

If you have more than half of

THE WEIGHTING GAME
Whatever your age, sex or build, making sure your weight distribution is correct benefits your game. Most of your weight must be on the left foot through impact. This action helps you hit down and through the ball – essential if you want the satisfaction and enjoyment of hitting crisply struck iron shots.

WEIGHT WATCHERS

①SHARED EQUALLY
Make sure your weight is evenly distributed – position your feet about shoulder width apart for a solid base. If you get it right at address you make life easier when parts start moving. Note how the arrows show the small amount of sway needed for good weight transfer.

②HALFWAY BACK
Sweeping the club back long and wide naturally pulls your weight away from the ball. From an evenly balanced position at address, more of your weight is on the right than the left – even at this early stage in the swing.

⑤CONTROLLED POWER
A good weight shift helps generate power at impact. The left leg is firm and supporting more than half your body weight. Both arms are fully extended, driving the clubhead low toward the target. The ball is propelled forward on a penetrating flight.

⑥RIGHT TO LEFT
The body faces the target and the left leg is straight – note the position of the right foot indicating how little weight is on that side. When the weight transfer is as smooth as this you can maintain perfect control from start to finish.

(3) TOP OF BACKSWING
Notice how the head has tilted slightly to allow an uninhibited shoulder turn, yet it has moved sideways very little from its original position. If your head does move too far, there's every chance something else in the swing has also done so.

(4) SMOOTH DOWN
The shift of weight back towards the target should start before you pull the club down. This helps set the club on the correct path down into the ball and also guards against flailing with your hands only.

your weight on the right side at address there's every chance you sway too far away from the ball on the backswing.

RIGHT FROM THE START

Your backswing is the key move. A wide takeaway acts as a trigger to help you transfer your weight on to the right side. Achieve this and you naturally pull your upper body into a coiled position.

Your right leg acts as a brace at the top of the backswing. The leg should be comfortably flexed yet firm to resist any tendency to sway backwards. This puts you in a strong position to support your body weight.

Think of tempo at the top and make sure you transfer your weight smoothly towards the left side on the downswing. As well as promoting a pure strike, it helps you achieve the classic balanced followthrough so recognizable with good golfers.

If you leave your weight trailing behind, you probably find yourself scooping at impact. It's impossible to strike correctly if you're

toppling back away from the ball. The likelihood is you hit plenty of thinned shots.

When you analyze your swing, remember that weight transfer is not the same as a sway. It's important to understand the difference between the two.

A very slight sway away from the ball on the backswing is fine and encourages weight transfer. So if you study your swing in a mirror or on video, don't feel anxious if you do sway a little on the backswing. The important point is that your weight shifts towards the ball on the way down. An excessive sway is potentially disastrous – it's definitely a problem that must be addressed.

TRANSFER TRAINING

A simple exercise can help you appreciate the importance of weight transfer. When you're next on the practice tee, adopt your normal stance with your weight equally distributed on both feet. A 5 iron is the best club to use.

Hit a couple of shots while making a deliberate attempt to

keep your feet firmly planted on the ground – almost as if there's glue on the soles of your shoes. This makes it impossible to transfer your weight correctly during the swing – particularly through impact. You're certain to hit almost every bad shot imaginable so don't continue this drill for too long.

Now revert to a more orthodox action. Concentrate on transferring your weight on to the right foot on the backswing and on to the left on the downswing. Right away you should strike the ball with more power and authority.

pro tip

Supporting role
An accurate way to check you're in a good followthrough position is to try to stand on your left leg immediately after you complete your swing. If you can, it means your balance is good and that you're transferring your weight correctly both on the downswing and through impact.

OFF BALANCE

▲▼ AVOID REVERSE PIVOT
Weight transfer is best demonstrated when you see good and bad together, viewed from behind (above) and from the front (below). Leaning towards the target on the backswing is a typical example of poor weight transfer. You create none of the width in your swing that is so crucial to striking the ball well. It's a weak position at the top and difficult to imagine a good shot following. The ideal top of backswing position (red outline below) has the body coiled away from the ball and just over half your weight on the right foot.

▲▼ FALLING AWAY
Toppling backwards on the downswing is disastrous because you're bound to scoop at the ball. You may catch it heavy, or produce a thin, but you're unlikely to hit a good shot. Rigid legs are often the root of the problem – if you can't drive your legs through towards the target, weight transfer is hard to achieve. When you transfer your weight on to the left side on the downswing (red outline below) the benefits are enormous. This position helps you generate clubhead speed and strike powerfully.

Perfecting your balance

The golf swing is an exercise that has an uncanny knack of upsetting an otherwise impeccable sense of balance. Staying firmly planted on your own two feet sounds simple enough, but it still manages to elude many club players.

The fault is so common because many golfers regard balance as an unimportant aspect of the swing – therefore they don't feel the need to work on it. They're so tied up with straight left arm, head down and coiled upper body that they forget about the movement of their feet and overall balance. It's an attitude that cannot possibly produce consistent results.

Don't make striking the ball more difficult than it already is. Be sure that you pay at least as much attention to perfecting your balance as you do to any other part of the swing.

ON AN EVEN FOOTING

There are times when keeping your balance is not easy, so you need to know how to cope. Even golfers who appear rock solid over the ball and during the swing can be prone to a slight wobble. Wild and windy days on an exposed links are often the cause of the problem – gusting breezes buffet you as you fight to stay steady.

In these testing conditions you need to work doubly hard at main-taining your balance – not just over the full shots but from close range too.

Widen your stance a fraction to give yourself a more solid foundation over the ball. Shorten your swing to make it more compact and less vulnerable to a battering from the wind – this has the added benefit of helping you hit the ball lower than normal.

If you have a long, willowy swing you're especially likely to suffer from balance problems in the wind. Bear in mind that the more compact you make your swing the better it stands up in gusty conditions. Picture Ian Woosnam's swing for example. Solid, straightforward – he's one

▶ STUMBLING BLOCK
The tell-tale signs of poor balance are easy to spot. All the body weight moves away from the target instead of flowing on to the left side. This technique destroys all hope of striking the ball correctly because the clubhead is on an upward path at impact. You're likely to block the ball out to the right. The cardinal rule of iron play is to strike down on the ball – impossible to achieve if your balance is so out of control that you topple backwards on the downswing.

◀ BALANCED FINISH
Good and bad together is an excellent combination when trying to identify specific faults. This is a fine example and highlights the benefits to be gained by keeping your balance. You can transfer your weight smoothly on to the left side which enables you to strike down and through the ball. The classic finish you achieve is an additional benefit – while it's too late to influence the path of the ball it still looks impressive.

KEEP IT COMPACT IN THE WIND

1 STABLE ADDRESS
Every golfer is exposed at some time to strong winds, so make sure you practice the techniques and shots that are best suited to these testing conditions. The low punch shot is a precious stroke – it keeps both the ball and your score down when the wind is straight in your face. Forget the distance you usually hit your approach shots – a 7 iron can be used from the 100yd (90m) mark as long as you stay in control. Place your feet wider apart than normal with the ball central in your stance – this looks and feels like a compact address position.

2 STEADY START
From a stable position at address you're in perfect shape to make a good takeaway – essential to the overall success of the shot. Sweep the club back and concentrate on making a one piece takeaway. Resist the temptation to become very wristy – this is a trap that many club golfers fall into when playing in the wind. If you pick the club up too steeply you're likely to strike down on a similar angle of attack which generates too much backspin. The ball starts low, but climbs too quickly and falls short of the target.

3 SHORT AT THE TOP
Control is the name of the game when you play this type of shot, so stop the club well short of horizontal at the top of the backswing. This serves a dual purpose in that the shorter you swing the club the more likely your technique is to stand up well in the wind. Remember, you should be doing all you can to resist buffeting from the breeze. Try to think of this as a shortened version of the full swing – note how the shoulders have turned and the weight is mostly positioned on the right side.

④ TOP TO BOTTOM

The split second that it takes to go from the top of the backswing to impact is such that you cannot deliberately link the moves together – it all happens too fast for the brain to react. It's vital to start the downswing correctly – you then give yourself the best possible chance of arriving at a good impact position.

As you pull the butt of the club down, slide your knees towards the target to help shift your weight on to the left side. Feel your hands leaving the clubhead behind – this guarantees they're ahead of the ball at impact to promote crisp contact.

⑤ PUNCHED FOLLOWTHROUGH

The ball is on its way but there's still work to do. You need to punch the clubhead through low towards the target. To help you, imagine a small coin about 12in (30cm) in front of the ball along the intended line, then visualize the clubhead traveling directly over that point.

Concentrate on staying down on the shot – your knees play a vital role in achieving this by remaining comfortably flexed through impact. With most of your weight now on the left side you can complete the swing the way you started it – simple, compact and perfectly balanced.

DRIVING IN CALM CONDITIONS

① ROCK STEADY
Even when there isn't a breath of wind you still need to concentrate hard on maintaining your balance. This is especially true when you have the driver in your hands – it's this more than any other club that causes golfers almost to throw themselves at the ball, which ultimately results in a loss of balance.

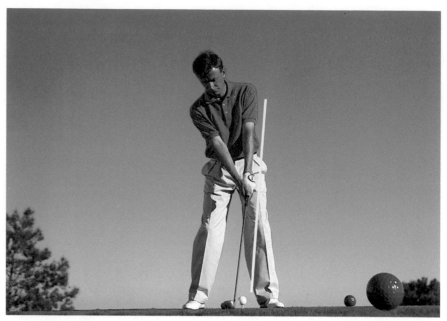

② ADDRESS TO TAKEAWAY
Sweep the club back close to the ground for at least the first 12in (30cm) of the backswing – this is one of the more popular pieces of advice because it concerns one of the most important moves in the swing. The straight line formed at address by your left arm and the shaft of the club should have altered very little at this stage of the swing.

③ SWING ACTIVATOR
This is the first clear sign of the swing starting to take shape and is a fine example of one good move leading to another. Taking the club back low to the ground sets the necessary wide arc – this in turn pulls the upper body into a coiled position and starts to shift your weight towards the right side.

4 TURNING POINT
Halfway through the swing you should feel in complete control of your balance. Whether you reach horizontal at the top of the backswing is really a matter of personal choice – a lot depends on how supple you are. Just short is a good position because it gives you time to turn fully and yet still remain in control.

5 BALANCING ACT
A smooth transfer of weight on to the left side helps you keep your balance in the hitting area. Note the good extension through the ball – clubhead speed should almost pull you into the followthrough. If ever golfers suffer from poor balance it tends to be at this stage of the swing – usually caused by a frantic lunge from the top.

6 HAPPY ENDING
This more than any other part of the swing is where you can spot the difference between good and bad balance. It's the followthrough position achieved by every professional and is something you can learn from and copy yourself. You can only finish the swing in impressive fashion like this by transferring your weight correctly and maintaining your balance.

of the finest wind players in the world.

When you have to play a shot from a viciously sloping lie, you need to counteract the imbalance by slightly altering your weight distribution.

As a rule you need to go against the slope. With the ball well below the level of your feet, shift a little more of your weight on to your heels to prevent you toppling forwards when you swing. Move your weight more towards your toes to help you cope with a ball above your feet.

BALANCE OF POWER

In calm conditions on reasonably flat ground there are no excuses for losing your balance. For the full shots you must maintain good balance because it helps you transfer your weight with control throughout the swing.

Your weight moves away from the ball on the backswing and on to the left side through impact. When you carry this out smoothly you enhance your power. But if your balance is slightly out, you upset both your rhythm and timing. This is certain to have a disastrous effect on the strike.

Perfect balance also consistently helps you keep the clubhead on the correct swing plane throughout.

When you see a golfer with poor balance, look at the direction the clubhead travels during the swing – it's unlikely to stay on the same plane from start to finish. A more likely scenario is that as the player topples from one poor position to another, the clubhead is unavoidably thrown out of plane.

Your swing plane in turn has an effect on the path of the clubhead through impact. When the plane is consistent you can more accurately control the direction of the clubhead as it meets the ball – one good move results from another earlier in the swing.

> *pro tip*
>
> ### Short game stance
> Windy conditions often play havoc as your ball flies through the air, but don't imagine the problems come to an end there. When you move closer to the hole there are other difficulties you need to contend with.
>
> The key to holding your short game together in strong winds is keeping still over the ball and staying balanced. To achieve this, take every step possible to build a solid and compact stance for both your chipping and putting.
>
> Stand with your feet slightly wider apart than normal. This establishes a good foundation and helps prevent any unwanted movement over the ball. You probably know from experience how important this can be to the shot. There's nothing more distracting than feeling a strong gust of wind just as you're about to start your takeaway.

Fall over backwards
Toppling backwards is a very common fault among handicap golfers. Sufferers are bound to be plagued by inconsistency and disappointment.

If your weight moves away from the target on the downswing you can forget about hitting the ball well – even from a good position at the top of the backswing. More often than not the shot goes horribly wrong.

The fault happens because the arc of your swing moves backwards along with you. This immediately destroys any good work you may have done earlier such as setting up to the ball correctly. As you come down there is little hope of making good contact – the clubhead either thuds into the ground before the ball, or travels up at the point of impact resulting in an ugly, thinned shot.

Remember, a slight sway from the target is fine on the backswing. But you must transfer your weight on to the left side on the downswing – failure to do so can only end in poor strikes.

GOOD BACKSWING

SWING ARC CHANGES

WEIGHT SHIFTS ON TO RIGHT SIDE ON DOWNSWING INSTEAD OF LEFT

CLUBHEAD MAKES CONTACT WITH GROUND BEFORE BALL

Tempo and rhythm

To be a consistent striker of the ball your swing must have good tempo and rhythm. Tempo is the speed at which you swing the club while rhythm is its fluency.

Good tempo and rhythm allow every moving part of your body to coordinate as a single unit. Although your head, shoulders, arms, hands, hips, knees and feet have their own function, they must work together during the swing. If your tempo is too fast or erratic, this doesn't happen and you don't make a solid strike.

Even if your set-up is perfect and you swing the clubhead along the correct path, you only play effective golf when your tempo and rhythm are relaxed and smooth.

DEVELOPING YOUR TEMPO

Most players with poor tempo and rhythm swing the club too fast in a vain attempt to work up power and distance. A quick or rushed swing doesn't allow each individual movement enough time to perform its task and your action is jerky.

To find your natural tempo and rhythm concentrate on swinging the club smoothly. Start with a half swing. Only when you achieve a solid, consistent strike should you lengthen your swing to three-quarter and then full.

Developing your ideal tempo and rhythm takes practice as well as natural ability. Once they improve you can build a repeatable swing.

It is vital you concentrate on keeping a good tempo and rhythm when playing a round. Once

SWINGING SMOOTHLY
Good tempo and rhythm allow each individual movement within your swing to work correctly and help produce a perfect swing path. If your swing is too quick your body hasn't enough time to rotate properly and the clubface isn't square at impact.

UNDERSTANDING TEMPO AND RHYTHM

① TAKEAWAY
The takeaway dictates the speed of the swing. If you rush it, the rest of your swing becomes too fast and erratic. Concentrate on taking the club away smoothly.

② THE BACKSWING
Your backswing must have a smooth and even rhythm. This allows your hands, arms and shoulders to move as one, and helps you to feel the clubhead throughout the stroke.

③ TOP OF BACKSWING
Allow for a slight pause at the top of the backswing to ensure that you complete it. This prevents you from rushing the downswing.

you've selected the club to fit into your game plan, your only thought should be making a smooth swing. Visualize your swing as a whole. Avoid analyzing any specific movement within your swing just as you blot out hazards on the fairway.

RECOVERING LOST TEMPO

No player – even leading professionals – consistently maintains perfect tempo and rhythm. Regaining your timing isn't difficult – as long as you go back to basics.

Once you establish a regular distance with each club, recover lost tempo and rhythm by playing to a shorter target. Reduce the distance you try to send each shot by about one-third. This automatically slows your swing down, allowing each body movement enough time to function.

By slowing down and reducing the length of your swing you

④ **THE DOWNSWING**
The downswing must have the same tempo and swing path as the backswing. To help you swing the club on the same line, the start of the downswing must be smooth.

⑤ **IMPACT**
To make a solid strike your tempo and rhythm must be perfect. Your swing movements must coordinate properly so that the clubface is square at impact.

⑥ **FOLLOWTHROUGH**
Your swing slows down as smoothly as it increased at takeaway. Good tempo and rhythm look effortless and should become natural and consistent with regular practice.

SHORTEN YOUR SWING

 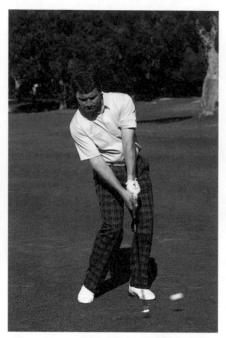 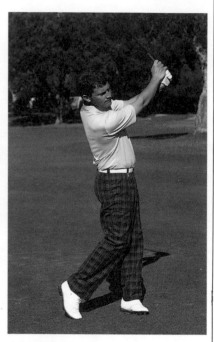

One of the best ways to improve – as well as understand – tempo and rhythm is to practice a three- **quarter swing. By shortening your swing you slow it down and it is easier for its individual movements** **to coordinate correctly. A three-quarter swing also increases clubhead feel.**

lessen tension and develop greater clubhead feel. You also hit the ball further than you expect because you achieve a more solid strike.

With a slower action it is easier to identify any faults in your set-up and swing – and then correct them. From here you can increase your tempo until your swing combines rhythm, consistency and power.

FEET TOGETHER

Another exercise for finding good tempo and rhythm is to hit the ball with your feet together. Because your center of gravity is higher than with a normal stance you must reduce the speed, length and power of your swing to avoid losing balance.

The best way to understand and appreciate tempo and rhythm is to watch top players – either at tournaments or on television. Although they all swing the club differently their tempo and rhythm are perfect.

Take an image of their swing on to the practice range or course and try to copy it. It's amazing how you can improve your own swing – and your game – by trying to imitate top players.

REDUCE YOUR DISTANCE

If your swing is too fast, slow it down by reducing the distance you try to hit each shot. For example, if you normally expect to strike a 5 iron about 150yd (136m), go to the practice tee and aim at a target 100yd (91m) away. This makes you reduce the length, speed and power of your normal swing, and helps you develop a smoother action.

3

SHOTS AROUND THE GREEN

There is no reason why you cannot develop a good touch around the green; consistency from 60 yards and in will reflect in lower scoring and less frustration. Many players place great emphasis on hitting the ball out of sight, while neglecting the all-important short game. You will come across a variety of situations around the green that will force you to vary your choice of shot, therefore club selection combined with feel and imagination are all points to consider for good chipping.

A deft chipping touch

Every time you tee up at a golf hole, whatever its length, shape or type, you have to aim for the green at some stage.

No golfer – regardless of ability – hits the green every time with the approach shot. Although many shots are accurate, some fall wide, some short and others beyond the putting surface.

Good golfers acknowledge that this happens to every player, so they pare down their score by showing deadly accuracy from just off the green. The flag is always put under threat whether they're chipping or putting.

Be prepared for wayward approach shots. Develop a delicate, confident touch when chipping.

▼ CHIPPING WITH CONFIDENCE
Work on a sure chipping stroke and know which type of shot to play. If you're confident from around the green – however ticklish the lie – you can attack the pin just as easily as if putting.

WHICH CHIP TO PLAY?

Playing the proper shot to give yourself the maximum chance of a makeable putt needs careful thought. After assessing if there is a hazard or rough in the way, and how flat the ground is, make your choice of shot and stick to it. Doubt leads to tense muscles and a duffed shot. Whatever the lie, there's usually a solution.

5 IRON – LESS LOFTED CLUB FOR PUTTING-TYPE ACTION

PUTTING ACTION FROM FRINGE
Lie: good
Club: 5 iron
Ball position: towards back of stance
Stance: slightly open
Clubface aim: at the flag
Grip: your putting grip, at the bottom of the rubber
Swing: short, slow and even, with no wrist break
Points to note: a putter might be easier to play but the longer grass makes the stroke hard to judge – a 5 iron lifts the ball cleanly and onto the green

CHIP AND RUN OVER APRON
Lie: a little fluffy
Club: 7 iron
Stance: slightly open
Ball position: towards back of stance
Clubface aim: at the flag
Grip: lower than usual
Swing: no wrist break – backswing and throughswing of equal length, with the left wrist staying firm through impact
Points to note: it's an easy option to take a putter but confidence with a 7 iron means you rule out hitting the apron with its less even surface – bounce the ball off the green for consistent speed

7 IRON – LOFTED TO LIFT AND RUN BALL ALONG GREEN

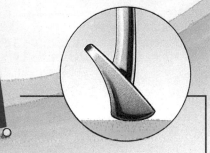

WEDGE – LET THE LOFT DO THE WORK

pro tip

SHORT CHIP OVER HAZARD
Lie: good, in grass long enough to tangle
Club: sand wedge
Stance: open
Ball position: central, with hands ahead of clubhead
Clubface aim: at the flag – aim to drop the ball on the top of it
Grip: lower than for full wedge
Swing: early wrist break to create steep backswing and downswing
Points to note: be positive – too delicate an approach puts the ball in the sand in front of you

Hands down the grip
You can improve your feel for the clubhead – and your control over the shot – by gripping further down than usual. Awareness of the clubhead is vital to a delicate greenside touch.

CHIP OVER A BUNKER

① **WHERE WILL IT BOUNCE?**
Decide where you want the ball to bounce; concentrate on that spot – not on technique, which should be unfussy. Imagine you're going over smooth grass. Align left to give the sand wedge plenty of loft and aim the clubface at the flag.

② **SHARP PICK-UP**
You can't run the shot because of the bunker, so you need to float it high and drop it quickly on the green. You have a lot of loft – now pick the club up sharply and at a smooth tempo, cocking your wrists early.

③ **CRISP STRIKE**
The clubhead moves down to the ball on a steep path. Keep your tempo even as you make contact – quitting on the stroke and slowing down the club leads to a thinned shot. Let the clubface loft lob the ball gently to the green.

Know which club to take and what sort of shot to play.

Begin by experimenting with different clubs. Many high handicappers restrict themselves to a wedge when they're just off the putting surface because they feel that the short distance to the pin rules out clubs with less loft. But this restriction limits the possibilities open to you.

KNOW YOUR SHOT

Learn to create shots with clubs of varying loft. Open the clubface to increase loft – keeping the clubface square to the ball-to-target line and opening your stance has this effect. Close the clubface and bring the ball back in the stance to decrease loft.

Size up the shot you have to play – take into careful account any hazards or obstacles along your ball-to-target line. Do you need to float the ball over them, or can you take a 5 iron and stroke the

ball along the ground – as if with a putter?

Whatever shot you decide to play, make sure it's appropriate to your golfing level. Be creative, but make sure you don't overreach yourself. Around the green, keep it simple is a very effective rule to follow.

Don't waste time worrying about the finer points of technique – you'll tense your muscles and thin the shot. The fewer moving parts you concern yourself with, the fewer are likely to move out of turn. Trust your instincts; rely on muscle memory. If you've honed your skills on the practice tee, all you know should come out naturally in the stroke.

KEEP IT CRISP

While most professionals do not hold up play, top players take their time over visualizing a chip – they examine every contour along the ball-to-target line. But when they

stand to the ball they strike right away, making sure of good, crisp contact. There should be no fancy flourishes or dallying when you chip.

Swing back and through evenly. Look down at the lie after the ball has left the clubface – this stops you lifting your head too early, which is likely to cause a thinned shot.

Judge the bounce
When you chip you may find that you either overshoot the flag or leave the ball short. Solve the problem by assessing where the ball will bounce first – this helps you gauge the rest of its path.

Visualize the shot quickly but clinically – stick with your choice and strike crisply. You may prefer the ball to run through the fringe to slow it down. Or you might attempt to stop it quickly near the pin.

Fringe play

Even top professionals don't hit every green in regulation, so they spend hours practicing the art of fringe play. They fully appreciate that the ability to get up and down in two is just as important as striking the full shots well.

Fringe grass is evenly cut and similar in length to light rough. A chip from the fringe is a short shot – there's seldom more than 30yd (27m) between you and the flag.

Unlike most other shots in golf, there are no obstacles in front of you to worry about.

STROKE SAVERS

There's more than one way to play a chip from the fringe and every one is a potential stroke saver. It's vital that you understand which club is best suited to any given situation, so try not to restrict

CHIP AWAY AT YOUR SCORE
Intelligent club selection and knowing how the ball reacts from different lies are just as important for the short game as a correct technique. A low running chip is a safe shot likely to give you consistent results. Don't lob the ball high into the air from short range unless you have very little green to work with.

CHIP AND RUN OFF FRINGE

1 SQUARE ON
When there's plenty of green between you and the flag the ideal shot is the chip and run. Select a spot on the green where you intend to pitch the ball. The ball is in contact with the ground for most of its journey, so consider the speed and slope of the green – the roll of the ball is influenced by both. Stand square to the target with the ball central in your stance. Keep your hands ahead of the clubhead at address – they should remain that way throughout the swing.

3 NUDGE FORWARD
The left hand leads the clubhead down on a shallow angle of attack into the bottom of the ball. Keep the hands ahead of the clubhead at all times to prevent the dreaded scooping action at impact. Don't worry about getting the ball airborne – the loft of the club does this for you. This is a simple back and through movement with the hands and arms. Don't hit down sharply at the ball – neither height nor backspin are required for this shot.

② **SLOWLY BACK**
Take the club away from the ball smoothly and break the wrists only a little. The length of backswing determines the length of the shot. Feel your left hand in complete control of the club – the right hand acts mainly in a supporting role for a shot as short as this.

④ **BALL RUNS UP TO HOLE**
Long after the ball is on its way to the hole your left hand should be held ahead of the clubhead. Concentrate on keeping the clubface pointing at the target. The ball pitches less than halfway to the flag and runs up to the hole. A successful chip leaves you a very makeable putt for your next shot.

HIGH AND SHORT

1 HANDS AHEAD
When the ball sits down in fringe grass and there's very little green to work with, a sand wedge is the club for the job. Adopt an open stance with the ball back in your stance and your hands forward.

2 STEEP BACK
Break the wrists very early in the backswing – the sideways movement of the hands is tiny but the hinge effect of the wrists gives you enough length on the backswing.

yourself to a personal favorite.

Check the lie of the ball, the distance between you and the flag and the ground conditions on the green – these three factors determine the club you should use. Let your imagination work in your favor – select a spot where you want the ball to pitch and visualize it running up towards the hole.

Take a couple of practice swings to develop a feel for the shot you've chosen. These swings help you focus your mind on the task in hand and prevent you rushing in too hastily.

FLOAT SHOT

When the ball sits down in a fluffy lie and there's not much green to work with, you're faced with a difficult chip. But a sound technique and sensible club selection help you out of trouble every time. You need to generate clubhead speed to avoid the duffed shot while at the same time taking care not to overhit the ball.

Reach for your sand wedge and stand open to the ball-to-target line. Lay the clubface open in your stance so that it aims squarely at the flag. Adopt a weak left hand grip to prevent the clubface closing during the swing. Break the wrists quickly on the backswing and cut down across the ball from out to in. Like taking sand with a bunker shot, you rely on the grass acting as a cushion at impact. The ball pops up in the air, lands softly on the green and runs very little.

If you're fortunate enough to find your ball in a good lie, this is altogether a much easier shot. The ball may fly up a little higher – and so run less – but exactly the same techniques apply.

LOW RUNNER

When there's plenty of green between you and the flag, a shot with a lower trajectory is required. If the lie is good use an 8 iron – you want the ball to travel in the air for less than half of its journey to the hole.

Select a spot on the green where you aim to pitch the ball. Gauge the slope of the green – the ball runs along the ground for most of the way and takes any breaks in the same way as a putt. Set up fairly square to the target and position the ball towards the center of your stance.

Swing your arms back and through, keeping the left wrist firm and dominant. The ball is lofted over the fringe on to the putting surface and runs smoothly up towards the hole.

From a poor lie use a more lofted club, perhaps a 9 iron. The techniques which served you well from a good lie help you again in this slightly trickier situation. Address the ball in exactly the same way. Make sure your hands are ahead of the ball – all types of chipping faults can stem from positioning your hands behind the ball.

Swing back with a small amount of wrist break and accelerate the clubhead down into the bottom of the ball. Grass comes between the clubface and the ball, so don't concern yourself with backspin. The ball comes out quite low and runs a long way.

3 RETURN TO ADDRESS
Grass acts as a cushion at impact – as sand does on a bunker shot – so accelerate on the downswing. The importance of a correct set-up becomes clear as you return to exactly the same position as address.

4 SOFT TOUCH
This is a perfect example of the paradox of hitting down on the ball to gain height on the shot – the natural loft of the club pops the ball up in the air. Your head remains perfectly still throughout.

Rules check
With a putter in your hands it's easy to mark and lift your ball simply out of habit – but you risk breaking the rules if you do so when your ball has come to rest on the fringe.

Most courses allow you this luxury only when winter rules are in force, so check the noticeboard in the clubhouse before you step on to the course. An infringement of this rule costs you a hole in matchplay and 2 penalty shots in strokeplay.

5 LEFT IN CHARGE
Notice how dominant the left hand is even though the ball is well on its travels – at no time in the shot is the clubhead allowed to overtake the hands. The ball lands softly on the green and runs very little.

CLOSELY CUT

The apron tends to be only a few paces wide and skirts around every green between the fringe and the putting surface. The grass is just slightly longer than you find on the green – for this reason your putter is usually the most effective club. The ball is always in contact with the ground, so you eliminate the risk of an uneven bounce.

If the apron is damp from early morning dew or rain, a shot with a 7 iron using your putting stroke can produce excellent results. Your stance, grip and ball position remain the same as if you were holding a putter. A smooth stroke gently lofts the ball over the apron, preventing any dampness slowing it down.

FRINGE BENEFITS

More than half of your shots in a round of golf are chips and putts, so at least half of your practice should be devoted to this aspect of the game.

You can spend hours practicing your short game and not become in the least bit tired – chipping requires little physical effort.

To make your practice enjoyable vary the type of shot you play. Experiment with different clubs and learn to understand how the ball reacts.

In the winter months you can also practice your putting indoors – and even some gentle chipping with an air ball. With enough practice you are certain to develop into an accomplished chipper of the ball – your scores are bound to tumble as a result.

Reach for an iron
If your ball is nestling down slightly in the fringe grass you can use any club from a 7 iron to a pitching wedge. The club you choose depends on the amount of green you have to work with. A good maxim to remember is less green/more loft, and more green/less loft.

Don't putt
Even if you're close to the flag, rule out any hope of using a putter from this lie – it usually leads to disaster. The straight face of the putter is totally unsuited to playing from the fluffy grass on the fringe. Pace is almost impossible to judge so take a lofted club instead.

APRON PUTTER

Not all putters are suited to apron play. Use one that gives a smooth roll – if the ball jumps into the air on impact it's likely to pull up short.

An **offset** putter lofts the ball slightly at impact – though the ball is briefly in the air it rolls smoothly once on the green.

A **mallet** putter isn't suited to apron play. The ball hops at impact – speed is lost and the putt pulls up short of the hole.

A conventional **blade** putter is ideal. Struck from the sweet spot the ball runs smoothly along the ground towards the hole.

Avoid a **center shafted** putter. The ball jumps into the air and you can't judge pace accurately.

Offset ✓

Mallet ✗

Blade ✓

Center shafted ✗

Short game slopes

There are three types of sloping green – each one presents its own set of opportunities and challenges. A few key thoughts can equip you with a game plan to handle the most severe slope.

You always need to be conscious of subtle borrows and gentle undulations on putting surfaces. This is especially true when you have to chip on to a sloping green – you should be aware of the borrow on the green before you take your putter out of the bag.

If slopes aren't too severe, they're easy to cope with and shouldn't present problems as you attempt to chip close. However, some course architects have a nasty sense of humor – wicked, sloping greens can wreak havoc before you even set foot on the putting surface.

The first point to remember is that chipping isn't just about holing out at all costs. Even professional golfers don't hole too many shots from off the green.

For this reason turn your attentions towards making your first putt as easy as possible – on a sloping green this means leaving the

SLIPPERY SLOPE
Be careful when chipping down a slope with water lurking the other side of the green – it's a potentially dangerous situation. Always play this shot with a sand wedge to ensure a soft landing – there's less risk of the ball racing away into trouble. A straighter faced club generates too much pace on the shot – if the ball comes out of the rough better than you expect, you may find yourself getting your feet wet.

LOW CHIP UPHILL

1 BACK IN YOUR STANCE
When you have to chip up a green that slopes uphill from front to back, look to your straighter faced clubs for the best results – a 5 iron is perfect. Your main thought should be to give the shot as little air and as much run as possible. Make sure you grip further down the club than normal to enhance your control. Stand comfortably – slightly open is ideal – and position the ball back in your stance. Remember, your left arm and the shaft of the club should form a straight line down to the ball. Just because you're close to the flag, don't immediately think of your pitching wedge. It's hard to judge a high flying shot uphill – you need make only a slight error and your ball struggles to climb the slope.

2 COMPACT TAKEAWAY
The backswing for a low chip and run couldn't be more straightforward – this is the strongest argument for using the technique whenever the situation allows you. Your weight should be slightly on the left side rather than central – this promotes a crisp, downward blow. Take the club back low to the ground and fractionally inside the line. This is really just a hands and arms shot – there shouldn't be too many other moving parts. Keep wrist break to a minimum to help eliminate the risk of striking the ball poorly.

3 GENTLE LOFT
A good downswing and crisp contact are products of a compact backswing. You need concentrate only on one key thought on the downswing – making sure the back of your left hand faces the target to keep the clubface square and stop you scooping at the ball. Try to ensure that you push the clubhead through towards the target and as low to the ground as possible. Note also how your arm and the shaft of the club should return to a similar position to that of address – a straight line – which helps guarantee you make contact with the ball before the ground.

4 HILL CLIMBER
The slight amount of loft on a 5 iron means the ball stays in the air for only a brief moment. You also generate very little backspin – this has the significant benefit of making the ball roll smoothly once it's in contact with the green. It all adds up to a shot that is tailor-made for coping with an upslope, giving you the best chance of getting up and down in two and the slimmest chance of failing to climb the hill at all. You can also use this shot when you have to chip up a two-tier green. This should stop you having to negotiate the step twice in the space of a few minutes – a putt up a severe slope is no less frightening than a chip from the same position.

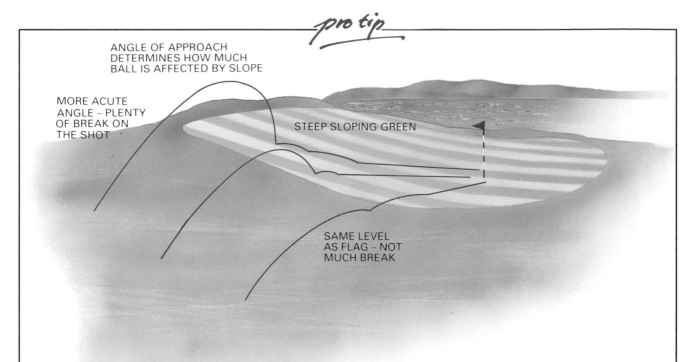

pro tip

ANGLE OF APPROACH
DETERMINES HOW MUCH
BALL IS AFFECTED BY SLOPE

MORE ACUTE
ANGLE – PLENTY
OF BREAK ON
THE SHOT

STEEP SLOPING GREEN

SAME LEVEL
AS FLAG – NOT
MUCH BREAK

Roll-on effect

Judging a chip on to a green that slopes from one side to the other can be a tricky business. A lot depends on the angle of your approach – it's not just the trajectory of the shot that you need to think of.

In general, the closer you are to the level of the flag, the more you can afford to choose a direct line. You still need to allow for a bit of break once your ball lands on the green, but it's a gentle borrow rather than a severe swerve to the right or left. A low chip and run is likely to serve you best on this line.

If your ball has most of the slope to negotiate, you need to allow for much more borrow. This is a situation where it's even more important to visualize the shot and identify the exact spot where you intend landing your ball. A slightly higher trajectory is required to ensure your ball rolls almost sideways down towards the hole.

If you choose too straight a line, your ball is certain to be swept away from the hole on the low side. No matter how high you play the shot, or how soft you try to land the ball, there's no way you can threaten the hole or finish close.

Try to find a green on your regular course where you can experiment a little and judge for yourself how best to tackle each shot.

ball below the hole and never above it.

You may complain of three-putting all the time, but the problem can often be caused by chipping into a poor position above the hole rather than by any serious flaw in your putting stroke.

BACK TO FRONT

The green that falls away from you is perhaps the trickiest of all. You need a delicate touch to tickle the ball down close to the hole. A lofted club is generally best suited to playing this shot.

It's fraught with danger though – if you overdo it slightly the ball can easily run away from you. Suddenly another opportunity to get up and down in two slips through your fingers.

But it's better to be too long than too shy – at least you then have an uphill putt. You must avoid leaving the ball short because you're then faced with a very difficult putt.

UP A SLOPE

Chipping uphill provides an excellent opportunity to attack and most golfers feel confident at giving the ball a good run at the hole. Don't be reckless – if you go well past the hole it's a treacherous putt coming back.

When a green slopes uphill, there's every chance that a ball coming to rest just short of the putting surface also lies on a slight upslope.

This effectively increases the loft of the club and means the ball flies a little higher – even from very close range. The ball also stops quicker than from a flat lie.

To combat this abnormal lie, select a straighter faced club to chip with. Play the shot with as little wrist break as possible – almost like an extended version of the putting stroke.

This generates a lower flight, less air time and a smoother roll on the green. It's the easiest type of chip shot to judge and should enable you to get up and down in two.

SIDE-ON VIEW

A green that slopes from one side to the other tends to look harder than it really is. The first mental adjustment you need to make is to forget about the position of the pin – this is no longer the actual target line.

Visualize the shot and try to judge how much the slope is likely to affect the roll of your ball. Then look to aim at a point – an imaginary flag if you find it helps – where the slope starts to sweep your ball down to the hole. From that point on the shot is all about pace.

Once again, more crucial than anything else is to leave yourself an uphill putt coming back. It's vital if you're regularly to get up and down in two, because you can attack the hole with an uphill putt. Downhill putts are trickier.

FLOATING DOWNHILL

① OPEN AND RELAXED
With the green sloping away from you and water the other side an entirely different shot is called for. You need plenty of clubhead speed to slide through the rough, but a soft, floating trajectory so that there's not too much pace on the ball when it lands. Play the shot with your most lofted club. It's very much like a greenside bunker shot in that you need to combine a slightly open stance with the clubface square to the target – this produces a cut up shot that lands softly and runs gently toward the hole.

② LONG BACKSWING
Despite the short distance between you and the flag, you need to make quite a long backswing. Take the club back along the line of your body – this is fractionally outside the line in relation to the target and helps create a slight out-to-in swing path. Keep your rhythm nice and smooth all the way to the top – this improves your overall control of the clubhead.

③ CUSHIONED IMPACT
Maintain a smooth tempo on the downswing and feel your hands ahead of the clubhead all the time. Another similarity with the greenside bunker shot comes at the point of impact. The rough grass acts as a cushion between the clubface and the ball – this means there's very little backspin generated, but that's not a problem because you want the ball to roll rather than stop quickly.

④ COMFORTABLE FOLLOWTHROUGH
Your hands should finish lower than normal when you play a cut-up shot with the sand wedge. The abbreviated followthrough position is a result of sliding the clubhead across and under the ball, keeping the back of your left hand facing the target for as long as possible. The flight of the ball should be rather like that of a gentle underarm lob. You can expect a soft landing on the green. Then let the natural slope of the ground do the rest as it sweeps the ball down to the hole.

Chipping down to a two-tier green

One of the hardest shots to control in golf is the chip down a split-level green. Often the back section of a two-tier green is higher than the front section. If you overshoot the green with your approach shot when the flag is on the lower tier, it's tricky to get close to the hole with your next.

DELICATE TOUCH

To play this shot you need a different technique from that used for chipping up a two-tier green.

You take a straighter faced club for going up the green because you need run to get the ball on to the top tier. Use a delicate chip with a lofted club for the shot down the green. In this situation run is not important as the slope provides the pace on the ball.

The art of the shot is to put enough speed on the ball so that it almost comes to rest at the top of the downslope. From there the slope takes the ball down the bank and towards the hole.

What makes the shot harder is the fluffy grass usually found at the back of the green. It is easier to control a shot from the front of the green because you play off either fairway or a short fringe. It's harder to judge from the back as you can't get backspin and the ball runs on.

Play the stroke with a normal grip unless the ball is only just off the green when it's easier to use a putting grip. Use a short, crisp swing. Throughout the stroke your weight should favor the left side. The key to success with this shot is practice.

FEEL, TOUCH AND CONFIDENCE
The shot requires a lot of thought, a sure touch and a little luck.
Visualizing the shot well is half the battle, as where the ball lands and how far it runs are important. Be confident and play positively.

DEFT DOWNHILL CHIP

① COMPACT STANCE
Adopt a narrow and slightly open stance. Grip your sand wedge about 1 in (4cm) from the top, and position the ball back in your stance. Your weight should be slightly on your left side.

② LOFTED SHOT
Play the stroke firmly and don't quit on the ball. The natural loft of the sand wedge throws the ball up and it lands softly on the green. The thicker the grass you play from the more the ball runs.

③ JUDGING THE SLOPE
You should have judged the shot so that the ball rolls just to the edge of the slope. Play the ball higher with a more open clubface if the downslope is close – then you need as little run as possible.

masterclass

Laura Davies: power and finesse

Any top professional, whether male or female, must have a good short game, and Laura Davies is no exception. She is best known for her immense power, but she also possesses a great touch when she plays delicate chips on to the green.

Many women pros make up for their lack of length from the tees with deft chipping and putting. But Laura Davies has used both her tremendous power and great finesse to win many big events, including the 1987 US Women's Open.

④ LET THE SLOPE WORK
If you judged the shot properly the ball reaches the step at a slow pace and then runs downhill towards the hole. Take into account the steepness of the slope in judging how you play the shot.

Sand wedge around the green

Balanced downhill stance

Most amateurs use their sand wedge around the green from only a bunker or rough grass. But there is great scope for a variety of shots to be played with the same club. Instead of using clubs from the 7 iron upwards for different situations, it's possible to manufacture every greenside chip shot with a sand wedge.

It's not for everyone, but the advantage of using the same club for nearly every situation is that you can cultivate good feel and touch. By regularly playing the sand wedge you know instinctively how the ball behaves whatever way you use the club. This helps your confidence. Chipping with a different club each time

HAZARDOUS LOB
Because the sand wedge is the most lofted club in the bag it's perfect for delicate lobs. Facing a chip over trouble from a downhill lie, position the ball slightly further back in your stance – to help avoid the thin – and choke down the grip. Try to tilt with the slope and push your weight forward to be sturdy. If the slope is steep, press on the inside of your back foot for balance. Pick the club up quickly with plenty of wrist break (above) to follow the contours of the slope. A steep attack also helps the ball to gain height.

makes judging the shot tricky – shaft length and loft vary with each club.

Playing the sand wedge in most situations also forces you to be creative each time. It helps you to visualize shots effectively, not only around the green but in every department of your game.

CHANGING CHIPS

The various sand wedge shots – perhaps a chip and run or high lob over trouble – are easy to play. Slightly alter your ball position, stance, clubface loft and type of swing.

The **long chip and run** shot is usually associated with a straighter faced club like a 7 or 8 iron but a sand wedge can be used just as effectively. Place the ball well back in the stance and push your hands forward, taking loft off the clubface.

Play the stroke with a firm wristed action – strike down crisply on the ball, and don't quit. The ball flies much lower than a conventional sand wedge, then checks on the second bounce and runs up to the hole.

Use the same technique for the **short chip over a fringe**. Most golfers opt for a putter, but sometimes there's a risk of an irregular roll through the grass and so pace is difficult to judge – especially on fast greens. A little bump off the back foot with a sand wedge lifts the ball just enough to clear the fringe and the ball rolls toward the pin. You may be surprised how often you hole out once you have thoroughly practiced this technique.

The **low running** sand wedge can also replace the 8 iron for a bump and run up a slope to a flag cut just on the green. Instead of pinning trust on the ball bouncing several times up the slope, you can play a sand wedge so that it bounces only once or twice, lessening the risk of the shot taking bad hops. But the sand wedge shot has to be played precisely so practice the stroke before you attempt it on the course.

The one time you should hit another club is when you're faced with a chip off hard, bare ground. The danger of thinning or fluffing the shot outweighs any advantage gained. Reach instead for a straighter faced club.

ONE FOR ALL

BUMP AND RUN
Don't be afraid of using the sand wedge from just off the green instead of a straight faced iron or putter – it's a simple shot to play. Position the ball well back in your stance – opposite the right foot – and push your hands forward to deloft the clubface. Push your weight forward also. With a firm wristed putting action strike down firmly on the ball – it pops up to clear the fringe but flies low enough so that it runs on landing.

CHECKING CHIP
An 8 iron is a good choice for a chip over a medium sized fringe provided the target is far enough away – the ball rolls on landing. A sand wedge can be played like an 8 iron, but the shot checks more on landing. This gives you extra control but the ball still rolls, which is especially useful on fast greens or going downhill.

DELICATE TOUCH
A chip over a large fringe with little green to work with is a perfect situation for the sand wedge. A pitching wedge is fine but needs to be played very precisely for the ball to go close. The sand wedge gains more height and lands softly so you can afford to be slightly bolder. But think again about using the lob with the sand wedge if it has to be played from hard pan. The pitching wedge is then the better option.

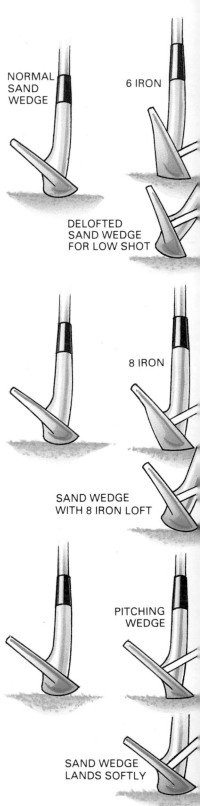

NORMAL SAND WEDGE

6 IRON

DELOFTED SAND WEDGE FOR LOW SHOT

8 IRON

SAND WEDGE WITH 8 IRON LOFT

PITCHING WEDGE

SAND WEDGE LANDS SOFTLY

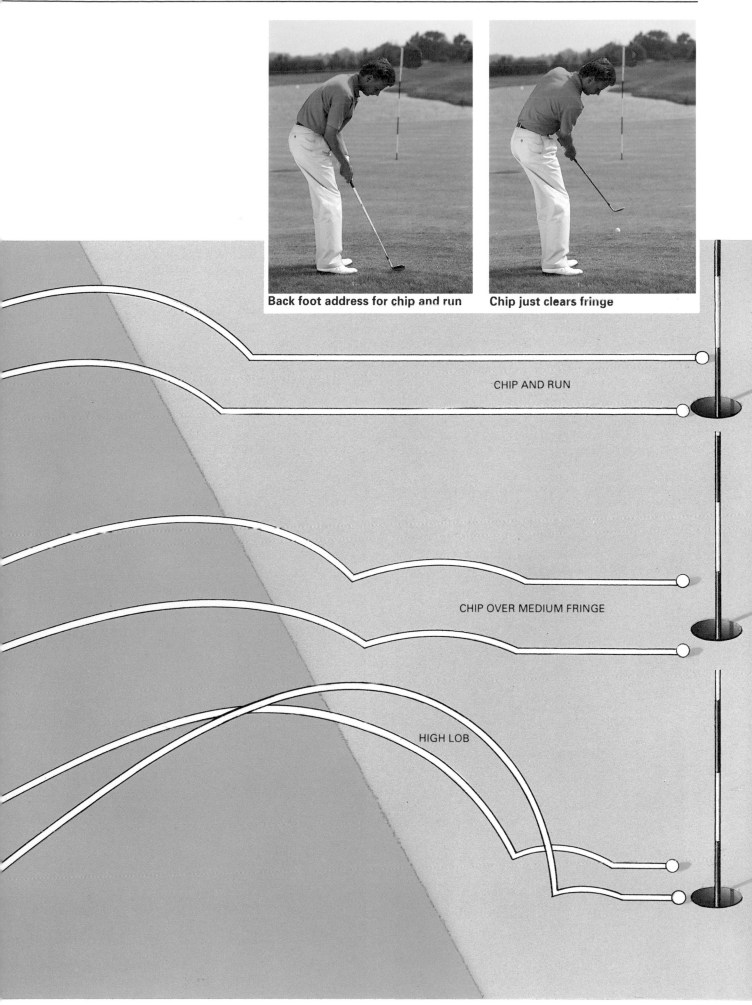

Back foot address for chip and run

Chip just clears fringe

CHIP AND RUN

CHIP OVER MEDIUM FRINGE

HIGH LOB

HIGH PITCH

The high, soft-landing lob is easy to play because the swing is almost full. With the ball forward in your stance, align slightly left allowing the blade to be opened up for extra loft. Your backswing should be steep and wristy but full. The length of your swing determines the distance you hit the ball. Swing down steeply and follow through fully – never flick at the ball or quit on the shot. Don't attempt this stroke off hard bare ground – thinning the ball is all too easy.

Make a steep swing...

...and full followthrough

masterclass

McNulty's versatility

Mark McNulty is superb around the green, getting up and down more often than not from any position. His great touch and confidence let him play the sand wedge when most other golfers would hesitate.

Even though the ball is just in the fringe and a putter could be used for the short distance to the flag, Mark opts to bump a sand wedge. The ball jumps just enough to clear the fringe but still rolls like a putt when on the green. This technique is ideal for coping with pacy greens such as those at Valderrama, the 1990 Volvo Masters venue where McNulty finished equal fourth.

pro tip

Sharpen your sand wedge

The feel, control and confidence you gain from playing a sand wedge creatively around a green can be found only by constant practice. An excellent way to develop this touch is to stand in the middle of the practice green and throw a number of balls around it – place them randomly by tossing them over your shoulder.

Without changing any of the lies or positions, work your way around the green playing each ball as you find it. You soon learn how to alter your set-up and swing to cope with every situation.

Applying backspin

When professionals play shots to the green, you often see the ball stop dead after only one or two bounces. This is because the player has applied backspin.

WHAT BACKSPIN IS

Backspin is particularly worth trying when you approach a soft or uphill green, as these accentuate the spin. The higher-lofted clubs – 7 iron to wedge – are ideal for backspin, because they give the ball height. Played with confidence, this type of shot improves ball control, which is bound to lower your scores.

With backspin the ball spins in a counterclockwise direction – this reverse spin helps to stop the ball on landing. The forward spin of a normal shot turns the ball clockwise.

For backspin, impact takes place during the downswing, as the club strikes down and through the ball. On contact the ball runs up the clubface causing a counterclockwise spin.

To make the ball spin back, you must hit down on the ball. Sharp contact with the clubface is vital, so make sure the clubface – particularly the grooves – is always free of dirt. Clean your ball at every opportunity as well. Even the smoothest swing cannot give you backspin if the clubface grooves are clogged or the ball is muddy.

HIGH AND LOW BACKSPIN

To hit the ball low with backspin, use no more than a half swing and keep your hands ahead of the clubface. Make sure you take a divot. This proves that you strike on the downswing.

To hit very high with backspin, you need to align left and cut across the ball by swinging on an out-to-in path.

Both types of shot can really lower your scores – but need confidence as well as practice if you are to play them successfully.

GIVING A SHOT BACKSPIN
Strike down and through the ball. A slightly open stance is necessary and your weight should be just to your left.

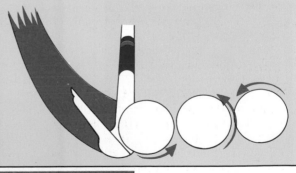

Backspin on the ball
As the club strikes down and through it, the ball collects spin by running up the clubface – though the distance is so slight it's not noticeable. This makes the ball spin in the opposite direction to the way it travels.

CONTROL YOUR APPROACH SHOTS

(1) BACKSWING
From an open stance, with your weight slightly favoring your left side, take the club away with your arms and break your wrists early to produce a sharp downward strike into the ball. Keep your weight transfer to a minimum.

(2) IMPACT
Your hands stay ahead of the clubhead through impact. This prevents you scooping the clubhead under the ball and helps to make a firm, clean strike. Feel your left arm pulling the clubhead through as you strike.

(3) THROUGHSWING
The club now moves back inside the ball-to-target line and so hits slightly across the ball. Your throughswing should be the same three-quarter length as your backswing.

Strike down to gain height
One of the oddities of golf is that you have to strike down to hit the ball up. When trying to give a shot plenty of backspin, it's important to strike down into the back of the ball.

Don't attempt to lift the ball with the club. Your weight is likely to stay on your right side, making you hit the ground with the club, or top the ball.

masterclass

Norman's target golf
Greg Norman has adapted better than anyone since Gary Player to the demanding target golf of the US Tour. This is partly because of his accurate approach shots.

On the undulating, lightning-fast greens of many American courses the ball has to land in the right place. Greg Norman has developed precision hitting because he tuned his wedge and high iron shots to a fine art. He knows that where his ball hits the green it stays. Greg can concentrate on selecting the right spot on the green for the safest or easiest putt, knowing his ball will be close to it.

High cut-up shot

UP AND OVER
With a rough covered bank between you and the green, a high cut-up pitch is the only shot that gives you a realistic hope of getting up and down in 2. It removes as many elements of chance as you possibly can in golf. Use your sand wedge, stand open to the ball-to-target line and make a smooth, full swing. The clubhead slides through the grass and the ball flies high over the bank. If you judge the shot well, you can expect a soft landing on the green.

pro tip

Take your pick
The key to good scoring is possessing a sharp touch around the greens. It's important to give yourself the best possible chance to excel in this department of your game, because it's the best way to knock strokes off your handicap.

Try carrying four short game clubs in your bag – a 9 iron, a pitching wedge and two sand wedges, one with standard loft and a second utility wedge with a few degrees extra. This range of clubs gives you great versatility around the greens.

Far too many club players' golf bags are heavily biased in favor of the long game. They might carry 3 different woods, plus a 1 and a 2 iron, but this is almost certainly too many long clubs. Analyzed closely, most golfers would probably find they rarely use some of them.

would for a longer shot.

Alternatively, grip further down the club – this means you don't have to make any other adjustments to your technique. Shortening the club narrows the arc of your swing which in turn reduces the distance you hit the ball.

If you feel you need to hit the ball hard to generate enough distance, you're probably too far out to play the cut-up pitch shot. It's impossible to maintain control of the ball if all you're thinking about is brute force.

There are a number of shots in golf that you play because there's no other way of finishing close to the hole. The high, cut-up pitch is a good example because it's often the only way to negotiate a hazard, hump, or other form of obstacle – situations where you cannot play a low flying shot.

With a high flight and soft landing, the cut-up pitch is extremely satisfying when you play it well. However, many club golfers fail to succeed with this shot because they think drastic changes in technique are required to produce spectacular results.

This is simply not true. You need to make adjustments to your overall set-up and swing, but they should be only minor and based on the fundamentals of your normal full swing.

TEMPO IS THE KEY

A smooth swing is essential when you intend lobbing the ball high into the air. The cut-up shot is all about finesse and touch – you must feel in complete control of the clubhead at all times.

To vary the distance you hit the ball with the cut-up pitch, don't vary your tempo in the slightest. As you move closer to the flag, simply shorten your backswing and keep the same rhythm as you

KEEP IN CONTACT

Aim to achieve normal ball to turf contact. You shouldn't feel you need to hit down any more with this shot – your change in set-up and technique should naturally take care of this.

A mistake that many golfers commit is attempting to dig out a huge divot with the sand wedge – mainly because they try to hit down on the ball too hard. The result is a heavy duff. You may see Ian Woosnam knocking doormat divots down the Augusta fairways, but the turf is different from the type you probably play on, and Woosnam is an extremely powerful and talented golfer.

Backswing basics
The full sand wedge is a poorly played shot among many club golfers. Often hit flat out, with the emphasis on taking a divot like a doormat, this shot is miss-hit far more than it should be. The main problem is almost certainly trying to hit the ball out of sight – an effective cure for this fault lies in your backswing.

On the practice green, find out how far you hit your sand wedge, but make only a three-quarter length backswing. Don't swing the club back all the way to horizontal at the top – that's when you start to lose control of the clubhead, and ultimately the ball.

Once you know the distance you hit your sand wedge, and the length of backswing required, you can play the shot with confidence when you're on the course. Never stray too far from this method – you can then develop a more consistent feel for distance from that crucial 100yd (90m) mark.

CUT ABOVE THE REST

1 SELECT YOUR SAND WEDGE
There's a steep rise in front of you, so you need to get the ball up quickly and land it softly on the green the other side. The cut-up chip is perfect, whereas other shots leave too much to chance. To play this master stroke, align slightly open and grip down your sand wedge for control. Make sure the clubface aims straight at the flag.

2 CLUB ON PLANE
Take the club back along a line parallel with your feet. When your hands are about waist high, the shaft of the club should point straight at the flag. Ask a friend to check this point for you – it's an indication that the club is on the correct plane at a crucial stage of the swing.

3 HOW FAR BACK?
Your top of backswing position should vary depending on the length of shot. From around the 50yd (46m) mark you should certainly take the club back beyond halfway – this ensures you can maintain a smooth tempo on the way down.

4 DOWNWARD ATTACK
Your first move from the top determines whether the shot is a success or a failure. You must pull the butt of the club down towards the ball – this sets the necessary angle between your left arm and the shaft of the club to ensure you strike down through impact and don't scoop at the ball.

5 SLIDE RULE
Imagine your left hand leading the clubhead through impact – you want to avoid releasing your hands so that the back of your left faces the target for as long as possible. From greenside rough you're not looking to strike the ball first – the clubhead slides through the grass, inflicting a cushioned blow at impact.

6 CHARGE HAND
Notice how the left hand pulls across the line from out-to-in through impact, not allowing the clubhead to pass the hands at any time. Make sure this is the way you finish every time you play the cut-up shot.

DIFFERENT PERSPECTIVE

VIEW FROM BEHIND
Every golfer knows how difficult it is to judge a shot when you can't see the bottom of the pin. It's a situation that often causes anxiety, which in turn triggers off a bad swing and a poor result.

Viewing the shot from another angle can make all the difference. From behind the pin you can see exactly what you have to do – note factors such as where to land your ball and how much green you have to work with. Visualize the flight of your ball. Once you have a clear picture in your mind you can then apply the necessary technique best suited to achieving the right result.

Be careful not to hold up play though. In a practice round with no one else present you can take as much time as you like, but when there's a group following close behind, show some consideration and avoid holding them up.

BLIND SHOT OVER HILL
DIFFICULT TO JUDGE

LOOK BACK FROM BEHIND FLAG TO
HELP YOU IDENTIFY LANDING AREA
AND VISUALIZE FLIGHT OF BALL

Dainty lob from downslope

Possessing a delicate touch around the greens can be your savior if you find a tight spot. You often need a gentle lob shot to keep the ball under control and give yourself a chance of getting up and down. But sometimes it just doesn't seem possible to land the ball softly enough to stop it near the flag. If you use a normal lob action, often it isn't.

Don't despair – there is one technique that pops the ball into the air so gently that it is hard to believe how softly it lands. It gives you the scope to play the daintiest of shots to even the tightest-cut pin. Added dangers such as having to play from a downslope over a bunker to a lightning fast geen shouldn't faze you either.

All it takes is a weakening of the left hand grip – every other aspect of your lob technique stays the same. This weak left hand enables the blade to be well opened up at impact and to stay so throughout the followthrough. There is no hint of the clubface turning over – which would make the ball fly lower than you want it to and run on landing. The blade stays square to the target throughout the throughswing.

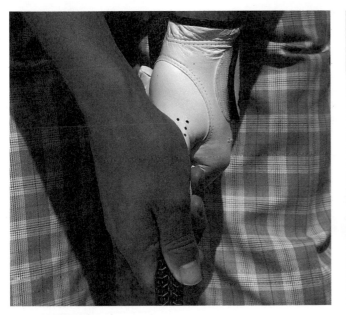

WEAKENED GRIP
Place your left hand as normal on the club then regrip by sliding it around into a weaker position. Now you should see only one knuckle at the most. For a really delicate chip it's best not to see any at all. Grip normally with your right hand.

DOWNHILL STANCE
Lean with the downslope by putting more weight than usual on your left side. Though you place the ball forward in your stance for a lob off a level lie, you need to position it centrally on a downslope to help avoid the thin.

WRISTY BACKSWING
Pick up the club quite quickly with a good deal of wrist to avoid clipping the ground behind the ball. But a steepish backswing is also needed for a wristy downswing, which in turn helps you to hit the ball high. How far back you swing determines the length of shot, and only experience can ingrain this feel into your mind.

LEFT HAND CONTROL
Swing down into impact leading with the left hand and working the wrists. This ensures you attack the ball on a steep enough angle to avoid hitting behind it, but you are still able to slide your blade underneath it. Make sure you keep your body steady to lessen the chance of a miss-hit.

OPEN LOB
Because your left hand is weak and tends naturally to return square at impact, the blade is slightly open and has almost maximum loft as you strike the ball. But this doesn't mean the ball flies off right of target. Because your clubface is so lofted the ball pops up with little sideways movement. It flies straight at the target along the line of your swing path.

HOLDING SQUARE
Hold your wrists firm through the ball. This action combined with your weak left hand stops the blade from closing. Though the clubhead is well through impact the blade is still square and faces skywards. This eliminates the risk of the clubhead turning over and you losing control of the ball.

CONTROLLED LOB
This controlled finish is the product of a firm, confident swing, but one that lofts the ball out very delicately. Keeping the wrists out of the throughswing stops you from flicking at the ball. If you continue through impact with the same wristy moves as your downswing you can easily thin the ball.

Seve's sensational touch

Many fellow pros and golfing pundits jokingly say that Seve Ballesteros should be made an honorary member of the Magic Circle. He is able to conjure up strokes of genius at will, often ones of incredible delicacy.

The Ryder Cup seems to bring the best out of the Spaniard, and those privileged enough to see the 1989 matches saw a glittering performance from him. He played several unreal shots but one chip stood out.

In the second day Seve – partnered by Olazabal – put in a body blow of a stroke at the 10th. He went for the short par 4 green with his tee shot but failed – only narrowly – to make the putting surface. Instead he found the banking to the back right of the green. To get at the flag, Ballesteros had to play an amazingly dainty shot from a downslope over a bunker – so there was no margin for error. Pitching one too short would either find sand or bounce forward off the downslope. To knock it close Seve had to play a high, gentle, soft-landing lob that pitched just beyond the fringe.

Seve being Seve, the ball floated onto the green and rolled out to the flag stopping an inch away from an eagle. But the birdie was good enough to win the hole and go 4 up on Mark Calcavecchia and Ken Green. His master stroke helped him and José-Maria notch up another famous victory, by 4 and 2, and add a vital point to the European team score, which proved to be just enough to hang on to the cup. The final score was 14 all.

Short and long pitch

Approach shots draw gasps of admiration – often tinged with a touch of envy – from the galleries at professional tournaments. Frequently finishing close and sometimes dropping in, the ball seems to have a magical attraction to the hole.

Take heart – any golfer can hit a good approach shot. You don't need bulging forearms, you don't have to possess awesome talent – you just need to have a grasp of the fundamentals. You then have a technique that you can apply to a variety of situations from 100yd (90m) and in.

The short pitch from around 50yd (45m) – often played over some form of hazard – is a shot that frightens many golfers into making a mistake. You need maximum height and minimum roll – there's potentially quite a lot that can go wrong.

Unfortunately it's one of those

CONFIDENCE AND CONTROL
From 100yd (90m) and in, you should find the green every time, get the ball close sometimes and miss the target altogether very rarely. Success from this range hinges a great deal on confidence. However, equally important is control – you must never hit an approach shot flat out. Call on the services of your 9 iron or pitching wedge, grip down the club slightly and make a three-quarter swing.

DOWNHILL APPROACH

WHICH SHOT?
When the fairway slopes downhill to the green and there are no obstacles in the way, you're in the pleasing situation of having a choice of shots. Try to think of a hole on a course you know where the contours are similar, and imagine you're just under 100yd (90m) from the hole. Probably the best shot – and certainly the most consistent – is a low flying, three-quarter stroke with a 9 iron. This controlled shot helps you find the correct line, judge weight accurately, and lets the natural lie of the land sweep your ball down towards the hole.

1 NO FRILLS TECHNIQUE
Golf is such a precise game that you should take every opportunity to keep your technique simple. There are situations when you need to be creative, but there's no call for heroics on this shot. A straightforward address position offers you a technique that is least likely to go wrong – feet, hips and shoulders square to the target with the ball central in your stance.

KEY POINT:
Distribute your weight equally on both feet.

2 EASY BACKSWING
You don't want too many moving parts in your swing here – play a hands and arms shot. Concentrate on a one piece takeaway and keep the club low to the ground. Never pick the club up quickly – you create too steep an arc and are likely to make a poor shoulder turn.

KEY POINT:
Keep it smooth.

③ CUT DOWN BACKSWING
For a full shot this backswing would be far too short for comfort. In this instance it's the perfect position. Your knees should be comfortably flexed and your shoulders almost fully turned. A little more than half your weight is now on the right side.

KEY POINT:
The left wrist should be firm and in control of the club.

④ CONSISTENT TEMPO
The most important point to remember at the top of the backswing is that you maintain the same tempo on the way down. Whatever you do don't rush it – this is a major cause of miss-hit shots.

KEY POINT:
Feel the back of your left hand guiding the clubhead.

⑤ LEFT SIDE IN CHARGE
Make sure your left wrist is firm through the ball. This ensures that the clubface remains square both into and after impact. A front view provides a good example of how you should retain your height throughout the swing. The head is at exactly the same level now as at address – there's no lifting or dipping at any time.

KEY POINT:
Most of your weight should be on the left foot at impact.

⑥ BALANCE PRACTICE
The hard work has already been done, but don't be lazy on the followthrough. Concentrate on key points such as good balance and a comfortable followthrough position. This helps improve your overall tempo during the swing.

KEY POINT:
Your upper body faces the target on the followthrough.

ON THE WATERFRONT

1 FLY THE FLAG
With water guarding the front the trouble is all too apparent. The mental fear rather than any degree of difficulty is the downfall of some club golfers. However, from only 60yd (55m), a shot at the flag can make you a contender – if you have the technique you can play a very attacking and satisfying stroke.

KEY POINT:
Grip down the club to enhance control.

2 OPEN FOR COMFORT
A slightly open stance is a good idea when you play this shot – your sand wedge is the ideal club. Both combine to produce a higher, more floating trajectory than you would normally wish for. Take the club back along the line of your body and break your wrists earlier than normal – this creates a slightly steeper swing arc which is essential when you play any shot from rough.

KEY POINT:
Keep your right elbow tucked in close to your side.

3 SHOULDER TURN
Even on a relatively short shot you need to be certain of making a good shoulder turn – although not quite as full as you would with a driver in your hands. You may be tired of being told to turn your shoulders, but if you don't, you can guarantee the club is way outside the line and on too steep an arc – it's impossible to hit a good shot from there.

KEY POINT:
Point your left knee in towards the ball.

4 UP AND DOWN
A view down the line gives a good indication of how the club should remain on a consistent plane throughout the swing. Note that the hands are in a similar position halfway through the downswing compared to halfway through the backswing. The angle of the club must be different though – almost lagging behind in a position known as a late hit.

KEY POINT:
Keep your head behind the ball – don't lunge forward.

5 STRIKE DOWN
You need lots of height on this shot, so remember to strike down firmly into the bottom of the ball. Compared with the full swing the legs are quite passive. However, they still have a role to play – drive your knees forward through impact to help move your weight on to the left foot. This promotes a sharp downward blow.

KEY POINT:
Keep your hands ahead of the clubhead at all times.

6 DANGEROUS FLOATER
The action of the clubhead sliding through the grass under the ball gives this shot the high, floating trajectory you desperately need. Practice it often – this is a shot that can help you threaten the flag in a host of potentially dangerous situations, such as flying over a hazard.

KEY POINT:
Push the back of your left hand through to the target for as long as possible on the followthrough.

shots that can ruin your score if you play it badly, so you must have the ability to get it right – at least to the extent that your worst pitch finishes very close to the putting surface.

Your sand wedge is the ideal weapon from most lies. Don't make drastic alterations to your technique. Simply open your stance slightly and position the ball further back than normal to ensure a downward blow and crisp contact.

The one exception to this rule is when your ball rests on hardpan. You need a club with a sharper leading edge – such as an 8 or 9 iron – to nip it cleanly off the surface. A sand wedge tends to bounce off hard ground.

PINPOINT ACCURACY

As you move a little further away from the pin, it doesn't necessarily become harder to pitch your ball close.

Professionals probably hit as many shots near to the flag from 100yd (90m) as they do from half that distance. There's no reason why you shouldn't either – although don't expect such a high level of accuracy.

The first point to remember is that it doesn't matter what club you use, as long as the end result is good. This means placing the emphasis on control. There's nothing impressive about bashing a sand wedge to 20ft (6m), if you can knock the ball closer with a comfortable 9 iron.

There are several factors that dictate the type of shot you should play. In calm conditions on a plain, featureless hole you have a wide choice of strokes open to you. In general though, never feel you're using anything more than a three-quarter swing.

FAVORED FLIGHT

It's easy to misjudge a pitch into a green that slopes uphill from front to back. Coming up short is usually the problem for most golfers. Keep backspin out of the shot – it doesn't favor you from this position.

The best policy is to take a less lofted club than usual so that the ball naturally has a bit of run on landing. Pitch it short, but still on the putting surface, and let the ball do the rest. This is your best chance of finishing close to the hole.

Try to avoid playing a high, floating shot in this situation. It demands a very precise stroke to finish close. If you pitch your ball only fractionally short, it's likely to come to an abrupt halt.

If the upslope is severe you may even spin the ball back towards you – particularly if the greens are soft and receptive. This is a disappointing result from a not particularly poor shot.

However, a high trajectory shot is ideal if the green slopes away from you. If you have a good lie you should be able to land the ball softly on the front of the putting surface and allow the slope to carry it gently down towards the hole.

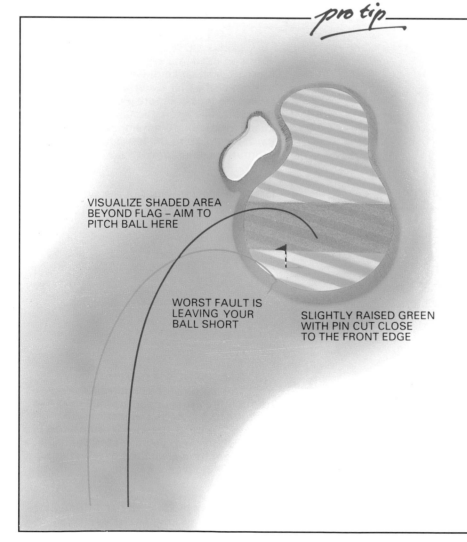

pro tip

VISUALIZE SHADED AREA BEYOND FLAG – AIM TO PITCH BALL HERE

WORST FAULT IS LEAVING YOUR BALL SHORT

SLIGHTLY RAISED GREEN WITH PIN CUT CLOSE TO THE FRONT EDGE

Percentage pitch
When you're playing well and feeling confident, anywhere under 100yd (90m) can seem like an open invitation to attack the pin. But there are times when it's best to play the percentage pitch.

Raised greens look simple enough and certainly don't inject the same amount of fear as a deep bunker. However, they're cleverly designed, making approach shots deceptively hard. You need to be careful if there are any raised greens on your course.

With the flag positioned close to the front of the green, it's a potentially dangerous situation. Visualize a shaded area just beyond the pin – this is where you should pitch your ball.

Fire too strongly and you finish at the back of the green – play the shot a little too tentatively and you should still find the putting surface. Either way you have a putt rather than a chip for your next shot.

The worst fault is leaving your ball short because you then have to negotiate the slope a second time with your next shot. This is the heavy price you pay for being too impetuous.

Chipping drills

At the end of the round it's the numbers at the bottom of your card that matter. If you want to score well your short game has to be in good shape. There are no prizes for hitting the ball brilliantly if your total doesn't match your striking ability on the day.

No golfer becomes a good chipper overnight, so take every opportunity to practice this part of your game – your short shots become sharper as a result.

As with all practice, it has to be constructive if you're to reap the full benefits from your efforts. There are probably more practice drills for chipping than any other aspect of golf, so it tends to be more enjoyable. The other advantage is you don't need a great deal of space to chip a few golf balls.

You may also have the boost of holing an occasional chip, which gives you lots of encouragement and spurs you on to hole even more. This form of practice has the psychological edge over hitting full shots – how often do you hole out from 150yd (135m)?

DEVELOPING DRILLS

The purpose of any chipping drill is to discover for yourself which shots work best for you. But there's always a lot to learn from the masters – both in technique and how to visualize each shot.

Tom Watson is a great believer in playing chip shots with as little backspin as possible. He feels that it's easier to roll the ball smoothly and judge pace when there's very little spin on the ball. Only when it's absolutely necessary does Tom aim to stop the ball quickly – for example when there's not much green to work with.

WIDE REPERTOIRE
The best way to learn about shots from close range is to regularly spend time around the practice green. Experiment with different clubs and play a variety of strokes. If you have more than one shot up your sleeve your options are never limited. Whatever the situation, keep your hands ahead of the ball at address and accelerate the clubhead into impact.

MAKE THE CORRECT CHOICE

LEAVE THE FLAG IN...
Every golfer aims to hole greenside chips. While you can't achieve this every time, you can increase the number of shots that finish close by leaving the flag in. This encourages you to be more aggressive on the stroke – you know that even if you hit the ball a little too hard, there's always the possibility of it hitting the flag and occasionally dropping in. This is particularly helpful for downhill chips where the ball often gathers speed towards the hole. Even at pace the ball seldom rebounds too far away, which means your putt is a short one.

...TAKE THE FLAG OUT
If you remove the flag when you chip, you have to judge weight very precisely. In the back of your mind you know the pace has to be spot on for the ball to stand any chance of going in. If you hit the chip too hard there's nothing to stop it – not even the back of the hole – and you're likely to be left with a long putt. You may also find that you leave a lot of chips short. Knowing the ball needs to be rolling gently if it's to drop prompts you to be tentative – which must be the furthest thought from your mind.

There's usually more than one way to play a shot from around the green – club selection is just as important as execution.

For every chip there are two targets you should consider – a precise landing area and the flag. The most accurate way to judge the weight of any chip is first to decide where you want to land the ball and then predict the roll. Don't make the mistake of concentrating *only* on the hole.

Select a hole on the practice green and play shots with a variety of clubs from the same spot. You quickly learn which club is best suited to the shot. You also find out which clubs make it hardest for you to chip the ball close.

An effective way to recreate an on course situation is to play shots to a variety of holes, all from the same spot. There are no second chances in a round of golf, so give yourself only one ball for each chip. This tests your ability to judge line and length at the first attempt. It's also a useful yardstick to assess the development of your touch and feel.

Another productive form of practice is to take a selection of

FLAG LEFT IN – PLAY AN
ATTACKING CHIP AT THE HOLE

BALL STOPPED BY FLAG – MAY DROP IN

CHIP SHOT HIT TOO FIRMLY – BALL
RUNS OVER HOLE

FLAG REMOVED

Playing for a price

One of the great advantages of golf is that you can practice on your own. But every now and then you need someone else around to help build a competitive edge into your game.

Chipping provides the perfect opportunity to bet with your friends. Playing for lunch or the first round of drinks is usually just the sort of incentive you need. The stakes aren't high, but no one likes losing.

Select nine different shots to play from around the practice green. The simplest game is playing closest to the hole – keep score as in a matchplay competition. Alternatively, treat each hole as a par 2 and play a mini strokeplay event with just your wedge and a putter.

clubs and a bag of balls and aim to pitch each shot on exactly the same spot. Place a tee peg where you intend landing the ball so you don't lose sight of your objective.

Pay close attention to the differences between each shot – the height generated by each club, the amount of spin on the ball and how far it rolls on landing. This quickly develops your knowledge of chipping and makes it easier to visualize shots when you're on the course.

KEEP IT COMPETITIVE

Even if you're on your own, try to be as competitive as possible in your practice and always set yourself goals. If hitting balls is aimless, you're unlikely to see much of an improvement in your short gamo – you soon become bored with practicing too.

Treat every chip as a potential matchwinner so that you put pressure on yourself to perform well every time.

Imagine you need to get up and down in two to win the most important competition at your home club. When it comes to the real thing you can look back on the hundreds of times you've been in that situation before – and played a good shot.

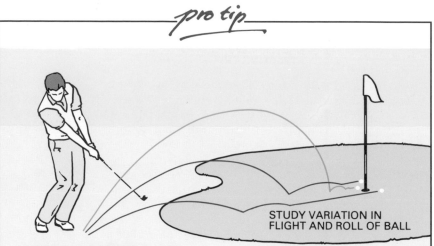

pro tip

CHIP WITH DIFFERENT CLUBS FROM THE SAME SPOT

STUDY VARIATION IN FLIGHT AND ROLL OF BALL

Choosing the right club

There's more than one way to play a chip shot. When you practice, take a dozen golf balls and play shots to the same hole with a variety of clubs. Only through a process of trial – and an occasional error – do you discover which shots give you the greatest success rate.

The higher the shot the less run there is on landing. This is ideal for floating the ball over trouble and is best played with a sand wedge. However, it's one of the more difficult strokes to play, so avoid the high chip unless you have no option.

Lower shots generate more run on the ball and are perfect when there's no trouble between you and the flag. Ideally, you want the ball running at the hole as smoothly as one of your finest putts. Any club from a 5 iron to an 8 iron gives you enough loft to clear the fringe with very little backspin, promoting roll.

Straight up

When you're just off the edge of the green, check that the flag is standing perfectly vertical in its hole. This makes sure there's a big enough gap for the ball to drop in.

If the flag is leaning slightly towards you it can prevent your ball going in. The rules allow you to straighten the flag so that you're fully rewarded if you play a good shot. But don't be greedy – you're not allowed to deliberately lean the flag away from you.

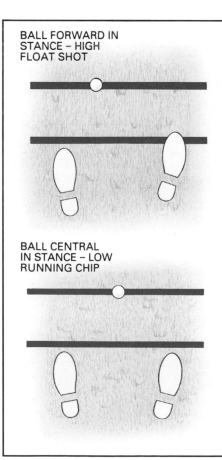

BALL FORWARD IN STANCE – HIGH FLOAT SHOT

BALL CENTRAL IN STANCE – LOW RUNNING CHIP

Altering ball position

Your stance and ball position have just as much bearing on a chip as the club you use. Subtle alterations to both enable you to vary your shots without changing your club.

If you want to float the ball high and stop it quickly, open your stance and position the ball just opposite your inside left heel. You can use your normal bunker shot technique to slide the clubhead under the ball, slightly out-to-in.

Playing the ball further back in your stance lets you use the same club to hit a lower shot. This is particularly helpful if the ball is sitting down in light rough.

Make sure the clubface is square to the target – this delofts the club and contributes to the lower trajectory of the shot. Break your wrists early on the backswing and strike down firmly with your hands leading into impact.

The low sand wedge

When faced with a pitch shot of 60-80yd (55-73m), it's an advantage to be able to play the ball either high or low. The loft on a sand wedge automatically sends the ball high if the shot is hit properly. But there are times when it's better to play low.

PLAYING A LOW BALL

The low ball is particularly useful when playing into the wind. By moving the ball back in your stance and keeping your hands ahead of the clubhead, you can produce a shot that bores decisively through the wind.

A lower shot is also effective when the ball is lying on a hard, bare surface. This is common on a links course. It's difficult to play a normal high pitch shot when there is no grass under the ball. If the shot isn't played to perfection, the clubhead tends to bounce into

HITTING THE LOW PITCH
Use the low sand wedge for playing into the wind or from a bare lie. You take the loft out of the shot by positioning the ball opposite your right heel at address, and by pushing your hands ahead of the clubhead. Align your body as normal, and grip the club about 1in (2.5cm) from the top. The clubface should be square to the target. For a normal pitch, the ball is central in your stance. In both cases you distribute your weight as normal.

BALL POSITION – LOW PITCH

BALL POSITION – NORMAL PITCH

PLAYING THE LOW PITCH

NORMAL PITCH

① THE TAKEAWAY
For the low sand wedge, your backswing should be a lot shorter than for a normal high shot. There is also very little wrist break. The stroke requires a firm left wrist throughout the shot. Compare this to the backswing for the normal sand wedge, and you'll notice that the club goes past the vertical, and the wrists have broken.

② THE DOWNSWING
Keep your wrists firm and lead the shot with your left arm – unlike the normal pitch where you use your hands conventionally and release into the ball. The main difference between the downswings of the two shots is the relative positions of the club and the hands. Even though your hands are in the same place, the clubhead positions are different.

③ THE STRIKE
Notice that the hands are once again in the same place, but the clubhead positions are different. You must keep the clubhead behind your hands during the stroke – unlike the normal shot – and resist the temptation to scoop up the ball. Try to strike the ball fractionally before the ground, nipping it off the turf. This creates the backspin.

④ THE FOLLOWTHROUGH
Keep your wrists and arms firm to ensure that your followthrough is short. The feeling of firmness throughout the stroke automatically reduces the loft of your sand wedge, and keeps the ball low. A full followthrough and conventional use of the hands send the ball high. Transfer your weight from the right side to the left during the stroke.

Playing into the wind

Because the natural loft of a sand wedge sends the ball high, it can be difficult to control into a wind. The danger of playing the shot normally is that the ball balloons up in the air and lands short of the target.

The low sand wedge lessens the effect of the wind. The ball pierces the wind, bounces short of the flag and hops up to the hole before biting. The technique for hitting the low wedge naturally creates a lot of backspin, helping you to control the ball.

Even though the ball flies low and looks as if it will go through the back of the green, the effect of the wind and the backspin stops the ball quickly.

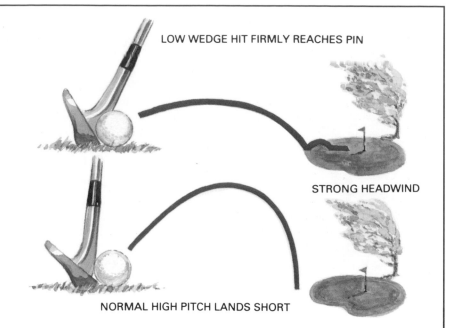

LOW WEDGE HIT FIRMLY REACHES PIN

STRONG HEADWIND

NORMAL HIGH PITCH LANDS SHORT

the ball, resulting in a thinned shot. But the technique you use in hitting the ball low prevents this happening.

CONTROLLED ATTACK

One big advantage is that the shot creates more backspin than normal, giving you greater control. The more control you have, the more aggressive you can be. The shot should be played boldly, and you must never quit on the ball. Failure to attack the ball results in a duffed shot.

When you play the stroke properly, you can be confident of the ball bouncing once and then biting. To onlookers, the shot may seem at first to be a miss-hit. They may feel that the ball is going to fly through the green. It is only when they see the ball checking on the green that they appreciate the shot. This stroke usually causes gasps from the crowd at a big tournament.

Because the shot is played low the ball doesn't stop immediately. You must try to pitch the ball short of the flag, and let it run up to the hole. The distance the ball pitches from the hole varies in different conditions.

If the green slopes towards you or is wet, the ball stops more quickly than normal. Aim to hit the ball further up to the hole. When the green slopes away or is hard, the first bounce should be well short of the flag, allowing the ball to roll up to the hole.

masterclass

Eamonn Darcy: skilful pitcher

The Irish Ryder Cup player is well known for his prowess near the green. From around 75yd (68m) he is very accurate, and he always gives himself a chance to get up and down in 2.

Darcy naturally hits the ball low, and his slightly stiff style means he is perfectly suited to playing this shot. His flair with the low wedge helped him to second place in the 1989 English Open at The Belfry.

Pitch with Rafferty

After a short but glittering amateur career, Ronan Rafferty has become one of Europe's leading professionals. A legacy from his unpaid days has held him in good stead ever since – an almost magical touch with the wedge.

To play at such a high level at so tender an age – Ronan was only 17 when he played in the Walker Cup – his short game had to be razor sharp to make up for his lack of length. Rafferty fine tuned his pitching, and from 50-90yd (45-80m) the Irishman is now one of the best on the Euro Tour.

Though Ronan has an individual style – quite a lot of hands and arms with a restricted leg action – you can learn lessons from his method.

His prowess stems from a superb rhythm. His swing is long, smooth and deliberate, but firm and controlled. Rafferty relies on his excellent timing and on the natural loft of the club to do the work – he never forces the shot.

CLEAN STRIKE

Unlike many of his fellow pros, Ronan's stock long range pitch takes little turf after striking the ball. He nips the ball off the fairway – a natural action, as the Irishman grew up on firm seaside fairways.

This clean, crisp striking method creates much backspin which heightens his control – even on the firmest of greens. But he does not hesitate to take turf if he needs to – perhaps for a punched pitch or out of light rough.

Rafferty stands fractionally open for every pitch. He feels that it helps him to keep the blade square to the target through impact, and he can resist releasing his hands too soon. This aspect of his method is one to copy – it improves your accuracy. Control the swing with your left hand, and guide the club with your right.

KEEP IT SMOOTH

Whatever type of pitch you play, try to keep balanced and steady. Excessive body movement and a snatchy action can only lead to a duffed shot. If you're too eager to watch the ball and come off the shot, it's easy to hit a thin. Trying to force a wedge can lead to a heavy shot.

Follow Ronan – stay still throughout the stroke and concentrate on a free flowing swing. Never attack the ball too aggressively – keep the rhythm the same for all lengths of shot. Simply vary the length of your backswing to judge the distance and use the same even tempo.

RONAN'S RISE TO THE TOP
Ronan Rafferty at last realized his full potential in 1989. Three tournament victories and several top ten finishes – including a 2nd place at the Dunhill British Masters at Woburn – helped him to grasp the No. 1 spot on the Order of Merit. He has an excellent all-round game with seemingly no weaknesses, but his strengths are definitely headed by his short game. Learn from Ronan's technique – you can add control and consistency to your short game by following his rhythmical action.

THREE-QUARTER LENGTH PITCH

① COMFORTABLE STANCE
Ronan is very relaxed at address. His arms hang freely with no hint of tension. Though his shoulders are parallel to the target line, his feet are slightly open to encourage a free throughswing with a square blade.

② TAKEAWAY
Rafferty looks a little unorthodox on the takeaway. He picks the club up with less wrist than normal so the blade is slightly hooded. This mostly hands and arms action gives him the feeling of control – something you must cultivate for confident wedge play.

③ CONTROLLED BACK
His backswing is shorter than normal to help his control – a too full backswing makes it harder to coordinate the downswing. Though Ronan stops well short of the top his shoulder turn is still full, but he has curbed any excessive movement of his legs.

④ EVEN TEMPO DOWNSWING
He swings down very smoothly with no hint of real force, trying to keep his rhythm in tempo with the backswing. Notice how his head has stayed perfectly still throughout the swing, his shoulders have returned square at impact and the left hand controls the strike – all keys to sweet, straight hitting.

⑤ RESIST RELEASE
Though Ronan is well through impact his hands have not yet released. He has resisted the right hand crossing over the left. This keeps the blade square to the target for as long as possible – a definite aid to accuracy and control.

⑥ SHORT AND CONTROLLED
Because Rafferty has controlled the shot with his left hand through impact, his finish is naturally shorter than normal. Even though his leg movement is more restricted than most players he still uses them enough to finish facing the target in a balanced position. Never stunt your followthrough – it leads to weak, off-line hitting.

Chipping up a two-tier green

S plit level greens have bamboozled golfers all over the world ever since they were introduced early this century by the famed course architect Alister Mackenzie. Time after time amateurs fail to get up and down when chipping up a tier. It's usually because of a poor choice of shot.

The players who struggle most are those who just look at the distance and hit their usual style of chip. You mustn't ignore the slope however small the rise – even a gentle bank can affect the ball dramatically.

If you hit the wrong type of shot you might have to putt up and over the bank again with your next. If you overshoot you could be faced with a tricky chip back – just a slight misjudgment and the ball could careen away back down the slope.

Understanding the correct club and shot selections means you can tackle the chip with confidence and avoid big scores.

DOUBLE OPTIONS

For the best chance of holing your putt you must make sure your chip finishes on the top level. The percentage shot is to play a straighter faced club – perhaps a 7 or 8 iron – and run the ball up the slope. The ball has more forward momentum than a high chip and so lessens the risk of the ball failing to reach the upper level.

STEP BY STEP
Practice and good visualization are the keys to understanding how to play up a two-tier green. You must know how certain shots behave if you want to overcome the slope. Try to imagine the path of the ball before you play a chip and run shot – it helps you gauge the pace. Always attack the shot confidently, as trying to be too cute can lead to disaster. Make sure that the ball reaches your target – 6ft (2m) past the hole is better than one that doesn't make the rise and rolls back towards you.

RUNNING CHIP

The low chip and run is easy to play and is the safest shot to combat a two-tier green. The risk of not reaching the upper level is lessened by a rolling ball which has momentum to climb the bank.

This type of shot is perfect for playing to a flag cut quite close to the step or downwind. Even if you have room to land a high wedge on the top tier, the ball may not stop because of the wind.

You can play the shot with anything from a 5 to a 9 iron. Your choice depends on the length of shot and how steep the bank is.

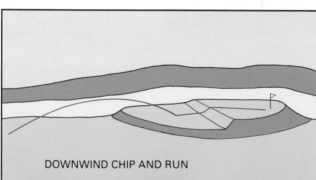

DOWNWIND CHIP AND RUN

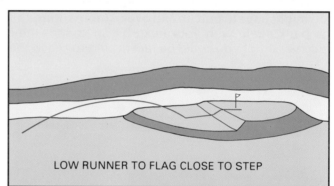

LOW RUNNER TO FLAG CLOSE TO STEP

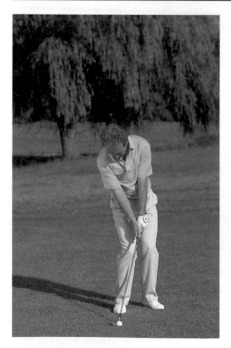

① PLACED BACK
Grip down the club and push your hands forward. Position the ball back in your stance to ensure a good strike.

② FIRM AND SHORT
Play the shot with a firm wristed action, and keep the backswing short. Lead the downswing with your left hand.

③ ABRUPT FINISH
Keep your hands ahead of the clubhead at impact, and stop short on the followthrough to help the ball stay low.

HIGH FLOATER

It's only wise to play the high lob when there is plenty of room on the top tier – so there's little danger of pitching on the bank – or if you're going into a strong wind.

The high chip floats on the wind and lands softly. You can afford to pitch the ball right up to the flag and be sure that it stops quickly. But if the green is firm, aim to land the ball short of the hole as it runs a little.

When the flag is positioned close to the edge, it's still probably best to play the chip and run even in a strong wind.

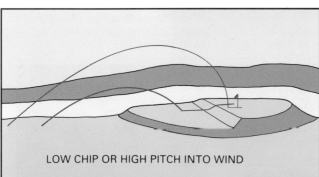

LOW CHIP OR HIGH PITCH INTO WIND

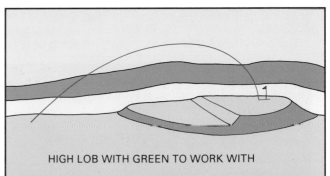

HIGH LOB WITH GREEN TO WORK WITH

1 WEDGE ADDRESS
Position the ball forward of center in the stance and square the blade. This creates extra loft which helps you to hit the ball high and soft.

2 WRISTY BACK
Take the club back smoothly with plenty of wrist break. The length of your backswing depends on how far you need to hit the ball.

3 FULL FINISH
Use your wrists on the downswing but don't flick at the ball – let the club do the work. Follow through fully – don't quit.

The chip and run shot is especially useful when the flag is just above the step or downwind. Trying to float a high chip up to the flag is dangerous and needs exceptional feel and some luck to hit the ball close.

TRY A HIGH ONE

If you don't quite judge it correctly the ball can easily pitch on the step and roll backwards or bound on through the green.

But there is scope to play the high, soft-landing chip. If the wind is against you or the flag is well on the top tier, you can afford to attack the flag and pitch the ball right up to the hole. The ball should sit down quickly.

CLEVER USE OF SLOPE

On the rare occasion that neither type of shot is called for – perhaps when the flag is cut just above a steep slope – you could use a combination of the two techniques. Using a lofted club, play a low shot off the back foot into the bank. The ball is slowed down quickly by the bump off the slope, so that it just creeps over onto the upper tier.

Playing a running shot up a steep slope makes it hard to judge the pace. But the bump shot doesn't completely eliminate the danger of the ball rolling back down the bank or overshooting.

You must hit this type of shot precisely for it to come off. It's a highly specialized stroke so you must practice it hard if you're to perfect the technique.

CAREFUL CONFIDENCE

Whichever shot you decide to play, you have to approach the stroke confidently. Careful thought and a weighing up of the slope are essential in deciding which shot to play and how hard to hit it.

Prepare yourself
With careful preparation and a good touch, chipping up split level greens shouldn't cause you too many problems. But beware, a mistake in club selection can cost you dearly, and even the greats of golf sometimes make that error.

The notorious 3rd green at Wentworth in England has caught out many amateurs and pros over the years. Once a two-tier green with a huge step, it now has three tiers, but is still tricky. Sandy Lyle shows how difficult it is to chip up this green by trying to fly the ball to the top level where the flag is.

Instead of playing a straight faced club and running the ball, Sandy chose a wedge. He makes a slight misjudgment and the ball fails to make it up the slope. If you're in two minds whether to pitch or hit a running chip, choose to run the ball. It is the safer shot and is more likely to reach the top tier.

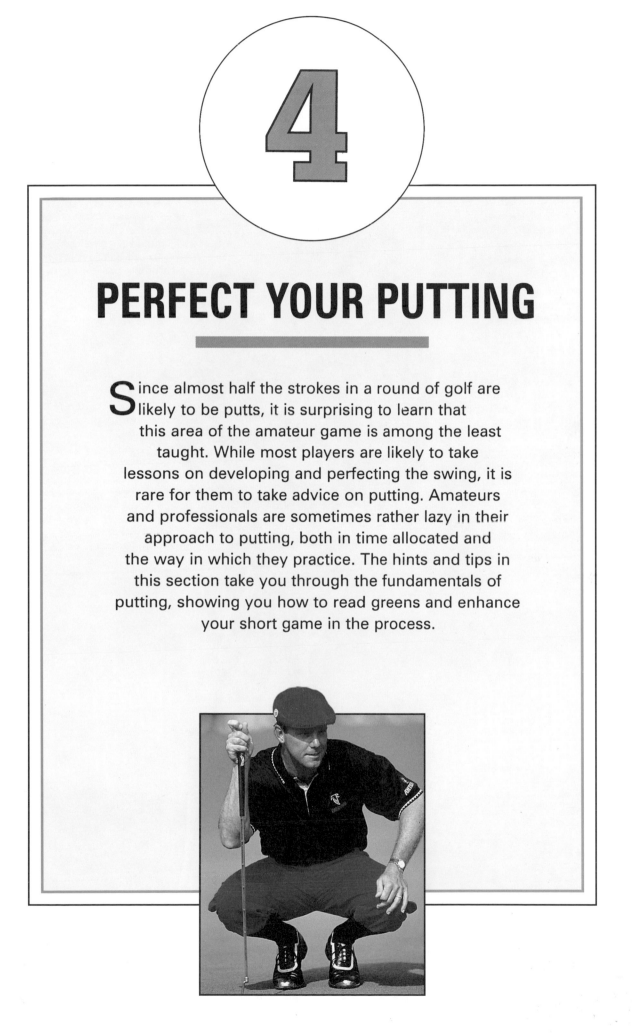

PERFECT YOUR PUTTING

S ince almost half the strokes in a round of golf are
likely to be putts, it is surprising to learn that
this area of the amateur game is among the least
taught. While most players are likely to take
lessons on developing and perfecting the swing, it is
rare for them to take advice on putting. Amateurs
and professionals are sometimes rather lazy in their
approach to putting, both in time allocated and
the way in which they practice. The hints and tips in
this section take you through the fundamentals of
putting, showing you how to read greens and enhance
your short game in the process.

Avoid green tension

Of all the strokes in golf, holing a putt just when you really need to gives you the greatest psychological lift. You know you can do it, but pressure has a nasty habit of undermining every golfer's technique at some time or other – no matter how good or confident the player happens to be.

If you can stay relaxed on the greens in a competition, your putting stroke remains with you all the way to the 18th hole of the match. Avoiding green tension is the key to putting well under pressure.

Cast your mind back to a couple of your best competition rounds – your putting was probably on song. On days like this – when the hole looks like a bucket – the putts

HOLING OUT UNDER PRESSURE

There are many ways to avoid tension on the greens – it's essential you have a system that works for you. If you can stay relaxed on the greens your putting is more likely to stand up to the most intense pressure. Whether it's a shortish putt on the 18th to secure a good score, or a curling left to righter to win a match, you can be confident of knocking it in.

SMOOTH STROKE

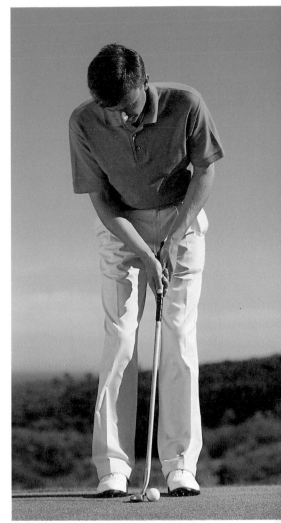

STRAIGHT AND NARROW

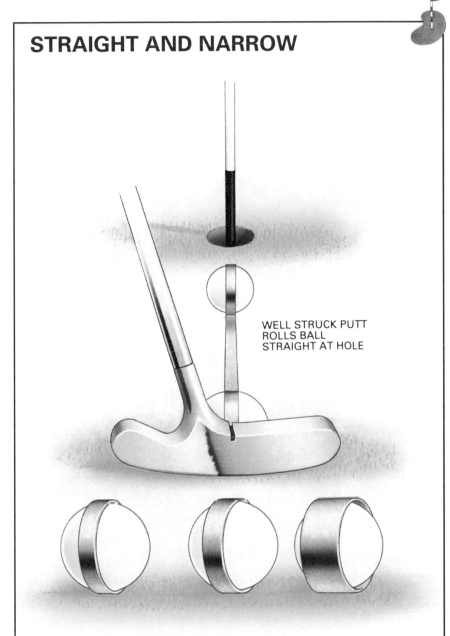

WELL STRUCK PUTT
ROLLS BALL
STRAIGHT AT HOLE

RAISED RIDGES VARY IN WIDTH
AROUND EACH BALL

The perfect putting stroke strikes the ball slightly upwards with the putter face square to the intended line – the result is a smooth roll on the ball.

A set of three golf balls is manufactured, each with a raised ridge around its circumference. The idea is to set each ball rolling perfectly straight without it toppling over to one side – achieve this and you know a putt is correctly hit.

Start practicing with the ball that has the widest ridge – this is the easiest of the three and gives you some early confidence. As you become more proficient move on to the next ball with a narrower ridge. If you perform this exercise successfully with the final ball, you can be confident that your putting stroke is in pretty good shape.

If you can't find these golf balls at a pro shop near you, paint a stripe around one of your practice balls. Take a putt with the stripe aiming straight at the hole. If it continues to point along the same line for its entire journey, you've struck the ball squarely and correctly.

Any sidespin – the ruin of every missed putt – is unmistakable as the stripe becomes more of a blur than a straight line.

① RELAXED OVER THE BALL
Staying relaxed at address is one of the keys to success over a long putt. Position the ball opposite your left heel – this helps you to stroke the ball slightly on the up to give it overspin. Your hands should be at least level with the ball – ahead is fine but behind is potentially disastrous.

pro tip

Shake to relax
Making sure your muscles are free from tension is essential when you're on the green. Relaxation promotes feel and touch – two vital qualities to good putting. If you struggle to achieve this, a simple exercise might solve the problem.

Before you address the ball, rest your putter against your leg and allow your arms to hang down freely. Loosely shake your hands a couple of times to relieve any muscle tightness – when it comes to standing over the ball you should be nicely relaxed.

② SMOOTHLY BACK
Maintaining a light grip, sweep the putter back low away from the ball. Make sure the triangle formed by your shoulders and arms remains the same as at address. For a putt of this length try to keep your wrists firm. If you allow them to hinge it's easy to lose control of the putter head – this upsets the angle of the clubface at a critical moment during the stroke.

③ DOWN AND THROUGH
Accelerate the putter smoothly into impact – the ball position at address ensures the clubhead travels up and generates overspin to set the ball rolling. If you hit down on a putt the ball usually hops into the air, making it extremely difficult to judge pace. Keep your left wrist firm to ensure your hands are in front of the putter head for as long as possible.

tend to drop at crucial stages in the round. This is the difference between a potentially winning score and an average one.

Because you have to be more precise on the greens than elsewhere on the course, tension is disastrous. It destroys the most important ingredient of any putting stroke – feel.

Your putter starts to behave erratically as you struggle to control the line and length of even the simplest of putts. You're in for a frustrating time as the ball keeps slipping past the hole.

TENSION TRIGGERS

There are several causes of ten-sion on the greens. On a **good round** in a competition there are many pressures on you to keep your score intact. Probably the greatest of these is remaining solid when it comes to the business of holing out.

When your **confidence is low** it's easy to imagine the hole is almost shrinking before your eyes – knocking in a putt of any real distance can seem like the hardest task in the world.

This doubt often stems from missing a short putt or two early in the round – your confidence has taken a battering.

The golfing muscles can also tighten at the prospect of a **difficult putt**. Every golfer has a ten-sion trigger – the one that breaks from left to right is the most commonly disliked.

Perhaps you find that putts from one particular range are the stuff that nightmares are made of. And a downhill putt on a slippery green is a real test of nerve, even for the professionals.

Whatever green experience triggers tension for you, don't be reconciled to disaster. Rather than expecting the worst, set out to break your run of missed putts.

Even if you've never felt the slightest bit nervous over a putt – which is unlikely – certain techniques promote a reliable putting stroke when it really matters. Striking your putt within a well rehearsed groove makes all the difference.

The hands play a vital role in the putting stroke, so first examine your grip. Do you feel in control of the clubhead? There's no right or wrong way to hold a putter – styles depend on individual taste and preference.

If you're a wristy putter – rather in the style of Gary Player – always grip the club lightly in both hands. The same applies if – like Tom Watson for instance – you're a shoulders and arms putter. Never grip the club too tightly – it restricts your feel for the clubhead, making assessment of weight tricky.

GRIP PRESSURE

Check your grip pressure is the same throughout the stroke. A consistently light grip helps you to make a smooth stroke and accurately judge the weight of a putt – it also reduces the risk of the putter face opening or closing.

To achieve success on the greens you need a sound putting stroke. Though you can copy certain fundamentals from the professionals, there should always be a personal touch to your putting if you're to be comfortable.

Only if a style is your own can you feel truly comfortable over the ball. A natural stance is a real tension beater – if there's a key to holing more putts, this is it. Sticking rigidly to one particular technique can hold back your putting.

PALMS FACING
You have the perfect putting grip when both hands work in harmony throughout the stroke. The reverse overlap – the most commonly used putting grip – is one of the best ways to achieve this. Both thumbs point straight down the shaft with the palms facing each other. A constant grip pressure encourages the hands to operate as one unit.

Making a good stroke
In the winter months greens are naturally more bumpy than in hot, sunny conditions. The grass tends to be a bit woolly which prevents the ball from rolling smoothly. You're bound to see the occasional good putt wander off line on an uneven surface.

In these conditions concentrate on making a good stroke at the ball and don't worry too much if the putts don't drop. It's easy to start doubting your putting stroke – thinking there's something wrong with you when often it's the greens that are at fault. Try to be patient and avoid changing your technique or your putter – good greens are usually just round the corner.

pro tip

Stroke of genius
Major championships are the ultimate test of nerve for professionals – some cope and others crumble. Few golfers experience such pressures, but you can learn a valuable lesson just by watching.

When Seve Ballesteros strode on to the final green in the 1984 Open at St. Andrews, he knew if he holed the 12ft (4m) putt the title was his.

Because Seve's putting style is his own he is able to feel comfortable over the ball. Even under intense pressure his stance is relaxed and his grip free from tension. A smooth, unhurried stroke saw the ball drop in the right edge of the hole – the claret jug was his for the second time.

When you're faced with an important putt, take time to compose yourself. Make a couple of practice strokes to give you a feel for the distance and, most important, to relax your muscles. Few experiences in golf are more satisfying than holing a putt when it matters.

Try out putting grips

All golfers go through periods of losing their putting touch and confidence on the greens. They may not twitch or yip the putts but just don't seem to hole as many as they should.

By experimenting with your putting grip you may find one that helps recapture your lost touch, and leads you to hole more putts. It's probably only a case of fine tuning.

CONSISTENT STROKES

The aim is to find a putting grip that is comfortable and helps you repeat your stroke consistently. This repetition of a smooth stroke is the most important part of a good putting game.

Remember that the hands play a passive role in the putting stroke. They must grip the club lightly yet hold the putter steady at all times – the hands shouldn't take any part in swinging the club. Adopt a grip that restricts any wrist action – a cause of much poor putting. Let the arms and shoulders swing the

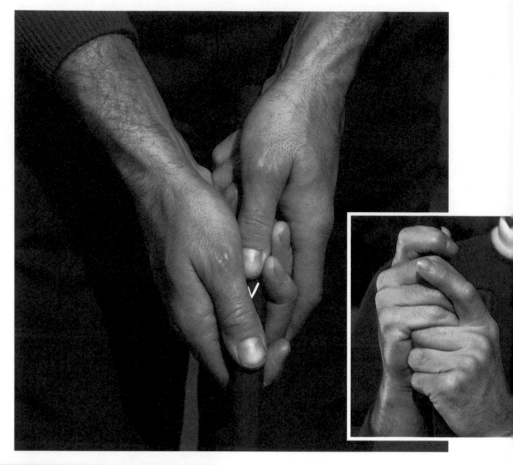

▲ STANDARD REVERSE OVERLAP
Try placing the forefinger of your left hand over either your little finger or all the fingers of your right hand. This restricts the breaking of the left wrist. Point your thumbs down the grip so your palms are square to the target. Players such as Crenshaw, Watson, Lyle and Nicklaus use grips very similar to this.

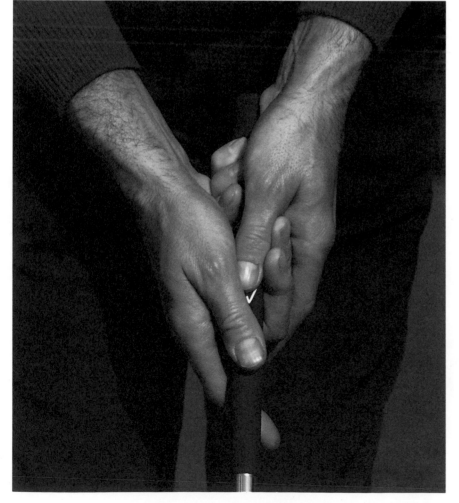

◄ OVERLAP CONTROL
Both Ballesteros and Faldo also favor the reverse overlap grip, with one variation. The forefinger of the right hand points down the grip and curls slightly underneath. This makes the right hand a little more passive, curbing the tendency to pull putts. Seve feels that this also gives him better feel and control on longer putts.

UNORTHODOX GRIPS

SPLIT HANDED

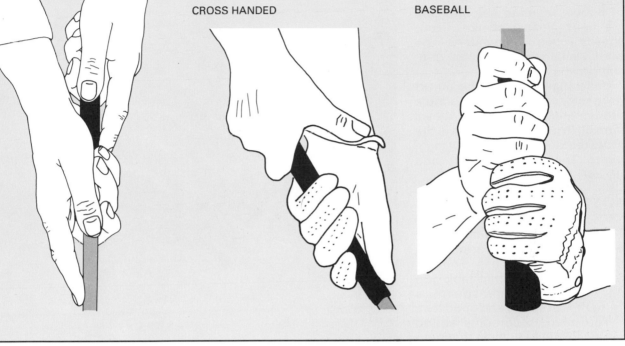

CROSS HANDED

BASEBALL

You may find an unorthodox grip works best. Try **splitting your hands** on the shaft – like Hubert Green – so that the right hand guides the stroke. Or try the cross-handed and the baseball grip. The **cross-handed** grip ensures that the left hand steers the shot and adds the power. The **baseball grip** is where all ten fingers are placed on the putter, giving the left and right hands equal prominence.

putter throughout the stroke.

Concentrate on holing out from around 10ft (3m) when you experiment with different grips. This is the crucial distance you must master to lower your scores. Try to find the grip that helps you to hole this length of putt more often – a good smooth stroke from this range should carry on to your longer putts as well.

Most of the world's top players have experimented with their putting grip at some time. The secret to their success is that they have found one they feel confident with, and can consistently reproduce a good stroke. But some players who have a history of troubles on the greens still constantly change their style, hoping their putting improves.

There are no hard and fast rules about which grip you should play with – it's what works best for you. But there are a few basic styles, which most amateurs and professionals use. These are well worth experimenting with until you find one you like.

masterclass

Langer's yip tip
The long hitting German has had his problems on the greens over the years – he has constantly experimented with different putting grips. A recent style is one Langer himself devised. He grips down the club with his left hand and then clasps the grip and his left forearm together with his right hand.

Langer turned to this unusual style to cure the yips. The left arm is locked on to the club making it impossible for the left wrist to break. He has had some success since turning to these drastic measures – he won the 1990 Madrid Open.

Crenshaw: master putter

The gentle Texan Ben Crenshaw is acknowledged by his fellow professionals and golfing experts as the best putter in the world. He studied the technique of Bobby Jones to help develop his near perfect stroke. Crenshaw's touch is legendary – he putts well on even the most difficult greens.

Believing putting to be an art not a science, Ben relies on simple fundamentals – he never allows himself to get bogged down in the more remote complexities of technique. The result is a pure and natural stroke.

PUTT PRIORITIES

The 1984 Masters champion recommends a putting style that suits the individual but is based on correct principles – a comfortable grip that keeps the blade square, a smooth arm swing and good feel.

You need to combine sound basic technique with an ability to read the greens. Ben accepts that speed determines the line when gauging a putt, and poorly judged speed rather than line is the cause of most three putts.

TEXAN TALENT
Ben Crenshaw combines a natural talent for judging slope and pace with superb technique, and is one of the game's finest putters. Both his long approach putts and touch around the hole are masterly.

Controlled comfort
Crenshaw holds the putter with a light and perfectly balanced grip. Both thumbs point down the shaft, leaving his hands square to the target line. His wrists stay firm throughout the stroke.

He believes every golfer should find a comfortable grip – one that works for the individual, rather than following a style that suits someone else. But try out the Texan's method, adapting it to your own game, if you're struggling to hole putts.

BOTH
THUMBS
DOWN
SHAFT

Trust your first instincts when reading greens is Crenshaw's advice. On long putts, worry about the weight of the shot more than the line – a putt that's the right distance is never far away. He treats short putts as 70% line and 30% feel. Keeping his head down until he hears the putt drop, he thinks about the stroke rather than the hole.

SMOOTH TEMPO

You can learn a lot from watching Crenshaw. He uses an arm rather than a wristy stroke. This makes his striking consistent – you must have perfect timing to putt well with a wrist stroke. Ben's action is smooth and the tempo is constant throughout the swing.

The Texan's grip is conventional – a reverse overlap. He points his thumbs down the shaft, ensuring that his hands are square to the target, and keeps the putter blade square throughout the stroke.

Like many top pros, he positions the ball opposite his left heel to promote a good roll. Although Crenshaw plays with a perfect pendulum stroke, his stance is slightly less standard.

Most top golfers position the ball so that their eyes are directly over it. But Ben putts with the ball further away from his body. He feels that this gives him the freedom to swing his arms rhythmically with no restrictions.

PUTTING LANE

When Ben visualizes a putt he doesn't just imagine a line, he sees a lane the width of the hole. This makes him feel more confident – he knows if he sets the ball off down the lane with the proper speed it has a chance of going in.

If you're struggling with your putting, go back to the basics. Even Crenshaw loses his surgeon's precision now and again, but he persists with the simple techniques he's always used. Don't despair if your putts aren't dropping – if they keep coming close they'll eventually go in.

Ben hasn't become the putter he is by just playing – he's worked for hours on the practice putting green to perfect his stroke. Follow his example – work out a practice routine involving both easy and difficult long and short putts.

PROVEN PUTTING STYLE

Use the basics but don't be afraid to experiment is Crenshaw's advice. The Ryder Cup player adopts a near standard technique on the greens. The only part of his set-up that is slightly unconventional is his ball position. Although he places the ball opposite his left heel – as many top golfers do to promote good roll – he plays it well away from his body.

Most golf teachers say that your eyes should be directly over the ball at address so that you can see the line easily. But Ben's method is effective, giving his arms the freedom to swing in a relaxed way. Crenshaw provides evidence that sound basics and an individual style are a powerful combination.

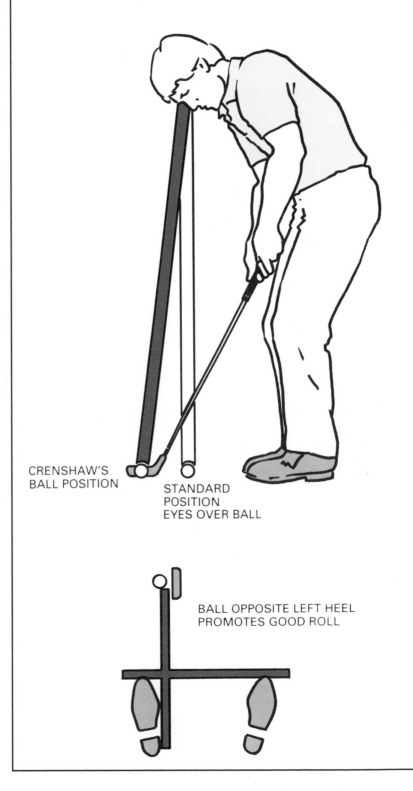

CRENSHAW'S BALL POSITION

STANDARD POSITION EYES OVER BALL

BALL OPPOSITE LEFT HEEL PROMOTES GOOD ROLL

Putting from off the green

A putt from off the green is probably the only shot in golf which pride prevents golfers from playing. Many players reach for a lofted club anywhere near the green. But if you think putting from off the green is a stroke only for beginners, you're making a big mistake.

Try telling Jack Nicklaus that it's a shot for novices. In his famous head to head with Tom Watson in the final round of the 1977 Open Championship, Watson rolled in an outrageous putt from off the 15th green. Many would have chipped, but Watson knew that a putt was perfect for coaxing his ball over the bone-hard Turnberry terrain. The shot proved to be a crucial turning point – he went on to beat the Golden Bear.

The beauty of putting from off the green is that it's very straightforward. There's no need to play a delicate chip with your sand wedge – a shot that can so easily go wrong, particularly if your con-

TAILORED TO YOUR NEEDS
Before you consider putting from off the green, you have to be certain that the ground conditions are just right. When they are, it's a tidy stroke that can help you get up and down with the minimum fuss. First, check the grass is closely mown so that your ball can roll smoothly all the way on to the putting surface. Then read the borrow – taking into account slopes before the green and on it. Pick out a precise line, set your sights and keep the stroke smooth.

fidence isn't sky high.

The technique for putting off the green involves more of a shoulders and arms stroke. In comparison to your normal putting style you should keep wrist movement to a minimum. Also make sure you grip lightly with both hands to help improve your feel for distance.

In the right conditions it's a deadly stroke and shouldn't frighten you in the least. So, when do you reach for your putter rather than one of your irons?

CLEAR RUNWAY

Putt from off the green if the grass between you and the putting surface is fairly closely mown. It doesn't really matter if there are humps, hollows and slopes along the way. As long as your ball runs over them quite smoothly, you can judge the pace on the ball – if the grass is too long, you can't possibly get the weight right.

Walk up to the edge of the green looking out for divots or any other obstructions which might get in the way of your ball. Don't just putt around them.

Be even more wary of a sprinkler head on your line. If your ball comes into contact with one of these it could shoot off at almost any angle. Chip if you're in any doubt about whether you can avoid these pop-up problems.

If your ball is on a tight lie, with

Stick in the mud
Putting from off the green is generally not a good idea in winter. All the conditions are against you – soggy ground under foot, damp lush grass, maybe even surface water which can be difficult to spot.

All these factors drag your ball to a premature halt – you may need to hit the ball so hard to allow for this that it becomes almost impossible to judge speed accurately. You're likely to struggle to get down in 2.

In extremely wet conditions there's always a better option than putting from off the green. A chip and run with a mid iron is probably the best of the bunch. It gives you enough loft to avoid any wet areas – and generates very little backspin, which encourages your ball to roll.

Leading edge
Some putters are better suited than others if you're considering playing the toe-poke shot from the edge of the fringe. It all comes down to whether your putter has the properly shaped head.

The putter used by Mike Donald in the 1990 US Open at Medinah is just about perfect for this delicate shot. The toe is fairly square, so there's less chance of the ball squirting off at a strange angle.

This is a good basis for your decision. If the toe of your putter is quite square, or the edges are well defined, you should have no major problems striking the ball correctly and accurately.

If the head of your putter is a more rounded shape, don't even consider playing this shot. It's almost impossible to stroke the ball consistently in the direction you want – instead it flies off at any angle from the curved edges.

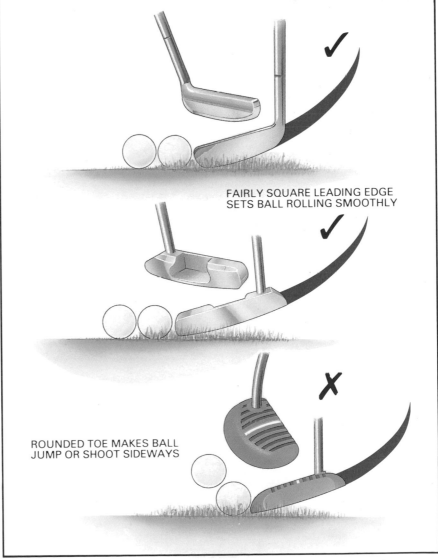

FAIRLY SQUARE LEADING EDGE SETS BALL ROLLING SMOOTHLY

ROUNDED TOE MAKES BALL JUMP OR SHOOT SIDEWAYS

PUTTING FROM THE FRINGE

① EASE THE PRESSURE
Many golfers find it difficult to play a chip shot when they're very close to the flag, mainly because you need an extremely delicate touch. This is when putting from fringe rough is a useful shot to have in your bag, particularly under pressure when you may be feeling a bit jumpy. However, you must be able to see the ball clearly. If the lie is any worse, don't attempt to use your putter.

② KEEP IT SIMPLE
One of the great advantages of playing this shot is that you use a very simple technique based on your normal putting stroke. Position the ball centrally in your stance – this helps you to strike down more than you do with a putt from on the green.

③ DISTANCE GAUGE
The length of your backswing depends on two important factors – the distance you are from the hole and the thickness of the fringe grass. Experiment with this in practice – through a process of trial and error you can play the shot during a round without nagging doubts concerning technique hanging over you.

④ FIRM THROUGH THE BALL
Notice how there is no sign of the left wrist breaking down – the angle you set at address remains the same through impact. Also make sure the back of your left hand faces the target until completion of the throughswing – this helps push the putter face square through towards the hole.

very little grass around it, a putt from off the green can be a sensible shot. You often come across these lies when the ground is baked hard – when you do, it can come as something of a relief to be able to take out your putter.

From a tight lie, striking the ball correctly with your putter is easier than trying to nip the ball cleanly with a lofted iron. This is true provided there's no great distance to cover. As a rule, anywhere under 40yd (36m) and you should be safe taking out your putter – any further and the benefits of putting from off the green start to diminish with every step back you take.

In fact, this shot starts to become quite dangerous from extremely long range. Most golfers find that it's easy to miss-hit a shot completely when making an incredibly long backswing with a putter. Once you're beyond a certain point, a comfortable chip with a 7 iron is a more reliable system.

pro tip

Creative putting

When your ball rests up against the fringe around the green, you can't place the clubhead behind the ball in the normal way. This in itself makes you feel uneasy and triggers doubts in your mind. It's also hard to deliver a good strike on the ball – grass is almost certain to deaden the blow.

These are the situations when you need to be creative. Try turning your putter around so that the toe points towards the hole (**1**). You find that the putter head sits closer to the middle of the ball, therefore boosting your chances of making a clean strike. This is difficult to achieve when the blade is at its normal angle.

Position the ball further back in your stance than normal. Other than that, don't introduce any major changes to your technique. Make a normal length backswing (**2**) and accelerate the putter head into the back of the ball. You may find the ball pops up in the air just after impact (**3**), but after that it should roll like a normal putt.

Every golfer knows how easy it is to make mistakes if you chip from this position, particularly under pressure. You can send your ball skimming through the green or make such feeble contact that you fail to move it at all. While striking with the toe of the putter may not be the easiest option, you at least get the ball moving forward at roughly the correct speed.

Sloping putts

Approaching a sloping putt well briefed and in the right frame of mind is the best way to hole it.

Many simple-looking holes are strengthened by heavily contoured greens, so make life easier for yourself by taking precautions.

ASSESS THE GREEN

Many parkland courses have relatively flat greens – you can deal with these fairly easily if you have a smooth putting stroke.

Heathland and links courses are a more complicated matter – their greens are designed to make you concentrate until your ball disappears into the hole.

When top players practice before a tournament, they size up the green from all angles. Putting from every part of the green helps them learn the best spot on which to land their approach shots – if they're on target they can look forward to a birdie putt.

You can make putting on sloping greens a lot easier by copying the pros. If you play the same course regularly, make a note of the best and worst parts of the greens. Aim your approach shots to the areas which offer the straightest putts.

Don't be content to hit the green anywhere – the most inviting spot may leave a three-putt.

GREEN SPEED

To assess how much the ball will move on a slope, you must get a feeling for the speed of the green. If the speed of the practice green

USE THE PIN
Play a sloping putt smoothly and confidently. Have the flag attended if it helps you gauge the slopes – though the pin must be removed after you've hit the ball.

Shade your eyes
To concentrate on the line of your putt, crouch down on your haunches and shade your eyes as you read the green. This helps give you a clearer, better defined picture of the putt you have to make than a wide and distracting view of the whole green – which disturbs your concentration.

PUTTING ACROSS A SIDESLOPE

READ THE PUTT
After you've read your putt play a smooth, straight shot along your imaginary ball-to-target line.

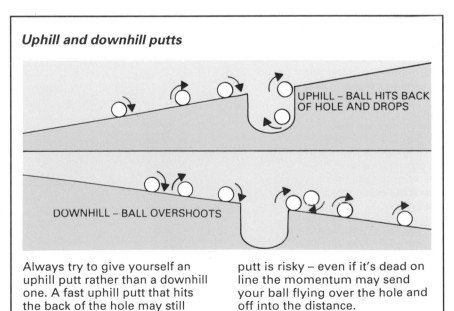

SPEED AND LINE
Some sloping putts have a huge borrow. Both speed and line have to be spot on if you're to get the ball close.

LET IT ROLL DOWN
Your ball-to-target line should account for the slope, so that a straight putt along your chosen path rolls down to the hole of its own accord.

is the same as the greens on the course where you play, spend some time putting beforehand. You'll putt far more confidently during your round.

The speed of your putt affects its line. A softly struck putt reacts to the subtle slopes more acutely than a firmly hit shot. If the green is fast, hit softly so that you don't overhit – allow for movement.

Bear in mind that a putt will not swing as far on a wet green as it does on dry grass. A putt on a wet green may leave a track in the grass as well, which gives an excellent indication of the swing.

Look at your putt from all angles to check the line – one view on its own could deceive.

Whatever the slope on your line, hit your putts straight. Let the borrow you've allowed roll your ball towards the hole. Never try to curve or spin a putt. Keep a positive image of the line in your mind and hit smoothly.

Uphill and downhill putts

UPHILL – BALL HITS BACK OF HOLE AND DROPS

DOWNHILL – BALL OVERSHOOTS

Always try to give yourself an uphill putt rather than a downhill one. A fast uphill putt that hits the back of the hole may still drop in. But a speedy downhill putt is risky – even if it's dead on line the momentum may send your ball flying over the hole and off into the distance.

Putting on two tiers

When your approach shot lands on one tier and the flag is on the other, you should still need no more than two putts. Learning to putt well on a two-tier green saves precious strokes.

Although the putting technique is the same as on a flat green, judging the bank is the key to playing well. Understanding how a ball behaves when it rolls over the step is half the battle.

Going straight up or down the bank is purely a matter of judging how hard to hit the ball. But when you're faced with a putt across the green and over the bank the line must be taken into account.

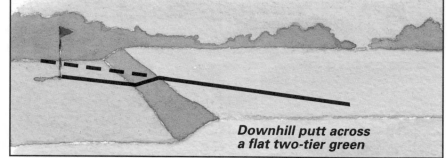

Downhill putt across a flat two-tier green

CHANGING PATHS

The path of the ball changes twice on its way to the hole. It first alters when the ball runs on to the bank between the tiers, and changes again when the putt reaches the other tier. The final path is parallel to the initial line.

For example, if you need to putt

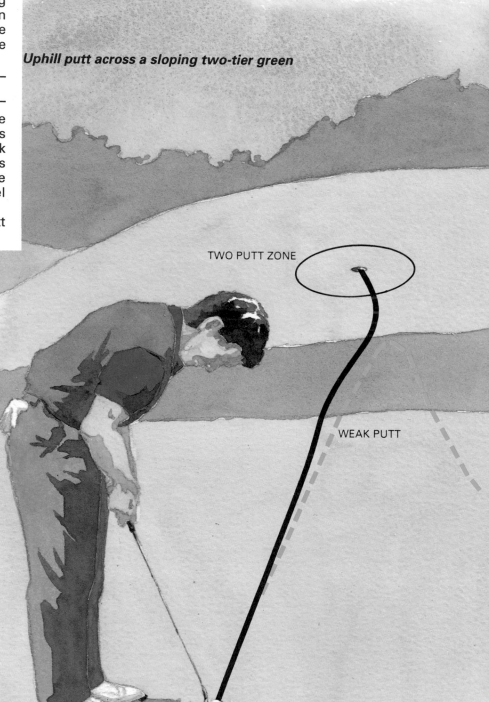

Uphill putt across a sloping two-tier green

TWO PUTT ZONE

WEAK PUTT

AVOID THREE PUTTING
Putting on split level greens needs careful thought to calculate the pace and line of the ball.

For a **downhill putt** going across a flat two-tier green from left to right you must aim to the right of the hole. The bank turns the ball left but it straightens out towards the hole on reaching the lower tier. The path the ball takes on the lower tier is parallel to the initial line if you judge the pace correctly.

When going **up the bank** aim to hit the ball into an imaginary two putt zone around the hole. Remember to take into account the cross slope on the top tier.

You must always get the ball on to the top tier with your first putt, even if it goes past the hole. Never hit the ball too weakly so it rolls back down the slope – a three putt is almost a certainty.

up and across – from left to right – a two-tier green, you must aim at a point wide and left of the hole. The ball moves to the right on the bank then straightens again when it reaches the top tier.

The amount the ball breaks depends on how high and steep the bank is, and the pace of the putt. The higher the bank, the more the ball moves off line, and the wider of the hole you must aim. The ball is less affected by the bank if it's rolling fast. If the green also slopes across, take this into account when choosing your line.

Once you have chosen your line you must judge the pace.

If you're **going downhill** pick a point on the edge of the bank and try to hit your ball over it. Imagine you're putting to a hole on the step. The strength of the putt should be just enough for the ball to trickle over.

Make sure the ball reaches the lower tier every time – a ball 10ft (3m) past the hole is better than leaving it on the top tier. If the hole is a long way from the foot of the bank, aim at a point on the bottom tier to make certain the ball reaches the target.

When **putting uphill** onto the top tier, choose a spot past the hole to counter the effect of the bank. Imagine you're playing to a hole beyond the actual flag. If you judge the pace correctly and take the proper line the ball should finish fairly close to the pin. You can lag your first putt to give an easy second.

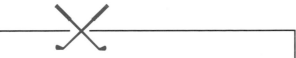

Judgement putting

When faced with a putt on a two-tier green you must make sure that you two putt – with practice it isn't that difficult. Fix your mind on avoiding the three putt – regard holing your first putt as a bonus.

To calculate the pace and line coming across the green and down a bank you must understand how the step and any slope affect the ball. Aim slightly right of the flag – visualize putting to an imaginary target at the top of the bank. The ball is carried away naturally by the bank towards the hole.

DOWN AND ACROSS
TWO-TIER GREEN

IMAGINARY TARGET

Canny Canizares

In the 1989 Ryder Cup match, José-Maria Canizares had two putts from 55ft (17m) on the 18th to retain the trophy for Europe. But he had to come downhill over a bank – judgement was all important.

He stroked the putt perfectly so it just rolled to the edge of the bank and then trickled down to within 3ft (1m) of the hole. He holed the next to beat Ken Green and secure the tie.

Plumb-bobbing

Greens are full of deceptive slopes and undulations, which make your putt more difficult. Plumb-bobbing is an effective way of measuring the slope of a green and is used by many top professionals to gauge the line of their putts.

The vertical line created by hanging the putter in front of you gives a useful pointer for the subtle slopes around you on the green. On hilly courses it helps you keep an idea of the true horizontal, as the humps and hollows can deceive.

ASSESS THE BREAK

You can also plumb-bob to assess the amount of break in your putt. Sometimes a putt can look straight but be affected by slopes that you can't see with the naked eye. Plumb-bobbing helps you to adjust your putt accordingly.

To plumb-bob correctly, you need to use your master eye. To find out which is your master eye, hold your forefinger at arm's length and look at it, aiming at a point in the background. Then look with each eye separately, closing the other as you do so. The eye which shows your finger nearest to the point in the background you're aiming at is your master eye.

Stand a few paces behind your

HOW DOES YOUR PUTT BREAK? Sometimes it's difficult to see the break of your putt with the naked eye. The technique known as plumb-bobbing gives a vertical reference to help you gain an idea of the correct borrow.

ball, on a direct line with the hole. Take hold of your putter with one hand and hold it at arm's length, opposite your master eye. The putter must hang straight in relation to your viewpoint. Make sure that the toe of your clubhead points directly towards or away from you.

Line up the center of your ball with the lower part of the shaft. Let your master eye come up the shaft until it is level with the hole. If there is a slope, the hole will be to the right or left of the shaft – adjust your borrow accordingly. If the slope is obvious, plumb-bob to confirm exactly how much.

Check the cut of the hole
Sometimes the last few rolls before the ball reaches the hole can have a marked effect on your putt. After plumb-bobbing, check how the hole is cut. Greenskeepers often pull up the hole cutter at an angle. This means that one side of the hole is higher than the other. For instance, if plumb-bobbing has shown you have a left-to-right putt, and the hole is cut higher to the right, you must adjust the line – the putt is now almost straight.

PLUMB-BOBBING TECHNIQUE

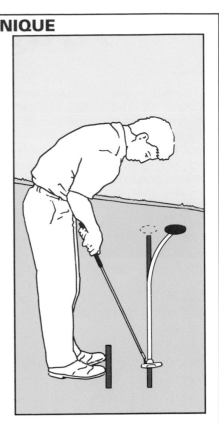

Let the club hang naturally. Make sure the toe of the putter is pointing either precisely towards or away from you so that it hangs vertical to your viewpoint. With the shaft lined up with the center of the ball, raise your master eye until it is level with the hole. If the hole is on the right of the shaft, aim left to allow for the borrow – and vice versa.

masterclass

Strange plumb-bobbing
In 1989, Curtis Strange became the first player since Ben Hogan, in 1951, to defend the US Open title successfully. As hearts were sinking elsewhere, Strange's use of plumb-bobbing gave him the confidence to go for putts. His final round over the tough Oak Hill course contained 16 pars – in part thanks to his smooth and positive putting stroke.

Judging the grain

Although reading the green correctly is essential, you can hole even more putts by judging the grain properly.

The grain is the direction in which the grass grows. In mild climates, grass grows straight up, so the grain hardly affects your putt. However, the grass is mown up and down, pushing it in one direction and then the other. These stripes give the same effect as natural grain.

EFFECTS OF GRAIN
The same putt varies according to the grain (the direction in which the grass grows or is mown). In warm climates, the natural grain can slow down, speed up or curve a putt. Mowing the grass can have a similar effect in colder climates.

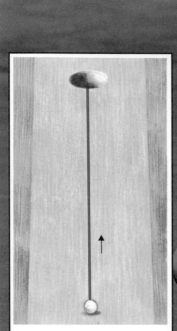

WITH THE GRAIN
If the grass is pale, you are putting with the grain, and your ball travels quickly.

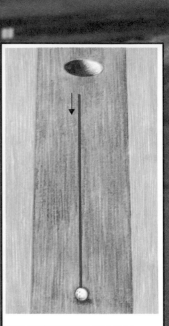

AGAINST THE GRAIN
The same putt hit against the grain runs more slowly and falls short of the hole.

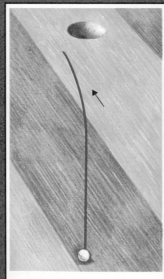

ACROSS THE GRAIN
As the putt meets the join it is almost like hitting a wall. The ball veers as a result.

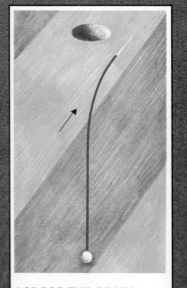

ACROSS THE GRAIN
The putt curves away as it strikes the join, along the left-to-right line of the mini "wall."

A green with a strong grain looks dull and dark when you stand on one side, and shiny and light from the other. When it looks light and shiny, you are putting with the grain, and the ball runs very quickly. With the green looking dull and dark, a putt is against the grain and runs relatively slowly.

In warmer countries, such as Australia, South Africa and the holiday areas of southern Europe, the natural grain is pronounced. Recognizing it and understanding what it does to the ball's path is as important as gauging the slope and line of your putt.

READING THE GRAIN

Golf courses in hot countries usually have greens laid with either Bermuda or bent grass. These are grasses which shoot up quickly in the sun and also grow in specific directions.

The direction the grass grows depends on where the green is – if there is sea or a natural lake nearby, it's very likely that the grain leads towards it.

Alternatively, the grain may point where the prevailing wind is heading, or it could lead away from mountains. Taking all these factors into account is vital if you are putting on grainy greens.

SLOPE AND GRAIN

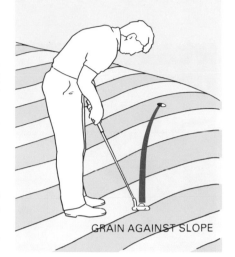

GRAIN AGAINST SLOPE

GRAIN WITH SLOPE

When the green slopes downwards and the grain runs against the slope, the putt is almost straight. If both the slope and the grain run in the same direction, the line of your putt becomes more acute. You must allow for even more break and aim well to the left of the hole.

The same goes for the stripes left by a mower. You need to assess the grass direction before you can judge the pace of your putt correctly. The ball has to roll over the join between each stripe, so you also have to allow for this making your putt break.

An uphill putt against the grain is extra slow. But the same putt with the grain may counteract the effect of the slope, and make a normal – or fast – stroke.

If the grain runs sideways across the line of your putt, it has the same effect as a sideslope. This means curving the putt with the grain.

If you have a left-to-right putt, and the grain runs in the same direction, the break becomes even more acute. When the line of your putt goes against the grain, its break is almost cancelled.

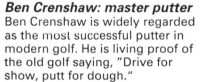

Ben Crenshaw: master putter
Ben Crenshaw is widely regarded as the most successful putter in modern golf. He is living proof of the old golf saying, "Drive for show, putt for dough."

On occasions, when Crenshaw's erratic swing isn't working too reliably, he stays in contention in many tournaments because of his beautifully tuned putting stroke.

Crenshaw putts so well because he perfected the firm-wristed pendulum action. He is also a superb green reader. Knowing that the slightest misjudgment can make a putt lip out, he studies the green and the grain from all angles until he is sure of his pace and line.

The confidence that comes from assessing the grain and slopes accurately is essential to playing a positive stroke.

Dry or damp?
A hot sun dries out the grass very quickly. If the green is sunken, or has trees overhanging it, parts of it may remain in shadow for longer than others. This means that sections of the same green can be either bone dry or damp.

Remember this when you assess your putt – damp grass can slow the ball down considerably, while dryness means a fast putt and a more acute break.

Green drills

Putting practice is vital, but still there isn't as much time spent on it as there should be. What can put people off is the boredom of hitting stroke after stroke at a hole.

You need to make putting practice enjoyable while improving your touch naturally. Using various drills and games helps you to become a better judge of line and weight, and to groove your stroke without unnecessary toil and boredom.

Many useful drills don't involve a hole at all, and some need more than one person to be of any use. Try to find the ones that you enjoy most, but also those that work on the worst aspects of your putting game – perhaps judgment of distance.

It's important to develop all facets of your putting game so you're solid from both short and long range – not just in a friendly game but when the heat is on and the pressure of competition is fierce.

MEASURED WEIGHT
To find your feel for distance it's best not to aim at a hole – it can be distracting. To gauge long range putts, simply press a tee peg into the practice green and try to lay every putt dead – within 2ft (60cm). Playing with a couple of friends helps as well – score a point every time you knock your ball closest to the tee. Perhaps even play for a small wager to help you cope with pressure.

To develop a touch for medium range putts, lay out three tee pegs in a line, the first about 15ft (4.5m) away and then at 10ft (3m) intervals. Hit two balls at each peg and keep repeating the exercise. This teaches you to take a putt on individually and judge the pace each time, which helps your touch.

▶ BOWLING GREEN

One of the most enjoyable ways to hone your judgment of pace and line is to play bowls. You need two or more players, three balls each and a jack – the target ball. Player 1 knocks the jack down the green, then hits his first ball towards it, trying to go as close as possible. Player 2 then has to beat his rival. Take alternate shots until you have hit all the balls.

To score, judge whose ball is closest. If you have the nearest ball award yourself a point. If two balls are closer than your rival's nearest, award two points. And if you are lucky enough to have knocked three inside your opponent's, claim three points. Play until one of you has reached 21.

masterclass

Allen's drill

US pro Michael Allen uses a very simple but effective practice aid to groove his putting stroke. He lays two clubs down parallel to each other – at just over putter head width apart – and aligns them at the hole, so that if he hits a straight putt the ball drops.

This means he has to take the putter back on a straight line or else it collides with the clubs on the ground. But he must also keep the blade square to target back and through the ball if the putt is to drop.

Allen's hard work on his putting finally paid dividends in 1989 when he won the Scottish Open. Five strokes back with one round to play he shot an amazing 63 to pip Ian Woosnam and José-Maria Olazabal. With 7 birdies and an eagle in the last 13 holes he needed only 22 putts.

He ended the year tied for 9th in the putting statistics – averaging under 30 putts per round – and carried this form to the US Qualifying School where he earned his card for 1990.

▼ ALL IN A ROW

Although trying to hole out every time isn't always a good idea – because you can easily become bored and lose your confidence – one drill works well on the short putts. Line five or six balls up on a flat piece of green about 12in (30cm) apart, starting from 3ft (1m) out.

Attempt to hole the first ball. If you do, move on to the next, and so on until you fail to hole out. When you fail, retrieve all the balls and start again. The object of the exercise is to hole out every ball one after the other. This drill helps your short putt stroke and does wonders for your concentration and determination. It makes you really want to hole out each time as you know you must start all over again if one fails to drop.

pro tip

Sweeten your touch

WEIGHTING GAME
To ensure accurately weighted putts, it's critical to cultivate your touch and feel from medium and long range. Your muscles rely on being sent a precise message from your brain about how hard to hit the putt.

To help you ingrain a sense of distance and weight into your game, forget about the line of your putts for a moment. Go on

to the practice green with about ten balls and position yourself 15ft to 40ft (4.5-12m) away from the edge. Then putt each ball towards the fringe – playing to a hole distracts your gauging of weight as you have to think about the line of the putt as well. Try to stop the ball as close as possible to the edge of the green without ever running up on to the fringe.

Play against someone else to make it more interesting – perhaps for a little wager – and score a point every time you knock one closest to the edge.

The action of putting to a band rather than a hole naturally helps your perception and feel for length. This drill should give you confidence to judge long range putts out on the course and avoid the dreaded 3 putt.

BLIND MAN'S PUTT
Putting without ever looking up to see where the ball has gone is a remarkably tell-tale drill. It gives you an accurate indication of your natural feel for weight.

With roughly ten balls, aim to a hole-free area. Take one ball at a time and try to stroke it to a point about 25ft (7.5m) away. Don't look up between shots, just roll the next ball towards you and repeat your stroke. Try to keep everything the same – the line, rhythm and strength. The idea is to finish up with the balls as tightly grouped as possible.

Only after the last ball is on its way may you look up. With putts of that length you should be able to throw an imaginary ring – about 2 ft (75cm) in diameter – around all the balls. Keep practicing until you succeed, then move on to a longer distance. For every 5ft (1.5m) you add to the length of the putt, the diameter of your target area should increase by 6in (15cm).

This drill is better than the usual blindfold exercise – putting with your eyes shut – since you can still concentrate on your stroke, and your ball striking is more consistent. Both your touch and putting stroke improve together.

How to beat the yips

No golfer with a heart would subject someone to a bout of the yips – not even their own worst enemy. Sufferers go through periods of sheer hell as one putt after another fails even to threaten the hole.

For those who have never been through the yips, it's a problem that's difficult to understand. The right hand tends to take over and jerk the putter head into the back of the ball. It seems like the club has a will of its own.

No matter how hard you try to stay in control of your stroke, the ball still shoots off in all directions. It can get to the stage where every short putt is a potential twitch just waiting to happen. And the faster the greens the more frightening it becomes.

ADDED PRESSURE

If you're unfortunate enough to suffer from the yips, missing three-footers is not your only problem. Poor putting also places enormous pressure on the rest of your game.

You start to believe that almost no putt is holeable. The more approach shots you hit, the more you feel you have to knock the ball stone dead to stand any chance of making a birdie. Finishing on the green – but a long way from the hole – is almost worse than missing the target altogether. As you walk towards the green all you can think of is three putts.

It's easy to see why players with the yips seriously consider giving up golf – it gradually eats away at their entire game. However, the problem can be cured – Sam Torrance and Bernhard Langer are proof of that.

And beating the yips doesn't necessarily mean carrying a broom-handle putter for the rest of your golfing days, although it works for some people. Nor do you have to call on the services of the nearest hypnotist or sports psychologist.

More conventional remedies can be found, but it's important to understand that the yips don't dis-

ANOTHER ONE SLIPS BY
Anyone who plays golf can sympathize with a player who regularly misses short putts – an affliction known as the yips. There is no worse feeling in golf, because it's difficult to know what went wrong. All you're left with is a sense of frustration and complete disbelief that you've missed from such close range. The problem is caused by both hands fighting against each other – once you get them to work in harmony you have a reliable system for holing out.

Hit and miss

Many golfers who suffer on the greens tend to miss putts in a fairly random manner. Left, right, short or long – on a bad day you might hit every one of these in close succession.

This is probably where putting differs most from any other part of your game. Every golfer hits one type of bad shot more than any other – a slice for instance. This makes it easy to spot the mistake when it happens and you can then work at correcting it. However, with putting, it's hard to identify where you're going wrong because putts tend to miss on different sides of the hole.

This is why your putting technique should be a style of your own – not some mechanical creation that you don't understand, adopted when cracks appear. Try to develop a stroke based on a combination of feel, individuality and five important qualities that are present in most successful styles:
○ Eyes directly over the ball;
○ Putter face square to the intended line;
○ A light hold on the putter with equal grip pressure applied by both hands;
○ A comfortable address position;
○ A repetitive stroke.

Look at these areas when you're trying to identify a fault in your putting. Never rule out a change of putter either. This is by no means the best cure – your equipment is seldom to blame for bad putting. But a change often uncovers a lack of confidence – this may be the problem rather than any serious technical flaw.

appear overnight. It takes time and you may have to experiment a little to find the system that works for you.

BACK TO SQUARE ONE

First, you need to go back to basics and look at what makes a good putting stroke. Two factors are common among great putters – a consistent angle between the left wrist and the shaft of the putter through impact, combined with a light, sensitive grip.

If you suffer from the yips, there's every chance that you're failing to perform one, or both, of these moves. So how do you go about building them into your putting stroke?

One of the most popular methods is a cross-handed putting grip. The main benefit of this technique is that it makes it easy to keep your left wrist firm throughout the stroke. It's very difficult to yip a putt if this move is part of your technique.

Another advantage of the cross-handed method is that it naturally pushes the back of your left hand through towards the hole. This keeps the putter face square and prevents the right hand taking over. These are two major steps towards eliminating a jerky putting stroke.

This is particularly important on the short putts, because once you're lined up correctly, you simply need a method that returns the putter face perfectly square to the ball at impact.

However, as you move further away from the hole, a square putter face isn't all you need. Good judgment of pace is just as important, because if you get the correct weight on a long putt, you're seldom too far away.

HOW FAR BACK?

While the yips usually refers to a stabbing movement into the ball, it's worth taking a look at the length of your backswing – particularly if you're struggling to find the correct length on many of your putts.

Bear in mind that the length of your backswing should determine the length of the putt. This allows you to accelerate the putter head smoothly into the back of the ball – the complete opposite of yipping

BAD CASE OF THE YIPS

1 GREAT EXPECTATIONS
The closer to the hole the more a golfer is prone to the yips. This is probably caused by expecting to hole short putts – worse still, so does everyone else – but no one presumes you should roll in one long putt after another. This poor state of mind often creates tension at address, particularly in your hands. As soon as this happens you're in danger of hitting a wide selection of very bad putts.

2 START OF YOUR PROBLEMS
This is a good example of one problem leading to another – if you're not relaxed at address it's extremely difficult to make a smooth backswing. It's more likely that you jerk the club back too quickly – at that precise moment you lose control of your putting stroke.

3 OUT OF CONTROL
A sure sign of the yips is the ball shooting off to the left the moment it leaves the putter face. This is caused by the right hand taking charge, which causes a hit rather than a stroke. Make sure you accelerate the putter head smoothly through impact – the ball merely gets in the way of your putting stroke.

4 MISSED AGAIN
This is a familiar – and extremely depressing – sight for any golfer stricken by the yips. The ball travels well left of the hole and often at speed. You should really aim to keep body movement to a minimum when you're over a putt – your shoulders, hands and arms are well capable of holding together your putting stroke.

a putt.

If your backswing is too short, you struggle to generate enough clubhead speed on the throughswing – you simply don't have time. This means you can forget about smooth acceleration into the back of the ball – you probably jerk the putter forward.

If you have too long a backswing you create a different set of problems. It's not a yip, but it leads to poor judgment of distance – and missed putts – because you decelerate the putter into impact. This is no less depressing than any other yipped putt.

Hover for a smooth start
The yips aren't confined only to the throughswing – often the problem stems from not taking the putter back smoothly. If you jerk the putter away from the ball it's impossible to control line or length – no matter how near you are to the hole.

This annoying fault is often caused by pressing the putter too hard into the ground behind the ball. It's easy to drift into this bad habit, particularly if

you're going through a crisis on the greens. Try a simple exercise – preferably in practice first – to help you cure this fault.

When you address the ball, hover the putter head just off the ground. This means the putter hangs more naturally – almost like a pendulum – and encourages you to start the backswing smoothly. It also helps you strike your putts on the up, which generates overspin and sets the ball rolling smoothly.

BEFORE AND AFTER
Bernhard Langer's putting problems are a legacy of his early golfing days in Germany. Slow greens – often in less than perfect condition – trained Langer to hit putts firmly at the back of the hole. He developed a truly magical touch and became a very good putter, particularly from close range. Even if the putts didn't drop he could blame the poor surface and not his stroke – Langer never suffered from a lack of confidence with his putting.

Moving on to the faster greens of the European and American Tours, Langer's orthodox putting stroke began to break down. Finding it hard to adjust to a

change in pace, his backswing remained far too long, almost as though he were still playing on slow greens. To compensate, Langer decelerated the putter into the ball to prevent him hitting his putts too strongly. This is when the yips began to set in.

Every time Langer is plagued by the yips he finds a cure – such as the cross-handed putting grip. It's unorthodox and it doesn't look pretty – but it works because his left wrist doesn't break down through impact. It also takes the right hand out of the stroke.

This is why you need to experiment a little if you're going through major putting problems. Finding a system that works is all that matters – not how it looks.

Torrance beats the yips

When Sam Torrance held his arms aloft as he rolled in the winning putt of the 1985 Ryder Cup at The Belfry, few imagined that within three years his confidence on the greens would be completely destroyed by the dreaded yips.

The yips is the name given to the involuntary and disconcerting convulsion of the muscles in the hands and arms while trying to hole putts. The golfer jerks the ball way past the hole.

Many famous golfers have been affected by the yips over the years, and some of them have never fully recovered. Peter Alliss and Ben

Hogan both retired from playing because of their inability to hole out on the greens.

Bernhard Langer also suffered from the yips. While he has done well to regain some of his form, he is far from the putter he was when he won the Masters in 1985.

But while Langer's putting has never been his main strength, Torrance was considered to have one of the smoothest strokes on the tour. When the yips came, his silky stroke was replaced by a jittery jab. He began to miss cuts and plummeted down the money list.

After a good 1987, when he finished ninth on the order of merit, he was hit by the yips and he

THE NEW SAM
The Scottish Ryder Cup star has turned to using a revolutionary new putter to combat the yips, which affected his performances in 1988. At 48in (120cm) the broom handle putter is considerably longer than any other on the market. This means Torrance can keep it steady with his chin throughout the stroke.

TORRANCE'S METHOD

1 THE ADDRESS POSITION
Sam aims the putter as normal. While gently holding the top of the putter with his left hand, he places the butt of the shaft under his chin. His right arm hangs relaxed down beside the shaft. He then places his right hand on a grip lower down the shaft. He lightly grips with his thumb and index finger, while his forefinger points down along the grip.

2 THE TAKEAWAY
With the left hand and the chin stabilizing the putter, Sam makes a slow, deliberate backswing controlled by the right hand. His head and body remain perfectly still, while his eyes are directly over the ball. There is no sign of a loop, often a cause of missed putts.

(3) THE STROKE
Sam accelerates through the ball with a smooth yet firm stroke as any good putter should do. The right hand guides the club, and also adds the force to the shot. But notice how lightly he holds the shaft with just his thumb and forefinger, giving him more feel and control. Throughout the whole movement Sam's head and body are quite still.

(4) THE FOLLOWTHROUGH
His putter head swings through on a straight line towards the target. Sam's followthrough is the same length as his backswing, whatever the distance of the putt. His visor position shows that his head remains in exactly the same place throughout. He looks up only when the ball has gone.

slumped to 51st in 1988. Tension and nerves were to blame.

BROOM HANDLE

Sam is a fighter and he doesn't give up. After trying all the accepted ways of curing the ailment, he searched for a club that he could keep steady at all times. This led to the invention of the broom handle putter.

The putter has been a huge success for Torrance. His results improved dramatically. 1989 saw Sam regain his Ryder Cup place, and a very creditable 11th position on the money list.

Australian Peter Senior also benefited from this style of putter. He rests the butt of the shaft on his chest instead of his chin. He used it to win three events in quick succession in 1989 after having problems on the greens.

There has been some doubt about the legality of the putter. But the R and A, who control which clubs can be played, have given Sam's brainchild the all clear. And to avoid getting an unfair advantage, the players on the European Tour have agreed not to use the putter to gain relief when dropping the ball.

So Sam's invention seems destined to become one of the best ways to cure the most feared affliction in golf.

▲ CROSS HANDED
Sam tried all the accepted methods of curing the yips. He turned to using the cross handed grip, still favored by Bernhard Langer. This style has helped the German regain his form, but it did not solve Sam's problems.

◀ CONVENTIONAL STYLE
For many years Sam putted conventionally, and was very successful. He was regarded as one of the finest putters on the tour, by both his fellow professionals and the public. His skill on the greens helped him to win many big tournaments – until he became afflicted by the convulsive jerky stroke known as the yips.

Try it for yourself
If you have problems with jerky putting, it may be worth your while trying a broom handle putter to steady your stroke. In price, these putters rank alongside the top of the range, so ask your local PGA professional if you can borrow a trial club. See whether it helps you to hole more putts before you go to the expense of buying one. The yips affect golfers in different ways – one player's cure may not work for everybody.

5

BUNKER PLAY

Generally placed to catch wayward shots, bunkers are obstacles that are either positioned cosmetically or are there to penalize you. Due to the variations in design from course to course, a greater knowledge of how to adapt to the many different lies you may encounter can only help to improve your score. This section deals with such situations, covering every aspect of technique, accompanied by clear illustrations and text to help you master the most feared shot in golf.

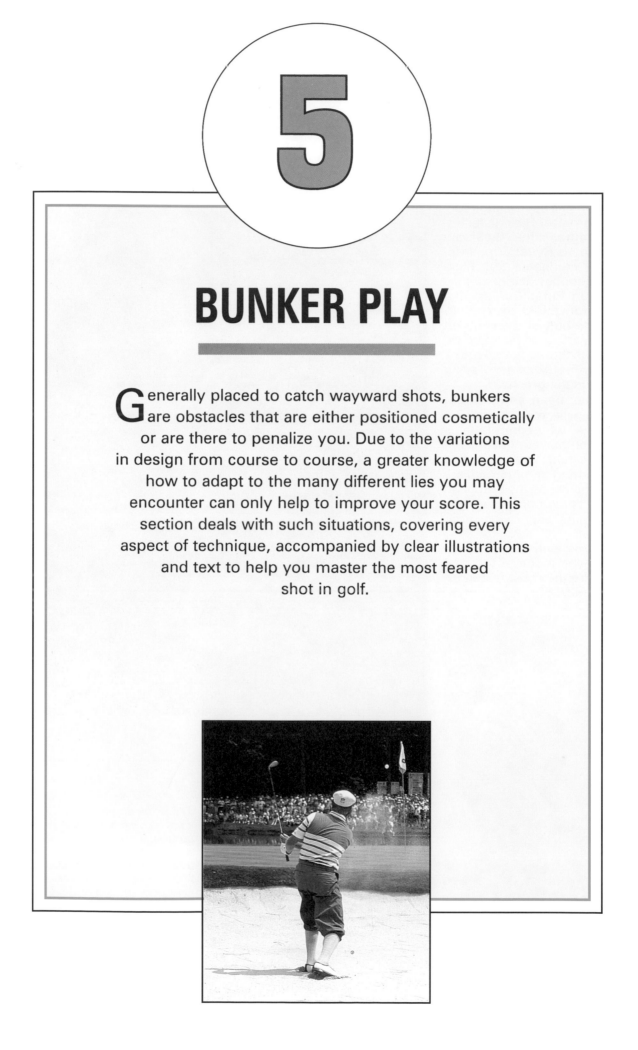

Bunker positioning

Every golfer has suffered a traumatic experience in sand before – either by being too delicate, or attempting too much and coming to grief. Whatever the cause, it always comes as a major disappointment. Avoid experiences like this by reducing the number of visits you make to sand.

The key lies more in your mind than in your golf bag. You need a cool, calculated approach – a strategy that prevents you doing just what the course designer wanted you to do.

SIDESTEP THE SAND

Fairway bunkers are designed to make you think off the tee. Instead of looking at them as a potential problem, use these bunkers to your advantage. Fairway bunkers can help you visualize a specific

CAVALIER APPROACH
If you're unfortunate enough to land in a bunker, don't lose heart – sand is a better proposition than water or out of bounds. When it's a fairway bunker you can afford to be adventurous – they're often shallow which means you can take a long club. Firing from long range, think of the club you would take from the same distance off grass and choose one more. Then enjoy the moment as your ball sails towards the green.

NOTHING TO GAIN

▶ **Many short par 4s are cunningly designed to catch you out. The holes look innocent enough, but the lack of length is often more than made up for by cleverly placed bunkers. Play the percentages to make sure you don't fall into the course designer's trap.**

Off the tee, select a club that guarantees your ball pulls up short of the fairway bunkers – even if you hit your Sunday best drive. This means the sand poses no threat. A good shot leaves you a straightforward approach into the green and sets you up for an excellent birdie opportunity.

If you risk all off the tee, you've very little to gain and everything to lose. Even with your best drive you still need an element of luck to avoid the sand and the chances of finding the green are slim. If it's not your day the ball may plummet into the sand, leaving you a medium range bunker shot – one of the hardest strokes in golf. What looks like a birdie opportunity on the card suddenly turns into a careless dropped shot.

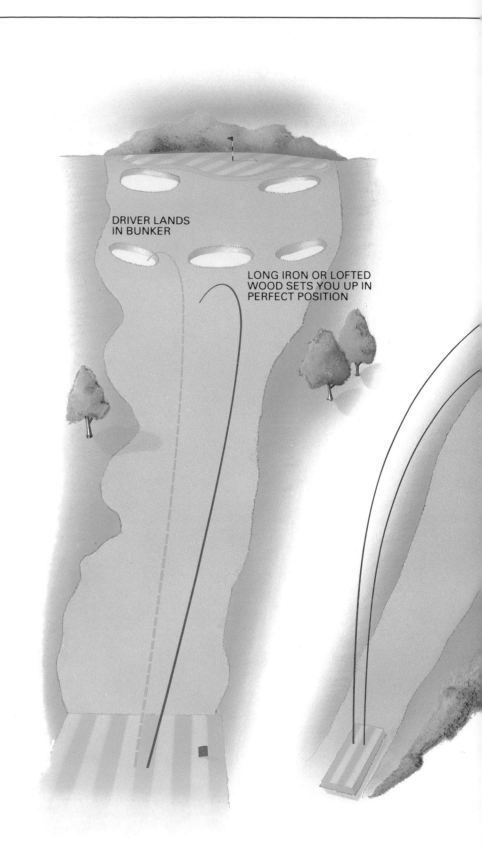

DRIVER LANDS IN BUNKER

LONG IRON OR LOFTED WOOD SETS YOU UP IN PERFECT POSITION

shot.

Also bear in mind that on most courses fairway traps are usually quite shallow and easy to escape from. The exceptions to this rule tend to be links courses where deep pot bunkers pose a serious threat to your score.

If you're sensible about club selection you should always be able to avoid cross bunkers. Positioned at the distance most golfers hit their drivers, there's usually no going around them – the only choice you have to make is whether to lay up short or try and carry them.

Whatever your decision, always give yourself a bit of leeway. If a 3 wood lands you perilously close to the sand, choose a more lofted club just to be safe. Only decide to carry cross bunkers if you can achieve it without forcing the shot.

An isolated fairway bunker you know you can comfortably carry is an ideal marker to help you line

up. Find a spot on the tee that lets you fire straight over the bunker to achieve perfect position on the fairway beyond.

Bunkers in the distance can also play a useful part in the lining up process. If they're out of reach, set your sights on the sand and fire away. Aiming at a specific mark in

the distance is a good habit to build into your game.

Often when there's a clear fairway ahead, it's easy to blast away merrily thinking it's impossible to find trouble. This is the sort of careless approach that leads to your sloppiest drive – disaster is usually lurking just round the corner.

IN THE DRIVING SEAT

ONLY ADVENTUROUS DRIVE
CLEARS SAND TO OPEN UP
GREEN FOR SECOND SHOT

AFE TEE SHOT
ULLS UP SHORT
 THE BUNKERS

◀ The temptation on a long par 4 is always to drive the ball out of sight – after all, the closer you are to the green the easier your second shot. But this is only true if you're on the fairway – there's no advantage gained if your ball ends up in sand.

When fairway bunkers guard the landing area on a par 4, it's wise to lay up short of them with a lofted wood. Even though you leave yourself a longer shot into the green, at least you can play off grass. If you're 20yd (18m) nearer the green but in the bunker, the shot is a lot harder. It may even be impossible to reach in two.

If you're feeling adventurous reach for your driver and fire past the bunkers. The reward is great – a shorter shot at the flag. But the price of failure is a high one – little or no chance of reaching the green in regulation.

HAZARDOUS PAR 3

SLIGHT MISS-HIT
LEAVES YOU CHANCE OF
SAND SAVE FROM BUNKER

TAKE PLENTY OF
CLUB TO PITCH ALL
THE WAY TO THE FLAG

NOT ENOUGH CLUB OR
BAD MISS-HIT LANDS
YOU IN DEEP TROUBLE

▶ Bunkers are a major problem on many holes, but on a treacherous par 3 they're often a secondary hazard. When water threatens the front of the green, seeing your ball finish in sand can almost come as a relief. Several bunkers surrounding the putting surface also accentuate the shape of the green.

Club selection is absolutely crucial on holes like this. Always take plenty of club to give yourself some margin for error – particularly if you're firing at the pin. Play a good tee shot and you fully deserve the birdie chance that awaits you. Even if you unintentionally draw the ball to the left, there's enough carry on the shot to clear the water. Hitting sand is far from disastrous – you still have a reasonable chance to make par.

But if you don't take enough club, or catch the shot a little heavy, your ball is destined for a watery grave. You then have to hole a shot almost as long as your last just to make par – for one loose shot this is a severe punishment.

OPTICAL ILLUSION

PLOT YOUR PROGRESS

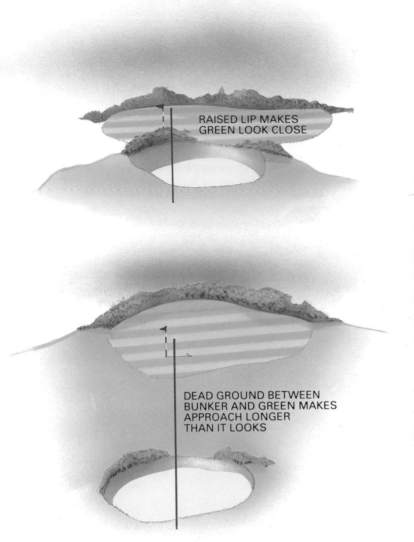

RAISED LIP MAKES
GREEN LOOK CLOSE

DEAD GROUND BETWEEN
BUNKER AND GREEN MAKES
APPROACH LONGER
THAN IT LOOKS

STUDY YARDAGE CHART
TO KEEP OUT OF SAND

50yd (45m)

100yd (90m)

140yd (130m)

180yd (165m)

Be sure of the shot you want to play before you take your stance. As well as the physical obstacle that bunkers present, they have a nasty habit of playing tricks on the eye. The front lip of a bunker can easily conceal dead ground – particularly if the fairway is flat all the way to the green.

You may think the flag is positioned just over a bunker, when in fact there can be as much as 50yd (45m) of dead ground between the sand and the putting surface. If you're not aware of this, your approach shot is certain to fall short of the mark.

Optical illusions cause nightmares when it comes to club selection. It's the sort of situation where a yardage chart proves invaluable – both off the tee and for your second shot. You can successfully plot your way along the hole, avoiding the traps that lurk up ahead.

On a hole where bunkers scatter the fairway, your mind should immediately turn to accuracy rather than distance. Choose your club wisely – a long shot off grass is usually easier than a shorter one from sand.

For your approach shot, don't be fooled by the dead ground over the bunker. While the eye might tell you it's a 7 iron, try to ignore your instincts. Trust the yardages on the card and choose your club accordingly.

SAND AROUND THE GREENS

Greenside bunkers tend to be positioned around the front half of the putting surface. They're inevitably harder to avoid than fairway bunkers because you have no choice but to flirt with them.

When bunkers eat into one side of a green, caution is the best policy. Aim to pitch your approach shot on the safe half of the green.

This gives you some margin for error should the ball leak to the right or left.

If you need to fly over a bunker to find the green, it's essential to play an attacking stroke. Take plenty of club and imagine the ball pitching on top of the flag – this encourages you not to be short.

You'll soon be pleasantly surprised how often you finish pin high rather than long. And you don't find many bunkers behind

greens, so as long as there's no other trouble at the back, it's better to be long than short.

The biggest mistake you can make is to take too little club and try to force the shot. A heavy handed approach seldom generates the distance you're looking for. You probably find yourself playing your next shot from the bunker in front of the green – which is exactly what you were striving to avoid.

Shallow bunker shot

In theory the shallow bunker shot should be the easiest stroke there is from sand. There's almost no front lip to negotiate, so height isn't a major consideration. You usually have a choice of shots.

This is certainly true from a shallow fairway bunker – a clean strike is essential but you're free to choose just about any club in the bag, depending on how far you are from the target. However, if the same bunker is close to a green, it often seems to create a problem rather than present an opportunity.

Often you become too tentative – the result is that you fail to escape from shallow bunkers at the

APPROACH WITH AUTHORITY
The shot from a shallow greenside bunker looks so simple – no front lip, perfect lie – that it's easy to think nothing could possibly go wrong. But this shot is only as easy as you make it – you can't afford to be sloppy. Mistakes creep in when you fail to treat the situation with enough care. Play the shot with conviction because you must generate clubhead speed to achieve success out of sand.

✓ THE GREAT ESCAPE

1 BALL OPPOSITE LEFT HEEL
Your stance in a shallow greenside bunker should almost be a combination of two different techniques – a splash bunker shot and your standard full swing. Stand with the ball opposite your left heel, align fractionally open to the target and position your weight a little more on the left foot than normal. Even though a high flight is not essential, your sand wedge is still the club best suited to this shot.

2 SET IN MOTION
Concentrate on making a smooth one piece takeaway – very much in the way you would with a full shot. This should prevent your wrists breaking too early and helps you take the club along the line of your body. Keep your weight fairly central throughout the backswing – it's dangerous to shift your weight too far either way when you're in a greenside bunker.

3 LONG BACKSWING
You probably seldom need to hit this shot more than 30yd (27m), but it's essential you make an almost full backswing. Note how the shoulders are nicely turned away from the ball – this doesn't vary too much from a normal shot off the fairway. The main difference is that your wrists should hinge a little earlier – this helps create a slightly steeper arc in your swing which promotes the correct angle of attack on the downswing.

4 LATE HIT
One of the major benefits of making a near full backswing is that you can start the downswing in a smooth, unhurried fashion. This gradually generates clubhead speed and helps you coordinate all the moving parts in your swing. Note how pulling the bottom of the club down with the left hand creates an action known as the late hit – this is a key move when you need to strike down and ensures the clubhead doesn't overtake the hands before impact.

5 SPLASH DOWN
Concentrate on a mark about 2in (6cm) behind the ball and imagine the clubhead entering the sand at that point. Stay down through impact – keeping your knees flexed is often an effective way to achieve this. Try to delay the release of your hands for fractionally longer than you would for a full swing – this guards against turning the clubface over too early which often causes the ball to fly to the left.

6 HIGH FLIER
You generate lots of clubhead speed during this swing but look at the early flight of the ball – it's clearly not traveling any great distance. This is the way it should be – the clubhead travels through the sand under the ball rather than inflicting a solid blow. Much about this position resembles a normal followthrough – weight on the left side and the arms pulling your upper body round towards the target.

✗ SWING FAILURE

1 ROOM TO IMPROVE
There are no major problems at address, but a few points could be improved upon. Ideally your stance should be a little wider and the feet aligned slightly squarer to the target line.

2 GOOD START
The early part of the backswing looks to be in good shape. The arms and the club move in one piece to create the necessary arc away from the ball.

3 COMBINATION OF ERRORS
The shot starts to go seriously wrong at this stage. The club doesn't travel far enough on the backswing, there's an almost complete lack of shoulder turn and the wrists are hinged a little too much. These faults are certain to make it hard for you to generate the necessary clubhead speed through impact.

4 DIGGING DEEP
The poor downswing and disastrous impact position, where far too much sand is taken, are caused by faults that occur earlier in the swing. It's the hopelessly short backswing that causes the panic as you struggle to generate clubhead speed. As is often the case in this situation, the body lunges forward and tempo changes dramatically.

5 DEAD END
This clearly shows that taking too much sand can kill the shot completely. There's plenty of forward movement – head, shoulders, upper body – everything except the ball. Your head coming up too early is a tell-tale sign of anxiety.

6 SADNESS IN SAND
This is one of the most depressing sights in golf – the ball comes down hopelessly short of the target and fails to make a clean break from the sand. While you can take a couple of steps nearer the hole, this does nothing to ease the pain. The next bunker shot is at least as tricky as the last.

Lip reading

The most common fault that many golfers commit out of a shallow bunker is leaving the ball in the sand. This is almost certainly the result of being too tentative and failing to accelerate the clubhead through the sand. Because there's no front lip you're easily lulled into a false sense of security.

Playing a positive shot is the most effective cure, but you first need to be in the right frame of mind. Visualize an imaginary lip in front of you to help you achieve this goal.

This sets a more demanding test and forces you mentally to play a positive stroke – one that generates both height and carry – to guarantee you clear the imaginary front lip. Remember, escaping in one should be your first priority.

Once you can combine these qualities with a good feel for distance you have the recipe for success out of any bunker.

first attempt. However, it's important to understand that a shallow bunker shot is no different from most other strokes out of sand. The more you treat it this way, the better you're likely to cope with the shot.

INVISIBLE OBSTACLES

Because there's no physical barrier to overcome in the form of a menacing front lip, your largest obstacle is mental. There's really no short cut to approaching shallow bunker shots in a confident mood. You achieve this by playing them well in practice and then bringing the technique out onto the course with you.

You should always try to play the stroke that involves the least element of chance. The splash bunker shot technique is the one most likely to give you consistently good results.

This method makes the sand work in your favor – one of the keys to good bunker play. You can make a full swing, generate plenty of clubhead speed and yet watch the ball float at no more than a gentle pace towards the flag.

MAJOR MISTAKE

Because very little height is called for, many golfers are tempted to play a chip and run. However, this may be a simple shot from grass, but it's a different story out of a bunker.

Sand can be an unforgiving surface – trying to strike the ball without touching a single grain is extremely difficult. Catch the shot too cleanly and the ball races through the green. Make contact with sand before the ball and your next bunker shot may come a lot sooner than you thought.

Only when there's very little sand in the bunker should you consider playing a chip and run. Your pitching wedge is the best club if you do decide to play it.

PUTTING FROM SAND

Occasionally a putt from a shallow greenside bunker is a clever ploy. Think very carefully before you consider this shot – it's risky and all the conditions need to be heavily stacked in your favor if you're to succeed.

Most importantly, the sand needs to be hard packed and not at all fluffy – this allows the ball to roll relatively smoothly on the surface sand. The lip must also be almost non-existent. Even a ridge of 2in (6cm) – hardly a lip at all on first sight – is probably enough to bring your ball to an abrupt halt.

When you consider whether to putt or not, visualize the front half of the bunker as a ramp. If you can picture the ball rolling up this ramp, and not being stopped by the lip, a putt may well be the right shot. But if there's any doubt in your mind, your sand wedge is ideally suited to getting you out of trouble.

Bunker recovery shots

Recovery play from deep greenside bunkers involves a huge variety of trouble shots – no two are likely to be the same. You often need all your wits about you just to find a way out – precise placement is usually the last of your worries.

From time to time all golfers are faced with difficult bunker shots when there seems no escape. Negative thoughts can often crowd the mind – but be firm of purpose. Turn your attention resolutely to the task in hand.

Your first consideration is to try to limit the damage as much as you can. Your thoughts must be on safety – top priority is to avoid playing your next shot from exactly the same spot. Getting up and down in 2 shots isn't the main issue.

Often you can't take a direct

SAFETY FIRST
Bunkers have a nasty habit of testing your technique and imagination to the limit. You may be only a short distance from the green, but try to be realistic. Accept that you can't always aim for the flag from every bunker. Just concentrate on making sure your next shot is from grass and not sand.

UP AND OVER

① OPEN CLUBFACE
From this position you can at least be hopeful of playing for the green but it's no easy task, as the ball needs to travel almost straight up in the air. Align your feet, hips and shoulders left of target with the clubface open.

② WIDE TAKEAWAY
A weak right hand grip helps you keep the clubface open throughout the swing. Take the club away smoothly along the line of your feet and body and break the wrists halfway through the backswing.

pro tip

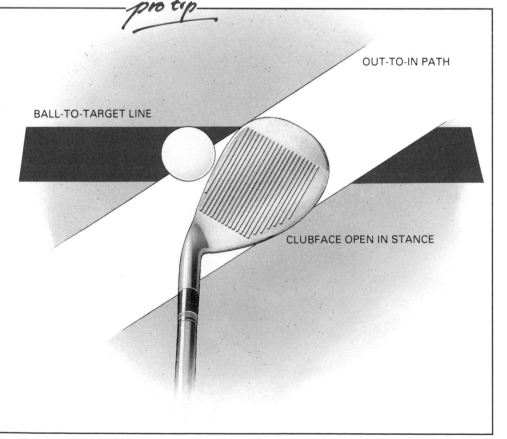

From out to in
Always strive for an out-to-in swing path when you play a greenside bunker shot – it is one of the fundamentals of a successful sand save.

Align left and swing the clubhead along your body line from out to in. The clubface lies open in relation to your stance to produce a straight shot. A small amount of sidespin is applied – this makes the ball pitch and spin right on landing.

OUT-TO-IN PATH

BALL-TO-TARGET LINE

CLUBFACE OPEN IN STANCE

3 FULL BACKSWING
Make a full shoulder turn and allow the club to travel near to horizontal at the top of the backswing. Your whole swing should feel unhurried and under control. Most of your weight is now on the right side.

4 CLUBHEAD SPEED
Your left hand dominates the downswing to set the clubhead traveling on a steep angle of descent. Visualize a spot in the sand behind the ball and imagine the clubhead splashing down on this mark.

5 SAND BLAST
Finesse doesn't play a part in this shot – generate as much clubhead speed as possible into impact. The explosion of sand throws the ball vertically into the air, avoiding the face of the bunker.

6 HEAD DOWN
The back of the left hand points skyward after impact, preventing the clubface from closing. Sand flying everywhere should help you keep your head down – never be tempted to look up too soon.

ESCAPE SHOT

1 NO WAY FORWARD
It's impossible to play a shot at the flag in this situation – the edge of the bunker prevents you from making a backswing or downswing. The only sensible alternative is to play out backwards away from the target.

2 FIRM FOOTING
The direction you're hitting the ball means that you can't place both feet in the bunker. Work your right foot well into the sand and flex your left leg. Position most of your weight on your right side.

3 STEEP BACKSWING
Pick the club up quickly on the backswing by breaking the wrists early – this action helps you to swing your arms on the upright plane needed for a high shot. Very little shoulder turn is necessary.

route to the hole so assess the options open to you. Think first of position – you want to make your next shot as easy as possible.

Look around the green and size up the shot carefully. There's nearly always a way out. Don't attempt anything foolhardy – settle instead for playing out sideways or even backwards.

If you're extremely unlucky and you simply can't see a realistic way out, take a penalty drop in the bunker. When the ball is plugged close to the face of the bunker it's better to drop rather than attempt an unlikely escape shot.

Before playing any bunker shot you must consider the texture of the sand. On links and heathland courses the bunker sand is fine and powdery. The clubhead slides through easily so the splash shot is ideal.

Sand on parkland courses tends to be heavy. While most of the bunkers are quite shallow, you still find deep traps eating into the side of some parkland greens. Your clubhead may dig in deep so don't be too delicate. The ball flies lower and runs further than a shot from soft, fine sand.

SAND TACTICS

Once you know in what direction you want to play the ball, think about the techniques required. The high splash shot can help you out of all sorts of trouble – particularly from deep bunkers. A sand wedge is the ideal weapon for the shot.

Adjust your stance to suit the slope of the sand – this is a key to successful recovery. You must put yourself in a balanced position which you can maintain throughout the swing. On an uphill or downhill lie position your shoulders as near to parallel with the sand as is comfortable.

Stand open at address with the clubface aiming square, or slightly open, to your chosen target. Work your feet into the sand to give yourself a solid base. Don't lock your legs rigid – keep them nicely flexed and relaxed. Stiff knees restrict your swing.

Swing high to hit high if the bunker lip in front of you is sizeable. Play the splash shot with authority and accelerate into the sand. You must generate lots of clubhead speed to avoid leaving

the ball in the bunker. Don't worry about hitting too far. The ball travels up as far as it moves forward and you very seldom overshoot the target.

Pick the club up steeply on the backswing by breaking your wrists early. Bring it down sharply on an out-to-in path into the sand – the clubhead cuts under the ball, and the explosion of sand at impact sends the ball almost vertically up in the air.

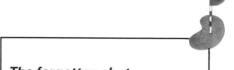

The forgotten shot
Bunker play is often neglected in practice routines – which doesn't help dispel its reputation as one of the most feared strokes in golf.

But playing off sand isn't all misery. It can be rewarding, particularly in practice. Experiment with shots from different slopes and lies in a variety of bunkers. You build confidence as you understand how to escape from the most difficult situation.

4 **AT THE TOP**
Stop your hands around chest height at the top of the backswing. Your wrists hinge as a result of picking the club up sharply earlier in the swing, and are perfectly positioned to help bring the clubhead down steeply.

5 **PULL DOWN HARD**
The left hand dominates the downswing, pulling the clubhead down hard. Most of your weight should be central – perhaps even a little on the right side. If you sway towards the ball you risk thinning the shot.

6 **SAFELY OUT**
Keep the clubface open as it cuts through the sand under the ball. The back of your left hand should face skyward long after impact. When the shot is played correctly the ball pops high out of the sand to safety.

Resign yourself

When your luck runs out and your ball finishes in a desperate lie, try not to lose heart – one bit of bad luck needn't destroy your round. Don't attempt a miraculous recovery shot – if it doesn't come off you risk taking more strokes in the bunker than you bargained for.

If you're not confident that you can escape at your first attempt, the rules allow you to declare the ball unplayable and take a 1 shot penalty drop. Select a spot that's nearer to the center of the bunker but still within two club lengths of the original position.

Drop the ball at arm's length and shoulder height. Although the ball may be further away from the pin than its original lie, a drop gives you a chance to play for the flag or the edge of the green. You can then comfortably escape from the bunker without disaster.

SAFE ALTERNATIVE

1 OUT OF REACH
A shot at the flag from this situation is possible only off your knees – but this is far too risky to attempt other than in practice. In a competition, simply choose the safest shot that's open to you.

2 SHOOT SIDEWAYS
It's easy to lose your balance with this awkward stance, so anchor your right foot firmly into the sand. Shuffle your left foot until you are comfortable – you must feel stable at address .

3 HEAD STILL
Break your wrists early and try to keep your right elbow close to your side on the backswing. It's important your head and body are as still as possible – sideways movement causes a thin.

4 ACUTE ANGLE
Pull the bottom of the club down almost vertically with your left hand to create an acute angle between your right arm and the shaft of the club. This action puts the clubhead on a steep angle of descent.

5 RETURN TO ADDRESS
Your left hand should lead the clubhead into the impact area, keeping the clubface open. Aim to strike the sand about a ball's width behind the ball – this guards against the possibility of a thinned shot.

6 SHORT FOLLOWTHROUGH
The splash effect of the sand throws the ball up and out of the bunker. This is one of the few shots where you don't complete your followthrough because the clubhead digs into the edge of the bunker.

Plugged lies

When your ball is sitting up in a bunker, you have a relatively simple shot. Plugged lies are another matter – extracting a buried ball from the sand is a tricky prospect.

Your ball could plug for a number of reasons. The texture of the sand is critical – newly laid sand can give you problems because it hasn't had a chance to settle.

Thick sand is likely to absorb your ball before the sand has time to thin out. When it does become finer, it acts as a cushion.

STUN SHOT

It's always the power of the club through the sand that blasts your ball out of the bunker – never try to play the ball itself.

With a ball that's lying well, you open the face, align left and use a fairly long swing. This provides height and backspin, so that the ball stops quickly.

The opposite happens when your ball is plugged. You set up parallel to the ball-to-target line with a slightly closed clubface.

That's why you can't expect height – the closed clubface digs

LESS HEIGHT THAN USUAL
Hitting successfully from a plugged lie is awkward because you don't get as much height and backspin as with a standard splash shot. Play a stun shot with a closed clubface to check the roll.

ESCAPING FROM A PLUGGED LIE

(2) HALF BACKSWING
Swing back about halfway, breaking your wrists right away. You need a steep angle of attack into the sand – the wrist break ensures it. When you play from a good bunker lie, your backswing is longer.

(1) CLOSE THE CLUBFACE
Stand parallel to the ball-to-target line with the ball central. Close the clubface – this helps dig out the ball. Set up differently from your normal splash shot address – for a good lie – when you align left with the ball forwards and open the clubface.

GOOD LIE

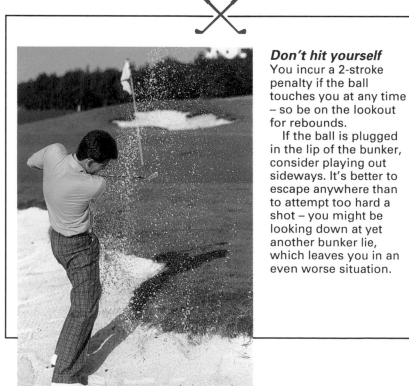

Don't hit yourself
You incur a 2-stroke penalty if the ball touches you at any time – so be on the lookout for rebounds.

If the ball is plugged in the lip of the bunker, consider playing out sideways. It's better to escape anywhere than to attempt too hard a shot – you might be looking down at yet another bunker lie, which leaves you in an even worse situation.

out the ball effectively, but with very little lift. The ball emerges with topspin and runs on landing to reduce further your chances of landing close to the flag.

To compensate for the strong roll, you must play a stun shot. This means having the confidence to cut short your throughswing, so that the clubhead does not pass your hands at any time.

Carefully assess the situation before you take up your stance, because the ball doesn't rise as well as from a good sand lie. You may not escape if the bunker has a steep face. If the face does look forbidding, play out sideways – at least you'll be out of the trap in one.

Strike firmly if you want plenty of roll. Trying for hardly any run on the ball is a riskier shot because you need to hit more softly – but

4 KEEP LEFT WRIST FIRM
Strike about 3in (7cm) behind the ball. At impact your hands should still be ahead of the clubhead with the left wrist – which mustn't collapse – taking the force of the shot. With a normal shot (right), the clubhead catches up with your hands at impact, but the role of the left hand is again vital.

3 HANDS LEAD THE CLUBFACE
Let your hands lead the clubface – exactly as you do when you're splashing out normally – and keep your left wrist dominant throughout the downswing.

not so softly that the club slows down, leaving your ball in the sand.

Although you strike with less power for the short hit, keep your left wrist firm. This helps to prevent slowing down the club as it enters the sand. When tempo is erratic, so is timing – and your shot is certain to suffer.

FIRM HOLD

Grip pressure is important. It should be firm for a long shot and more relaxed   though still solid – for a shorter shot.

It's worthwhile to spend some time in the bunker rehearsing strokes from a plugged lie. The more confident you are the more daring you can afford to be – but your top priority is to escape in one shot.

5 LOW CLUB AFTER IMPACT
Shorten the throughswing. This stunning action reduces the roll of the ball when it lands. From a good lie you don't need to lessen the followthrough, as the ball's height stops roll.

HOW'S IT LYING?

ASSESS THE SITUATION
When you enter the bunker, visualize your shot carefully. You can move man-made obstructions, but natural impediments must be left as they are. It's possible that you can move stones without penalty – check your scorecard for local rules. When you've played, leave the bunker as you'd wish to find it – litter free, raked and smooth.

CIGARETTE BUTTS
You can move cigarette butts, candy wrappers and the like – they're man-made objects.

FOOTPRINTS
You must play from footprints even though your ball can plug in them. Unfortunately you're paying for the lack of etiquette shown by another player.

RAKE MARKS
The ridges of sand created by the rake effectively plug your ball, but you can't claim anything under the rules.

LEAVES
If a stray leaf is lying next to your ball, you can't move it because the leaf is a natural object.

Bunker close-ups: good greenside lie

A sand's eye view of bunker play is the best way to understand and put into practice such well worn phrases as "lifted out on a cushion of sand."

Bunker technique is often shrouded in mystique and approached with fear. But seeing close up what happens at impact cuts through the theory and gets to the heart of sand success.

Once you understand how a ball reacts from sand you can form a clear mental picture of each shot you play.

SPIN BALL WIZARD

From a good greenside bunker lie the clubhead at no time makes contact with the ball. And while there's seldom any great distance between you and the flag, you can easily create backspin if you play a shot correctly.

The action of the clubhead sliding under the ball imparts the spin and sends it high into the air. You can be confident of the ball landing softly, which helps you play a positive stroke.

CONTROL THE SAND STORM
Many professionals would rather be in bunkers than in rough – particularly if the lie is good. They use the sand to help them control the ball – you can do this too if you know what to look for. Confidence out of sand soon filters through to your whole game. Once you can judge precisely how the ball reacts, and the amount of backspin you need (shown by red stripe), you can swing freely on a hole littered with bunkers, relaxed in the knowledge you're able to cope with shots from sand.

SOLVING THE MYSTERY OF SAND

① PSYCHOLOGICAL LIFT
There's never a good moment to land in a bunker, but if you find your ball lying well your spirits should immediately be lifted. A good lie means you can accurately judge how the ball behaves. The sand is fine so it's the perfect situation to play the splash bunker shot. Note that the red stripe is vertical at this point.

KEY POINT

Don't ground the club or touch the ball.

(2) **SPLASH DOWN**
The clubhead comes down steeply, cutting into the sand behind the ball. You must accelerate the clubhead into impact, otherwise the sand acts like a barrier, destroying the shot completely. It's the hitting down into the sand that pops the ball up in the air. Although your part in the shot is well under way, the ball is still motionless and the red stripe still vertical.

KEY POINT
Accelerate down smoothly.

③ BACKSPINNER
As the clubhead travels down, the ball is lifted up into the air on a blanket of sand. The red line shows clearly the backward rotation of the ball – this is the first sign of spin on the shot that stops the ball quickly on the green. You must play the shot precisely – as contact between clubhead and ball is indirect only total control gives you the spin you require.

KEY POINT
Feel the club sliding down and under the ball.

(4) **SAND BLAST**
The explosion effect of the sand is clear to see as
the ball is propelled upwards and forwards. The wide,
rounded sole helps keep the clubhead sliding through
the sand underneath the ball. At this stage the ball is
behind the clubhead and has rotated backwards 1½
times. It's important the clubface points at the target
through impact for as long as possible.

KEY POINT
Keep up clubhead momentum.

(5) **HEADING FOR SAFETY**
The clubhead leaves a shallow trough in the sand as the ball floats towards the target. The shot is played firmly and with authority – yet a soft landing on the green combined with backspin ensure the ball runs very little.

Practice makes perfect
If you usually take a practice swing before every shot, do the same when you prepare to play out of a bunker. Remember, the rules say you can't touch the sand with the club so stand outside the bunker and practice the swing you intend making. This helps give a feel for the shot – once in the sand you find you're more comfortable over the ball.

Player's bunker shots

Gary Player is generally regarded as the finest bunker player yet.

Early in his professional career he realized that his short stature would prevent him being a really long hitter. As he would be hitting longer clubs into the green than many of his stronger and larger contemporaries, he reasoned that he would often find sand. So he perfected his bunker play into a virtual art form.

The advice Player gives on bunker shots is particularly useful for women and junior players – or for anyone who hits short.

Player's success comes down to two factors: one mental, one physical. Unlike most players, he thinks positively about bunker shots. He never refers to bunkers as traps, as that immediately conjures up negative thoughts.

He also practices constantly. As a result, he knows how the ball will react from different sand textures and from a variety of lies, and can adapt his technique accordingly.

Many amateur golfers believe that the bunker shot requires a steep, chopping swing with the club swung back on the outside of the ball-to-target line. Player regards this as a recipe for disaster –

GARY'S POSITIVE APPROACH
Many golfers are happy just to lift the ball out of a greenside bunker. Player advises you to be far more ambitious – treat it like any other short game shot and aim to hole it.

IMPACT
Player sets his body in an open position so that his feet align to the left of the target. He strikes the clubface behind and underneath the ball. Because of his open clubface and the raised leading edge of the sand wedge, the club bounces rather than digs through the sand.

THROUGHSWING
Taking an explosion of sand with his shot, Player accelerates through the ball into a good, high finish. By varying the out-to-in swing path and the amount he opens his stance and clubface he can control the distance of the shot.

he still uses his basic swing for bunker shots. The changes in set-up create the necessary cutting action through the ball.

THE SET-UP

When faced with a shot from a greenside bunker, Player first wriggles his feet down to give him a firm stance. By doing this he also gets an idea of the sand's texture.

He then places his feet, hips and shoulders in an open position so that his body line is aiming left of the pin. The ball is opposite his left heel. Finally he opens the face of the club – a sand wedge – so that it is aimed right of the pin.

This set-up makes the swing follow the open body alignment – the path of the backswing travels outside the ball-to-target line and returns across it, placing sidespin on the ball. Player's body weight is a little more on the left foot as this helps the wrists to break earlier in the swing.

When using this method Player sees the shot as a skid through the sand. The splashing bounce

on the sole of his sand wedge counteracts the steep angle of attack. The club slides under and through the ball, which is thrown out with the force of the impact.

This technique works well for a good lie in the sand. However, for a ball that is semi-plugged in a bunker (a fried egg lie) he makes certain changes.

THE FRIED EGG LIE

Player still sets up to the ball with a fairly open stance but the ball is positioned more towards his right foot. His hands are well in front of the ball and his weight is firmly on the left side.

The set-up helps to create the right type of swing with a very steep angle of attack on the ball, so the club digs rather than splashes. This shortens the followthrough.

The amount of sand that gets between the clubface and the ball prevents backspin – and without backspin the ball rolls when it hits the green. To minimize the roll, Player always squares the club-

face to the ball. He never opens it as with a normal bunker shot, or the ball is caught thin and goes way beyond the green.

Player's method is worth copying – he is one of just four players who have won all four Majors.

Player's golden rules
For effective bunker shots Gary Player stresses four important points:
○ Open the clubface from a good lie, and square it from a buried lie.
○ Choose a club which has a deep flange – this creates the bounce on impact – and avoid using a pitching wedge, which has a sharp leading edge.
○ Do not try to chip from bunkers – the chances are the ball won't make it out.
○ *Practice, practice, practice* – as Gary himself has so often said, "The harder I practice, the luckier I get."

Downhill bunker shot

The downhill bunker shot – when the ball ends on the downslope – is one of the most awkward and feared sand shots to play. This lie occurs when the ball trickles into a bunker without enough power to run down to the bottom.

With any bunker shot it's important to hit the sand first. But with a downhill lie the downslope and lip of the bunker make hitting sand difficult. Practice the technique to avoid taking a penalty or playing backwards out of the bunker.

YOUR SET-UP

You might not be able to get into the bunker with both feet to take up your normal set-up – you may have to play with one foot on the fairway.

This position makes your upper body tilt in the direction of the slope. Though it's awkward and uncomfortable, practicing from this angle helps develop your downhill technique.

If you're really unlucky with the lie of the ball you won't be able to get into the bunker at all. In this situation you have to bend down on one knee – or perhaps both – and play the shot as normally as you can. Get as comfortable as possible, and be positive about your stroke.

Keep your clubface open as for a normal bunker shot but bear in mind that the ball may fly lower from this type of lie.

> ### Check the sand
> Sand texture is important for a good splash out from a downhill bunker shot.
>
> If the sand is soft and deep rather than wet and compact the shot is much easier – with wet, shallow sand there's a danger the clubhead won't slide under the ball. The shot may come out low with a lot of roll. Use a narrow-soled sand wedge to reduce the chance of a bounce, and be positive – hit firmly and with confidence.

KEEP YOUR HANDS AHEAD
At address your hands are ahead of the club – hold this position throughout the stroke to steepen your angle of attack into the sand.

BALANCE YOURSELF
A downhill bunker shot is made more difficult if you can't get both feet into the bunker. Lean forward from the waist to keep your balance. Your feet should be aligned left of target – an open clubface compensates. Position the ball further back in your stance than for normal bunker play to ensure that you take sand with the stroke.

ADDRESS AND ATTACK

1 GET COMFORTABLE
Open your stance and your clubface. You probably need to shuffle about a bit and rehearse the backswing to make certain you miss the back lip of the bunker when you start the swing.

THE SWING

Whatever way you have to tackle the shot, exaggerate the wrist break at the start of the swing so you pick up the club more acutely and avoid touching the bunker lip. This action also steepens your angle of attack which helps you hit into the sand behind the ball.

The quick wrist break moves your hands ahead of the clubface. Keep this position as you swing down and through the sand – have your right hand underneath the shaft as you strike through.

With your throughswing make a conscious effort to swing down and through the slope. This should be quite easy as you'll be leaning in the correct direction.

TRIAL AND ERROR

The downhill bunker shot is very much a feel shot – how the ball lies is a critical factor. Try shuffling back and forth to get comfortable. Experiment with how much you open the clubface at address and how acutely you break your wrists to start the swing.

Forget about reaching a respectable distance – be grateful to get out and hope for a good putt.

2 BACKSWING
Because of the acute angle of your upper body at address, you must pick up your club steeply to clear the back lip. Your open body position means you swing the club slightly outside the ball-to-target line.

masterclass

Alliss' natural ability
Peter Alliss – the all-around player and British TV commentator – shows his skill at tackling the downhill bunker shot. Very much a feel player, Alliss was able to attack the sand and lift the ball neatly out. Note how far back the ball is positioned to allow for the steep slope.

3 LEAD WITH HANDS
Let your hands lead the clubhead so that the face is open on contact with the sand. Don't be tempted to look up too early to see where the ball is going – your head movement could destroy the shot.

4 THROUGHSWING
Keep your right hand underneath the shaft as you swing through. The ball is thrown out by the sheer force of the clubhead hitting the sand underneath and behind the ball. Don't be too ambitious – be content simply to get out of the bunker from this difficult lie.

Mid-range bunker shot

One of the most feared shots in golf for both amateurs and professionals is the medium-range bunker shot. Some bunkers are strategically placed between 20-60yd (18-55m) from the green to catch any miss-hit shot. They are often found at par 5s where players are trying to get to the green in two.

If you find yourself in this situation, greenside bunkers between you and the hole often make the shot more difficult.

PRECISE STRIKING

An exact strike is needed if you are to get close to the flag. There are two common failings from this situation. If you take too much sand the ball lands short of the target, and may end up in one of the greenside bunkers. If you don't take any sand you strike the ball on the upswing and thin it.

The perfect way to play the shot is to take as little sand as possible – without thinning the ball – and to strike it clean with a square club-face.

THINK POSITIVE
Providing the strike is clean, playing from a bunker set 20-60yd (18-55m) from the green shouldn't ruin your score. Confidence is all important – don't be put off by more bunkers between you and the green.

The technique for playing the mid-range bunker shot differs only slightly from that used for a normal bunker shot. It's not essential to use your sand wedge – a pitching wedge is often better when you need the extra distance.

Judge the shot meticulously. Take time to walk up the fairway and view the scene from the side, so that you can visualize precisely what's needed.

When you play the shot correctly, the clubhead puts a lot of backspin on the ball. You can afford to pitch the ball right up to the flag and be confident of it stopping quickly.

If the lie is poor the flight and spin of the ball are affected. When the ball is sitting down in the sand you need a longer, more powerful swing.

Accept that the ball will run when it lands – though this can cause problems when the hole is cut just over a greenside bunker. In this case it might be better to take an indirect route to the hole.

Nick Faldo: bunker mastery
Faldo is acknowledged to have an excellent all-round game with no weaknesses. One of his strengths is his ability to play great shots from sand. He uses conventional technique, and produces sand saves from the most difficult of situations. He is confident of getting down in 2 from any bunker, even those at the awkward range of about 50yd (45m).

BUNKER PLAY

GREENSIDE SHOT

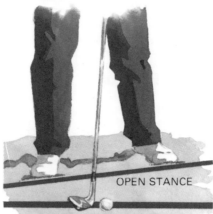

OPEN STANCE

BALL-TO-TARGET LINE

OPEN STANCE
When you play from a greenside bunker your feet, hips and shoulders should be open. Aim the clubface just to the right of the ball-to-target line.

OUT TO IN

OUT TO IN
Make a distinct out-to-in swing to help lift the ball high and stop it quickly on landing. You want height rather than distance with this stroke.

2-3in (5-7cm) OF SAND

SPLASHING ACTION
The clubhead slides under the ball, striking the sand about 2in (5cm) behind it. This action throws the ball high in the air and lands it softly on the green.

MID-RANGE SHOT

SLIGHTLY OPEN STANCE

SLIGHTLY OPEN
Position the ball in the middle of your stance and align your feet, hips and shoulders just left of the target. Aim the clubface square to the ball-to-target line.

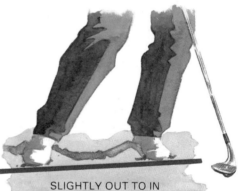

SLIGHTLY OUT TO IN

PITCH SWING PATH
The technique for this shot is very similar to playing a normal pitch. You are set up just open, so you swing on a slight out-to-in path, helping control the ball on landing.

CLEAN STRIKE

NIPPING ACTION
You must try to catch the ball as cleanly as possible without thinning it. Don't take much sand, or you reduce clubhead speed and lose distance.

In-out bunker shot

It's rare that you can't stand in the sand to play a bunker shot, but finding yourself in a tricky in-out situation shouldn't deter you from attacking the flag.

The most important element for a successful stroke is a sturdy and balanced stance. The way you address the ball depends on how far below your feet it is. If it's only just beneath your feet you can probably take a near normal stance by bending over from the waist a little more than usual.

You must make sure that you stay in the same position throughout the stroke – the tendency is to straighten up on the downswing

SPLASH DOWN
Concentration, confidence and a steady, rhythmic stroke are the keys to playing an awkward bunker shot – the in-out is no exception. This situation can arise at any time and on any course. Don't be afraid to play off your knees – it may look hard but a controlled splash shot is still possible.

UPPER BODY SWING

1 NEAR NORMAL ADDRESS
Adopt as near to a normal upper body position as possible – even if it means kneeling down. Make yourself comfortable and, if the cut of the bunker allows it, align slightly left. If not, align as best you can, perhaps even slightly right if you have to, as here. Position the ball forward in your stance as usual.

2 RESTRICTED BACKSWING
Swing with your hands and arms only. Pick the club up steeply to avoid clipping the sand, and try to make a full shoulder turn. Your top of backswing position should be shorter than normal – this lessens any lower body movement which can ruin your balance. Keep your head steady.

and it's easy to hit a thin. It helps to grip the club as far up as possible, lessening the amount you must bend to reach the ball.

ON YOUR KNEES

Sometimes you can't reach the ball no matter how much you bend at the waist or flex your knees. Either spread your legs wide or kneel. Kneeling is probably the

best choice because you are closer to a normal stance. It's also easier to swing from a kneeling position as you can turn your shoulders almost fully.

The only difference from a normal swing is that the plane is more upright and the movement of the lower body is restricted – you must play the shot with your hands and arms.

Because the plane is upright the

ball tends to fly off to the right so aim to the left of the hole if you can – sometimes the way the bunker is cut makes it impossible. If it helps to align left you may be able to have one leg in the sand and one out.

Whatever stance you adopt, make plenty of practice swings to see if the shot is on and to feel comfortable. Be sure not to touch the sand with your club – even

③ SAND BLASTER
Attack the ball with a smooth yet forceful action – don't quit on the stroke. Your impact position should be almost an exact replica of your address – especially if your posture is awkward. Moving to a different position impairs your striking – the clubface is unlikely to return to the ball correctly.

④ FOLLOWTHROUGH
Control the throughswing with your left hand to keep the blade pointing at the target for as long as possible – resist your right hand taking over. Follow through as far as you can without overbalancing – with your finish short and controlled, you should still end up facing the target.

though you're not standing in the bunker, the ball is in a hazard and you can't ground your club. If you do, you incur a 2 shot penalty or lose the hole in matchplay.

If the stroke is too difficult, it's best to find another route to safety. When in severe trouble with no obvious shot on, you shouldn't rule out taking a penalty drop – but don't forget you must drop in the bunker.

pro tip

Gripping changes
The way you set up to an in-out bunker shot dictates how you should grip the club. Move your hands up and down the grip so that you can set up as near to normal as possible. Standing above the ball and bending from the waist is easier if you grip the club near to the end – you don't

have to lean over so far, so the shot is simpler.

When kneeling to the ball you may have to choke down the grip so you can take up the correct upper body position. Gripping the club normally means your upper body is too straight and makes it difficult to swing.

KNEES BEND, ARM STRETCH

KNEEL DOWN TO KEEP
NORMAL UPPER BODY POSITION

The advantage of kneeling down to address an in-out bunker shot – instead of bending and reaching for the ball – is that your upper body stays in a normal position. This makes it easier to play the shot because you can use a near conventional swing. The one difference is that the swing plane is more upright than usual because the shot is played with the hands and arms only.

If you have to bend over from the waist to reach the ball, the danger is that you return to a normal position during the downswing and risk thinning the shot. Kneeling down lessens this risk as you can stay in the correct position more easily.

masterclass

Player's sand strength

Gary Player is one of the greatest ever exponents of sand play. His understanding of technique, and his balance, touch and confidence mean he can escape from the trickiest of positions – nothing fazes him.

Playing an in-out bunker shot poses few problems for the man in black – it is one of the rare occasions when Gary's lack of height is an advantage. A taller man finds it difficult to take a solid stance and still play a decent stroke. But Player – winner of nine majors – easily maneuvers his body into a relaxed and stable position to play the shot with control and assurance.

Long slider from sand

Knocking a ball into a deep-faced fairway bunker usually proves costly to most amateurs. Some try to be too adventurous and take a direct route with a straight-faced club and leave the ball in the trap. Others lack confidence and settle for a safe chip out, leaving just a glimmer of a chance to get up and down from long distance to save par.

But there is a technique that combines these two approaches and can be a true matchwinner. Hitting a long, sliding, left-to-right cut out of the trap means you can loft the ball out but still gain maximum distance.

The method is simple. If you align well left of target, keep the blade square and swing along the line of your feet, the ball starts left and curves back to the right.

This shape means the ball has more time to climb before meeting the face than if you fire directly

ESCAPING THE TRAP
Power play from sand is too often disregarded by amateurs, who think it is beyond their scope. But with a little imagination, a calculating set-up and swing, and above all confidence, you can pull off even the most difficult of sand recoveries. You can reach a green that most would believe to be out of range by hitting a cut out of the trap – where the ball starts way left and curves powerfully back to the target.

BLASTING CUT

① SLIDER'S SET-UP
Align as far left as you think is safe. Imagine the flight path of the ball – bearing in mind which club you have in your hand – to help you decide how far left you need to align. Don't forget it is more important to escape the trap than reach your target. Square the blade. Make sure that it is not too open in relation to your stance.

② SUBTLE CHANGES
Keep your action as normal as possible – swing along the line of your feet. You may want to swing on a slightly more upright plane than usual to help promote the fading flight. At the top, your club should point well left of target.

③ OUT-TO-IN FOR LEFT-TO-RIGHT
It's crucial to keep swinging along the line of your feet into impact. Trying to swing the blade straight at the target means the ball starts off on the wrong path and runs the risk of colliding with the bank in front of you. Because of your set-up, the downswing path is naturally out to in – this gives the ball its left-to-right shape.

4 EXACTING STRIKE
The strike should be quite clean with just a little sand taken after the ball. If you take too much sand you lose clubhead speed and the ball doesn't fly the full distance. But if too little is taken, a thin into the bank is often the result. Even though your swing is near normal you may hold the blade square through impact for a fraction longer than usual to help the left-to-right shape.

5 FADER'S FOLLOWTHROUGH
An upright throughswing plane is quite natural and a sure sign that you've given the ball a cut. The combination of this swing and an opened up clubface sends the ball high – even with a long iron – and it starts left of target.

6 FLOWING FINISH
A swirling finish is another indicator of a cutter's action. If you're in this position, you can be sure that the ball has started left before sliding back to the right. Provided your club selection and striking are good, you can be confident of an accurate result.

at the flag. Aiming straight at the green means you can't hit a club both to fly over the lip and still reach the target.

SHALLOWER SIDES

Often a fairway bunker has a crescent-shaped face – where the middle part of the bank is deeper than the sides. It means that the bank may be less steep to the left of the ball-to-target line, and because you are playing a cut shot the ball naturally flies higher than normal. Both these facts make the stroke much easier to hit.

It is safer to play this shot from the right side of the hole because you aim down the left side of the fairway. Even if the ball doesn't cut as much as you would like you should be safe enough. But you mustn't be frightened to play this shot from a bunker on the left.

If your set-up and striking are good, you can be confident of the shot coming off – despite sometimes having to fly the ball over trouble before it cuts back toward, the green.

STRIKE COMMAND

As striking plays such an important part in the success of the shot, you should practice hitting long irons from sand before you introduce the cutting shape into the flight.

Find a low-lipped bunker to fire from, and concentrate on catching the ball quite clean, so that you take little sand. And remember – always clip the ball before the sand to avoid the fat.

If the sand is soft you must not strike down too hard on the ball – this lessens the chance of a fat. But if the sand is firm you can afford to attack the ball as normal.

Don't try to lift the ball out of the trap or to catch it too clean, as a thin is the most likely outcome, and all the good work in your shot preparation would be ruined.

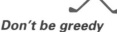

Don't be greedy
Even though the aim of hitting the long slider is to reach the green when it seems improbable, safety must come first. Never stretch the bounds of reality. Being too ambitious can not only ruin your score but may be a danger to your health.

It is not unknown for a player – who chooses too straight-faced a club and is greedy about their line – to come off second best. Quite often the ball comes rebounding off the bank and at best stays in the trap, but at worst inflicts a nasty blow. The pain is not eased by the fact that you also incur a 2 shot penalty in strokeplay or lose the hole in matchplay.

Be sensible about the shot. If there is a seed of doubt about the stroke coming off, settle for a safe pitch out.

masterclass

Mac the knife
Mark McNulty is more readily recognized as a steady, consistent performer, but he also has a cavalier spirit. Faced with a crucial long range bunker shot at the 1990 Wang Four Stars event, Mark showed what can be done by hitting the sliding cut.

Standing at 17 under playing the 72nd hole, he needed a par to take the clubhouse lead. But his drive came to rest close to the lip of a fairway bunker. After a careful visualization Mac settled into an open stance but kept his blade square and let it rip.

The ball missed the lip and came flying out to the left. But McNulty had made such a cutting swing that it flew back towards the green. His unbalanced finish is a sign of a slider's action. All his efforts were rewarded as he secured his par. A round of 65 meant he forced his way into a playoff with three others.

Unfortunately for Mark he was topped for the top prize by Rodger Davis.

Bunker shot from grass

Most amateurs dread the delicate shot over a bunker onto the green, especially when the ball is sitting in thick grass. To make matters worse the flag is often a short distance away, and there is only a small landing area between the bunker and the hole.

In this situation you need to hit a high floating chip with a sand wedge so that the ball lands softly on the green.

It's hard to apply any backspin when grass comes between the ball and the clubface. There is also a tendency for the club to become caught up in the grass and for the clubface to close. With little backspin and lack of clubhead control, it is difficult to achieve a perfect shot.

The technique is similar to the greenside bunker shot. Open your stance, and with a square clubface – opened up for extra loft – hit slightly behind the ball as if you are taking sand.

BE PREPARED

Take a little time to visualize the shot before you play. First assess the lie of the ball. The further it is sitting down the more grass is taken and the firmer you must swing. You should always walk up to the green and choose where you want the ball to pitch. Bear in mind that the ball rolls forward on landing.

Form a positive picture in your mind. Imagine the ball popping out of the grass and landing on the spot you chose. This helps you relax and feel confident when you play the shot.

At address check that the club doesn't get tangled in a clump of grass when you take it back. Always make sure the club can move freely away from the ball. Hover your clubhead above the grass if you can't move the club away properly after grounding it behind the ball.

Your backswing path must be outside the ball-to-target line, and your downswing out to in. This makes you cut across the ball, and because you have opened up the clubface for extra loft the ball jumps high out of the grass.

HAVE NO FEAR
At some time everyone finds themselves having to play a tricky shot – often when the ball is sitting down – from thick greenside grass over a bunker. If you use the right technique and are positive you can tackle the shot fearlessly.

GENTLE LOB FROM THICK GRASS

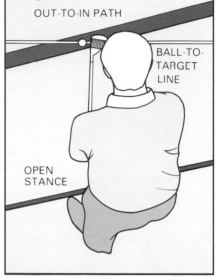

Open up
The key to the shot is in your alignment and clubface position. The combination of an open stance and the extra loft of the opened-up clubface produces an out-to-in swing path and a high lobbing shot that lands softly on the green.

OUT-TO-IN PATH

BALL-TO-TARGET LINE

OPEN STANCE

①OPEN ADDRESS
For extra loft open up the clubface and aim it square to the target. Grip down the shaft slightly and align your feet, hips and shoulders left of the target. Position the ball opposite your left heel.

②SHORT AND WRISTY
Allow your wrists to break early in the backswing, which is shorter than normal and outside the target line. The length of your backswing is determined by the distance the ball must go and whether it is lying well or badly.

3 FIRM AND POSITIVE
Your downswing
should be out to in and
the strike firm and
confident. Do not try to
hit just the ball – unless
it's sitting right up in the
lie, you must take grass
with the shot as you
would sand in a bunker.

**4 FULL
FOLLOWTHROUGH**
Make sure you don't quit
on the shot – swing
through fully. Never slow
down through the ball. As
in a bunker, failure to
swing through positively
results in a duffed shot.

HOW IS IT LYING?

masterclass

Jim Milligan's killer blow
In the 1989 Walker Cup at Peachtree GC in Atlanta, the Scot Jim Milligan was the hero. Great Britain and Ireland needed a half from the final singles to win the trophy for the first time on American soil.

Milligan was 2 down with 3 to play. After winning the 16th with a birdie he took the 17th by chipping in from a grassy lie. The miraculous shot using bunker technique ensured a famous win.

▲ ▶ The lie is very important to how the ball needs to be played. Often the ball is perched almost in mid air on top of the grass. In this case you shouldn't ground the club as you may cause the ball to move and pick up a one shot penalty. Hover the club behind the ball and try to take the shot cleanly.

If the ball is sitting down in the grass you can ground the club as the ball is less likely to move. You must take grass with this stroke or you may hit a topped or thinned shot.

The condition and type of grass are also important. If the grass is wet your clubhead is slowed down more than usual through the ball. You must hit the shot crisply as it won't go as far as a stroke from dry grass.

Swing firmly if you are playing in hot countries out of Bermuda grass – the club is more likely to get tangled than from the rough found in cooler climates.

BALL SITTING ON TOP OF GRASS   BALL SITTING DOWN

pro tip
Polished sand play

GO TO BOARDING SCHOOL

The mid range bunker shot – one of 25-60yd (23-55m) – is an awkward stroke for any level of player. However, one drill helps you to fine tune the correct technique, and become a confident and proficient performer from this tricky distance.

Because crisp striking is essential to gauge the weight of the shot correctly, you need to nip the ball cleanly off the sand. To practice clipping the ball crisply, lay down a wooden board about 45yd (41m) from the practice green – or play to an umbrella stuck in the ground. It doesn't have to be in a trap, but practicing with your feet in sand is realistic.

Place the ball in the center of your stance and align parallel to the target line – not left like a greenside bunker shot. You may want to play the shot with a pitching wedge to lessen the chance of bouncing the blade into the back of the ball. The longer distances are also easier to judge with a pitching wedge.

Concentrate on swinging with a smooth, easy rhythm, and attack the ball from a steeper angle than you would for a greenside sand shot. This ensures you catch the ball first and not the board. The ball flies out on a good trajectory with plenty of backspin. Clipping the wood first results in a duff or thin. Let the club do the work – don't try to lift the ball up.

If you can strike consistently well flighted pitches from such a hard and bare lie, you should have no problem nipping a ball off sand without fatting or thinning the shot. This improves your mid range bunker accuracy enormously and boosts your sand save percentages.

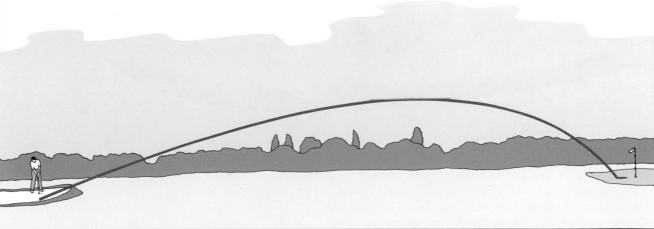

SLIDING UNDER

The blade of your sand wedge must slide under the ball to hit a controlled splash shot out of a greenside trap. You have to take sand, but it must be just the right amount. Too little and you're in danger of thinning the ball, too much and you fluff the ball.

Ideally you should aim to start taking sand about 1 in (4cm) behind the ball. The blade should continue through impact on a shallow path floating the ball out on a blanket of sand.

To perfect this technique, try either the tee peg or double ball drill.

TEE PEG DRILL
Push a tee peg into the sand 1in (2.5cm) behind the ball. Forget about the ball – concentrate only on the tee. Be sure you set up properly and then make your swing. Aim to scoop out the tee peg with a sliding action by hitting slightly behind it – so you

contact the sand at the critical 1½ (4cm) behind the ball.

If you have made the correct shape of swing the ball should naturally pop up into the air without you having to think about it. You can take this technique out on to the course by picking a spot behind the ball to aim at. Don't look at the back of the ball.

DOUBLE BALL DRILL
Another way to achieve the same effect is to try to splash two balls out with the same stroke. Place one ball directly behind another pointing at the target. Set up imagining the ball nearest the hole to be your target ball, but don't aim to hit it. Try to slide your blade under both balls.

Having to go under the first ball to be able to splash the target ball out naturally ingrains the correct technique into your muscle memory.

It's best to practice in a low-lipped trap – the target ball does not fly out as high as you would expect because it is bumped forward by the first ball. Keep your eye on the first ball as it lofts daintily out of the trap – this gives you a good idea how the target ball will behave when you use the same technique with only one ball.

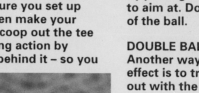

SLIDE BLADE UNDER TWO BALLS
FOR CORRECT SPLASH TECHNIQUE

6

MASTERING THE WOODS

The longest and lightest clubs in the golf bag, woods are designed to enable you to drive the ball the greatest possible distance, both off the tee and on the fairway. Harder to control than irons, woods need to be mastered if scores are to be lowered. This section teaches you the basics of wood play and takes an in-depth look at how to create maximum power within your swing.

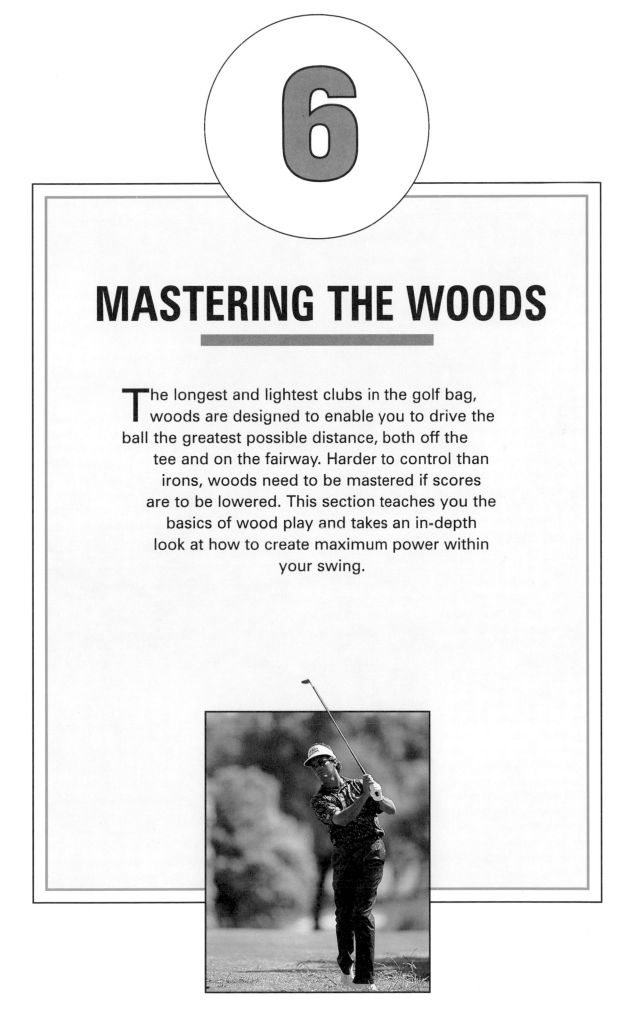

Using woods

You use the woods for maximum distance both on the tee and the fairway. Although woods are usually harder to control than irons, especially when you are new to the game, you should learn how to use them as soon as possible. Using woods to hit the ball long distances is an ability you must learn at an early stage to lower your scores.

A well-struck wood shot sets you up in the best possible way for the remainder of the hole.

The most commonly used woods are the 1, 3 and 5. They are designed to increase your distance and power without any extra effort.

While the size and shape of the clubhead provides the most obvious visual difference between woods and irons, it is the length of their shafts that helps you achieve the extra distance.

Shape, material and length combine with your technique to extract power from the club.

MORE POWER

When you swing a wood, the longer shaft gives a wider arc and this means that the clubhead has a greater distance to travel. If you swing a wood with the same rhythm and tempo as an iron, the clubhead travels around the arc in the same time, but it has to cover much more distance and this raises its speed. It is this increase in clubhead speed that provides you with the additional power to

WOOD AND IRON SWINGPLANES

SWINGPLANE OF IRON

SWINGPLANE OF WOOD

There is a marked difference between the swingplane of a wood and that of an iron. The swingplane of a wood (blue) is flatter, where you cause the clubhead to sweep through the ball at impact. The swingplane of an iron (pink) is more vertical, and the clubhead approaches the ball at a more acute angle. These differences are brought about by the length of the club changing your posture at address. Posture is more upright with a wood.

SWINGING WITH WOODS

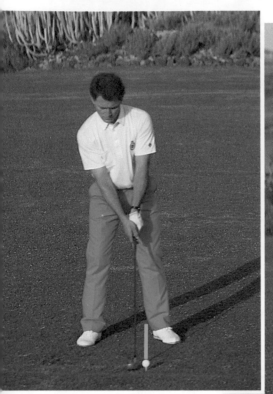

1 ADDRESS & TAKEAWAY
At address the ball is opposite the inside of your left heel. Take the club away slowly, keeping the clubhead low to the ground.

2 ROTATE TO THE RIGHT
Allow your upper body to rotate freely as your left arm swings the club back. By the two-thirds point in your backswing your weight has transferred from a central position at address to the inside of your right foot.

hit the ball longer distances. You do not have to speed up your swing and tempo to make the clubhead go faster. Your tempo should be the same for every "full" shot from driving to pitching.

While the longer shaft of the wood should not affect your timing, it does lead to changes in your address including stance, posture and ball position. It also affects your swingplane.

ADDRESS AND SWINGPLANE

With a wood, you stand further away from the ball than you would

with an iron because the shaft is longer. Your stance is wider so that you can maintain your balance. Your posture changes so that you address the ball with your back more upright and you position the ball opposite the inside of your left heel.

This upright posture triggers a number of other differences between woods and irons. Your swingplane is flatter, so the clubhead approaches the ball at a shallower angle. You sweep through the ball, which is struck at a later point in your swing. This is why the ball is placed opposite the inside of your left heel.

3 TOP OF THE BACKSWING
At the top of the backswing your shoulders have rotated 90° and your hips 45°. Make sure you complete the backswing before starting the downswing – a slight pause before the downswing helps. At the top of the backswing the shaft should point at the target.

④ STARTING THE DOWNSWING
Rotate your left hip to the left to start the downswing. This pulls your arms and hands into an ideal striking position.

⑤ FOLLOWTHROUGH
After impact, allow your weight to move across to the outside of your left foot. The left side of your body controls the entire swing – from takeaway to followthrough – while your right side remains passive.

Pick your wood

1 WOOD (DRIVER)
3 WOOD
5 WOOD

The wood you use depends on the shot you want to make and the distance you want to hit the ball. The 5 wood has more loft than the 3 and 1 woods and hits the ball higher. The 1 wood has the longest shaft and hits the ball furthest.

⑥ THE COMPLETED POSITION
Allow the momentum of your club to pull your right shoulder and your head to face the target. Your whole body should also face the target. At the finish you should be balanced with most of your weight on your left foot.

BALL POSITION AT ADDRESS

FORWARD IN THE STANCE
With a wood, place the ball opposite the inside of your left heel and stand with your feet about as far apart as a normal walking pace is long. With a medium iron the ball is near the middle of your stance.

DISTANCE FROM FEET
Stand further away from the ball when you use a wood than you do with an iron. You have to do this because the shaft of a wood is longer.

THE BACKSWING

Once you have understood the changes to your stance, posture, ball position and swingplane, the basic technique for using woods is similar to using irons. Your tempo remains the same, as do your grip, aim and alignment procedures.

From address, take the club away slowly, keeping the clubhead close to the ground for the first 6-9in (15-23cm). Your left shoulder is pulled across and your weight transfers from an even distribution at address to the inside of your right foot by the completion of the backswing.

PAUSE AT THE TOP

When you reach the top of your backswing, allow for a slight pause before starting the downswing. This pause helps create rhythm and improves timing by separating the backswing from the downswing. Many golfers believe that the backswing and downswing are one continuous movement. This is wrong, and to treat them as one movement only leads to a rushed swing and a poor strike.

THE DOWNSWING

Begin the downswing by smoothly rotating your left hip to the left. This pulls your hands, arms and the clubhead down to the halfway position where your arms and hands swing the clubhead through the ball. The momentum of the clubhead pulls your right shoulder under your chin. Your head rotates to face the target and your weight moves across to your left foot.

TEEING UP THE BALL

When playing a wood shot from a tee peg you have to place the peg at the correct height. The height varies from club to club, but the general rule is that the center of the ball should be level with the top of the clubface when the club is resting on the ground and the ball is on the tee.

Clubfaces on woods vary in depth, although within any one set, the lower the number of the wood then the deeper its clubface and bigger its clubhead. The 1 wood has the deepest clubface of all woods. The tee peg for a 1 wood should be higher than for a 3 wood, which in turn is higher than for a 5-wood. A ball teed at the correct height is easy to sweep off the top of the tee peg.

If you don't tee your ball at the correct height you lose both distance and accuracy or even mishit the shot.

TEEING HEIGHTS

When teeing up, half the ball should be above the top of the clubface at address. So, the deeper the clubface, the higher the tee peg should be set in the ground. Because the 1 wood has a deeper clubface than both the 3 and 5 woods, its tee peg should be higher. The 5 wood has a shallower clubface so the ball is teed lower.

If you tee-up too high you might hit the ball with the top of the clubhead and send it into the sky. If you tee up too low you might hit the top of the ball and send it a short distance along the ground.

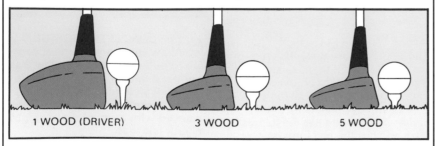

1 WOOD (DRIVER)   3 WOOD   5 WOOD

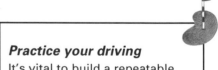

Practice your driving
It's vital to build a repeatable and consistent stroke with your woods. A long hit with your driver gives you the best possible chance of reaching the green of a long hole in few strokes. Practice with your woods until you are confident that you can hit long distances accurately. If you neglect any part of your game, the whole of your game is bound to suffer.

Swing well with a sway

One of the biggest myths in golf is that you must keep your head perfectly still at all times during the swing. To complete a proper swing there must be some slight movement of the head. It's almost impossible to make the right moves and hit the ball well when playing with a fixed head position.

You can't turn your shoulders fully or transfer your weight properly when you try to keep your head totally motionless. You tend to shift your weight on to the left side during the backswing – the reverse pivot – which is the opposite of what you should do.

You need to feel you are slightly moving off the ball on the backswing, and moving back on to the ball during the downswing. This slight swaying motion creates a freedom from which you can make a full shoulder turn during the backswing.

At the top of the backswing your head should have tilted slightly right so that you're looking at the ball with your left eye.

① SET-UP
Be conscious of the sway from the start of your swing. Note that the pole is placed behind the player's head to check any movement during the swing.

② SLIGHT SWAY
When you make a full shoulder turn and transfer your weight on to the right side, your head moves naturally a little to the right. Look at the ball through your left eye.

③ CENTRAL SHIFT
When you swing down your head must shift back to the central position. You generate power by moving away on the backswing and coming back to the ball on the downswing.

Start the downswing with the lower half of your body. This triggers a weight shift from your right side to your left, which in turn brings your head back to the central address position.

SWINGING A PUNCH

These movements are essential if you're to deliver the clubhead into the ball powerfully. It's rather like a boxer throwing a punch. To have any sort of power he must sway and transfer his weight on to his back foot before coming through with the punch.

This principle also applies to striking a golf ball – the rocking on to the right foot during the backswing provides the momentum for moving back through the ball with power on the downswing.

During the followthrough your left side continues to clear. Your head should move forward and up from the impact position, so that your body and head face the target.

Learn the correct sway technique, because moving in the wrong way makes it almost impossible to hit the ball well. Don't just shift sideways on the backswing without shoulder turn. And avoid moving too much to the right – it's then hard to co-ordinate your downswing and to strike with good timing.

Too far back
Too much lateral movement of your head and upper body on the backswing makes it impossible to finish your swing properly. From this position coordination and timing are extremely difficult.

masterclass

Strange sways to success
Curtis Strange dispels the myth that you can't swing properly if your head moves. On the backswing his head shifts about 7in (18cm) to the right. But he still makes a full shoulder turn and the correct weight transfer.

At impact his head returns to the central position. Strange moves through the ball with a flowing motion, finishing in the classic pose. This method gives him great rhythm and consistency – he won the US Open title two years running in 1988 and 1989.

Too far forward
If you sway too much on the downswing your head and hands are likely to move too far ahead of the ball. The result is almost always a shot that squirts off to the right.

Develop the power hit

Millions of golfers throughout the world constantly strive for more power and extra distance. Too many fail and become wild because they try to swing faster to gain more length.

Greater swing speed does not equal greater distance. Clubhead speed is the critical factor. This is generated by a combination of dynamic body action and fast hands. For maximum power you need to create a lag of the clubhead behind your hands on the downswing, and release into impact at the last possible moment – the late hit.

The world's most powerful golfers are all natural late hitters and have no need to force the hands to work. But luckily you can develop this power hit to a degree – without ruining your tempo, rhythm and control.

ANGLE HELD FROM TOP OF BACKSWING UNTIL HANDS ALMOST AT IMPACT POSITION

LATE HIT GENERATES MASSIVE CLUBHEAD SPEED

110 mph

HOLD ANGLE FOR LATE RELEASE
The key to a late hit is to retain the angle – formed between your shaft and left forearm at the top of the backswing – for as long as possible on the downswing. Ideally you should not start working the wrists until your hands are almost opposite your right thigh.

This means that the clubhead has to travel a good distance in the last fraction of a second before impact to return square. This creates the massive clubhead speed needed to hit the ball powerfully.

But you must never force the hands to work – they should be free and loose. Also never leave the releasing of the hands too late as it is almost impossible for the blade to return square. The likely result of leaving it too late is a huge carve out to the right.

However good your hand action, you must still combine it with good body positions to generate maximum power and still stay in control. You can't get the best from your fast hands unless you take the club away on a wide swing arc, make a full shoulder turn and drive into the ball with your lower body.

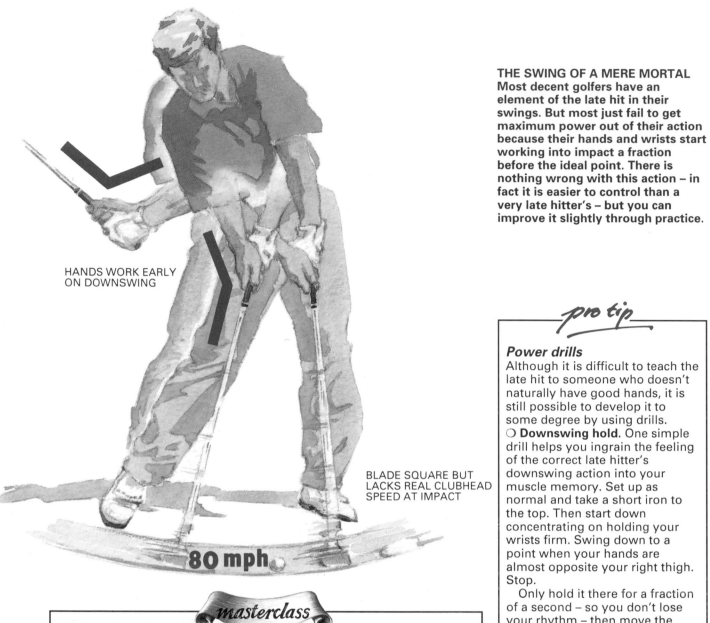

HANDS WORK EARLY
ON DOWNSWING

BLADE SQUARE BUT
LACKS REAL CLUBHEAD
SPEED AT IMPACT

80 mph

THE SWING OF A MERE MORTAL
Most decent golfers have an element of the late hit in their swings. But most just fail to get maximum power out of their action because their hands and wrists start working into impact a fraction before the ideal point. There is nothing wrong with this action – in fact it is easier to control than a very late hitter's – but you can improve it slightly through practice.

masterclass

Mighty Fred
If there is one golfer in the world today who perfectly illustrates the mix of an easy swing with awesome power, it has to be Fred "Boom Boom" Couples. The distances he smacks the ball are often unbelievable, because his swing is so languid, smooth and unhurried.

The slow tempo belies the fact that Fred's hands start working into impact extremely late, and so generate enormous clubhead speed. The lag he creates is astonishing, and even when his hands are almost at their impact position, the clubhead trails way behind.

This action comes naturally and Fred never forces the shot. This means he has control to go with his might – a potent combination that has lifted Couples into the world's top rank.

pro tip

Power drills
Although it is difficult to teach the late hit to someone who doesn't naturally have good hands, it is still possible to develop it to some degree by using drills.

○ **Downswing hold.** One simple drill helps you ingrain the feeling of the correct late hitter's downswing action into your muscle memory. Set up as normal and take a short iron to the top. Then start down concentrating on holding your wrists firm. Swing down to a point when your hands are almost opposite your right thigh. Stop.

Only hold it there for a fraction of a second – so you don't lose your rhythm – then move the club back to the top and repeat three times without ever unhinging your wrists. On the third swing continue past the stopping point and release your hands into the ball.

Keep repeating this drill. You should soon feel yourself creating a little more lag and power. Don't worry if you push the balls slightly to start with – in time you should naturally work your hands more, so that the blade returns square at impact.

○ **Bell ringer.** Many teaching professionals suggest using your imagination to help develop the power hit. Think of yourself pulling down hard on a bell rope from the top of the backswing. This action of trying to ring a bell automatically makes your hands pull sharply down and keeps your wrists from working too soon on helping you produce the late hit.

Beat driver phobia

T hose who dread the driver and steer clear of the club at all costs are missing out on one of the most uplifting experiences in golf – a good bash with a driver bites a large chunk out of most holes and is a tremendous boost to your confidence.

The problem for a lot of golfers is not always genuine fear of hitting this club, more a case of struggling to find a driver they feel comfortable with.

If you've ever felt this way you probably take the headcover off your driver very reluctantly. It's hardly surprising that some golfers store their drivers in the cupboard rather than the golf bag.

The search for that elusive longest club in the bag is rather like looking for your perfect putter – it often takes time and can easily mean experimenting with several makes and styles.

The driver is a very personal club – far more so than any set of irons you'll ever buy. Once you find one you like, stick with it through thick and thin. The club takes on a far less frightening appearance and at times you're likely to feel you can hit almost any shot – this is very important in a pressure situation.

DRIVING LESSON

Even with a club that suits you it's important to know how to drive before you can stand on the tee with total confidence.

Although it's mainly a distance club, never hit your driver flat out unless the situation is really desperate and crying out for you to take a gamble.

The well known phrase that you

TAKE THE EASY OPTION
Every golfer drives the ball badly from time to time – even the best in the world. Don't feel you have to slog your way through a slump with your driver – if you're suffering from a bout of low confidence it could take a depressingly long time. Move down to your 3 wood and swing the club just as you would a driver. You don't lose much distance, the club is easier to hit, and an upturn in morale is just round the corner.

SUBSTITUTE DRIVER

1) FIRM FOUNDATION
The 3 wood is much easier to hit than the driver and gives you almost as much distance, so if you're struggling off the tee, a more lofted wood is often the short term answer. Adopt exactly the same address position as you would for a driver – the only adjustment you need to make is teeing the ball fractionally lower to allow for the smaller clubhead.

2) FIRST STEP
Try to ensure that your first movement away from the ball is correct. Sweep the club back close to the ground for at least 12in (30cm). This serves a dual purpose – it prevents your wrists breaking too early and sets the club on a wide arc away from the ball. Both are essential for generating clubhead speed during the swing.

3) HINGE POINT
The importance of creating a wide arc is clear at this stage of the swing, as the left side is pulled into perfect position. The right leg acts as a brace supporting more than half your body weight. At about the time your right arm folds your wrists should begin to hinge – this helps ensure the clubhead travels on a consistent plane to the top.

4) ROCK SOLID
The top of the backswing is one of the most crucial stages of the swing, whichever club is in your hands. Look out for certain essential points – full shoulder turn; hips rotated about 45° from address; shaft of the club as close to horizontal as possible; and good weight transfer away from the ball.

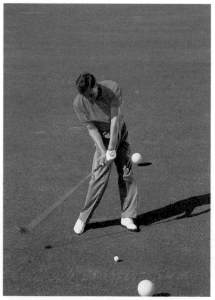

5) NATURAL PROGRESSION
The downswing is made that much easier when you work hard at getting your backswing right. The solid pose achieved at the top helps trigger the correct moves into impact. The body unwinds from a coiled position and the weight shifts onto the left side – each combines to generate clubhead speed.

6) TURN FOR THE BETTER
This fluid followthrough is the result of swinging correctly – you can't put yourself in a good position through the ball if you make mistakes earlier. Once you start to strike your 3 wood well, move up to your driver – you stand a better chance of hitting good shots with this club when your confidence is high.

CARDINAL POINTS

Many courses have practice greens that aren't big enough to hit a full driver. For many golfers the local driving range presents the only opportunity to practice with this club. If you're among this group of golfers, you must be aware of some helpful points to ensure you make constructive use of your time and money.

Most importantly you need to avoid the greatest temptation of all, which is to mindlessly thrash away as if you were in a long driving contest. You see this at every range with "aerosol golfers" spraying the ball to all points of the compass. It seems like a good idea – after all, knocking the ball a long way is fun and there's a full bucket of balls waiting to be hit – but this activity has a damaging effect on your game.

Swing within yourself and always take your time between drives. Never hit too many shots – about 20 or so is an ideal number. Only pull out the driver towards the end of a practice session and never at the beginning – you need to be properly warmed up to hit the ball well with this club.

You also have to accept that concentration can be hard at times when you're at a crowded driving range. With balls shooting from the bays like tracer bullets it's easy to get distracted. Try to ignore the blur of activity going on around you and look at it as good experience – if you can focus at a driving range you shouldn't have problems doing so on the course.

Bear in mind that the balls at a golf range are usually quite poor quality. They feel soft off the clubface and don't travel as far as the type you would use on the course. So don't feel miffed if your best drive falls well short of the usual mark. Another drawback of most golf ranges is the fixed rubber tees. If they're at a different height to those you're used to, don't hit balls off them. It's bound to feel strange and you may find yourself making adjustments to your swing. Use tee pegs if possible – otherwise don't hit drives at all.

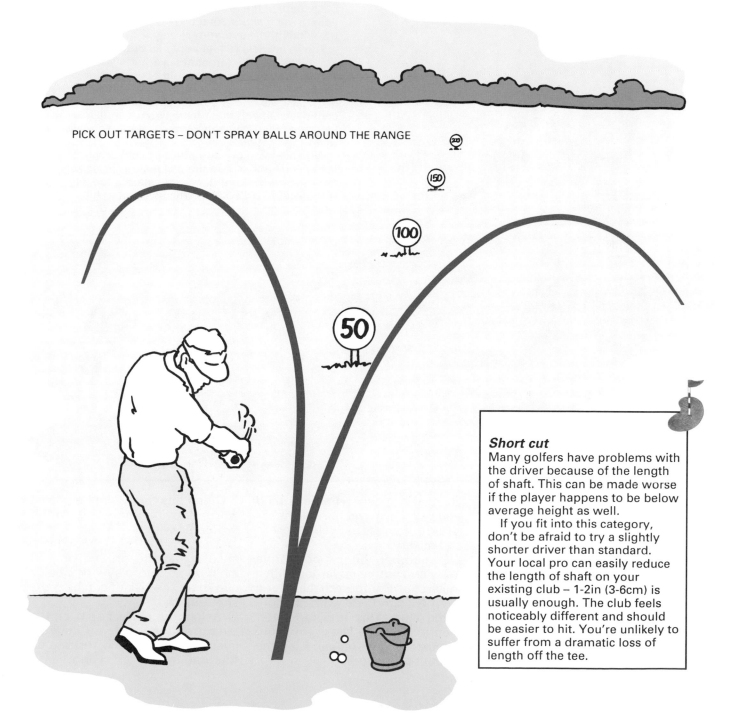

PICK OUT TARGETS – DON'T SPRAY BALLS AROUND THE RANGE

Short cut
Many golfers have problems with the driver because of the length of shaft. This can be made worse if the player happens to be below average height as well.

If you fit into this category, don't be afraid to try a slightly shorter driver than standard. Your local pro can easily reduce the length of shaft on your existing club – 1-2in (3-6cm) is usually enough. The club feels noticeably different and should be easier to hit. You're unlikely to suffer from a dramatic loss of length off the tee.

pro tip

TWO UMBRELLAS AT DRIVER DISTANCE

30yd (27m) APART – WIDTH OF AVERAGE FAIRWAY

Realistic aim

When you practice with your driver it's important you set yourself a realistic target to hit. Two umbrellas serve the purpose as well as anything. Stick them in the ground at the distance you hit your driver – about 30yd (27m) apart represents the width of the average fairway.

You're unlikely to hit every ball between the umbrellas, but the target at least gives you the sort of landing area you would expect to find on the course. If you're driving well you can achieve a good success rate and gradually build on your confidence. If you don't have two umbrellas, aim between two trees at the end – this is an equally realistic target area.

Whatever you do, don't try to pump drives at a lone pencil-thin tree in the distance. This is likely to destroy what confidence you started the day with because it's such a difficult target to hit.

TAKE YOUR TIME – SWING WITHIN YOURSELF

should swing your driver as you do a 9 iron is one of the finest single pieces of advice you can absorb.

Try to feel as though you're swinging at about 70% of full power. This gives you the distance you need and, more importantly, the control which is essential for consistently finding the fairway.

When you stand on the tee it's important to do all you can to put yourself in a positive frame of mind – how you feel over the ball makes all the difference between success and misery.

Remember, hit a good drive away and you're rewarded with a much shorter approach than if you were to play safe with a more lofted club. This is a far better mental attitude than worrying whether or not you can keep the ball out of the trees.

Other positive points are also worth drawing upon if you suffer problems with the driver:

○ Tee the ball high enough to ensure that the ground doesn't even come into play – this helps eliminate the risk of catching the shot heavy.

○ Select the perfect spot on the teeing area so that you have an even patch of ground and a good foundation for your swing.

Soft landing wood shot

The mark of a good player is the ability to pluck a specialist shot from his repertoire just when he needs it most. Think how often you've known the shot best suited to a situation, but didn't have the knowledge or the confidence to carry it through. It's a frustrating feeling.

The soft landing wood is a good example of a specialist shot you can use in several quite ordinary situations. You can play it with any one of your lofted woods, depending on the distance you intend hitting the ball. However, it's not a shot you should attempt with your driver.

The main feature of the soft wood is the control it gives you. While it won't be the longest shot you ever hit, it's likely to be one of the safest. Essentially a fade, it's perfect when you want your ball to land like a butterfly with sore feet.

PROS AND CONS

The soft wood shot is a useful alternative to hitting a long iron. The ball should fly higher and sit down quickly on landing. A lofted wood is also easier to hit and more forgiving to a poor strike. This means you can play it from a greater variety of lies – good or indifferent.

This shot is only as good as the situation you apply it to. You may have your sights set on a small and distant green, or a narrow fairway littered with bunkers – anyplace where no run on the ball can work in your favor.

On the negative side, a soft flight can easily wander off line in strong winds. And there are bound to be times when you want a low, penetrating trajectory, and the ball to run out on landing. The soft wood can't give you this result, so if you want to steer clear of trouble it's important to know when not to play the shot.

SOFT OPTION
When a tree blocks your path to the green, you need to conjure up distance and height – no easy combination, even from the fairway. A soft wood provides both and also lands the ball softly, allowing you to hold the green. It is also easier to hit than a long iron from the same position.

MASTER THE SOFT WOOD SHOT

1 ALIGN SLIGHTLY LEFT
The main characteristic of the soft wood shot is the floating, fading flight it produces. It's a tremendous asset in this situation because it enables you to fly the tree and stop the ball quickly on the green the other side. You must align slightly left of target – making sure the clubface is square – or you risk missing the green on the right.

3 SQUARE THROUGH IMPACT
On the downswing imagine the clubhead traveling along a line parallel with your feet. Due to your set-up and alignment, the clubhead moves very slightly from out to in through impact in relation to the target. Combined with a square clubface, this produces a shot that starts left and then fades back onto the green.

2 BACKSWING ON PLANE
Once you've set up correctly, a normal backswing places you in perfect position at the top. The angle of the back of the left hand in relation to the clubface indicates that your swing is on plane. Other points to concentrate on are a full shoulder turn and good transfer of weight onto the right side.

4 WELL BALANCED FINISH
By now you should be well aware how good the shot is. Perfect balance is an excellent sign and a good indication that you have swung within yourself with a high degree of control.

CHOOSE THE RIGHT SHOT

RAISED GREEN – TRICKY TARGET

FLOATED WOOD LANDS BALL SOFTLY – FINE CHANCE TO HOLD GREEN

HIT THE BULL'S-EYE
You find raised greens all over the world – playing to them is rather like trying to pitch and stop your ball on an upturned dinner plate. If the greens show any sign of holding, aim to pitch your ball all the way. This is one occasion where the soft wood shot works in your favor because it produces a more floating, less penetrating flight than a long iron. Combined with the fade on your ball, the shot is tailor-made for this testing situation.

Running your ball on to a raised green can be a haphazard affair. It's fine if you're chipping from close range, but from a distance you can never be sure how the ball is going to cope with the slope.

pro tip

Go to any lengths
The combination of clubs that you prefer to have in your bag may permit you to carry only one utility wood. But this shouldn't restrict you to using the club from one specific distance – the boundaries are far wider.

Grip down your utility wood to reduce the flight of the ball through the air – this gives you enormous versatility without having to change your swing. It's almost like giving yourself a 15th club to carry in your bag.

USE THE NATURAL ELEMENTS

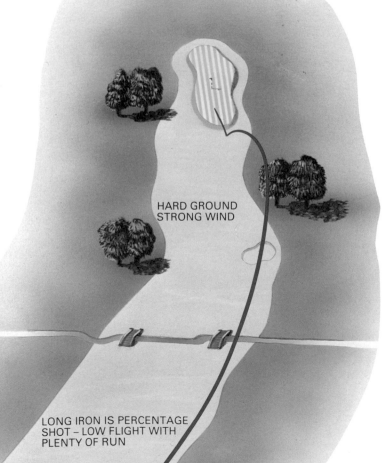

HARD GROUND STRONG WIND

LONG IRON IS PERCENTAGE SHOT – LOW FLIGHT WITH PLENTY OF RUN

GO FOR THE LOW RUNNER
On most courses there are plenty of opportunities to make the natural elements work in your favor – this becomes almost a necessity in strong winds. If the fairway is clear between you and the green, always favor a long iron which helps you keep your ball low.

Even a slight miss-hit should creep close to the green, because on firm ground there's lots of run on the ball. This is one situation where an average long iron is likely to produce at least as good a result – perhaps even better – than your best soft wood shot.

When there are no hazards to carry don't play high flying shots just for the sake of it – you allow your ball to be ravaged by the fierce wind. This is where the soft wood shot can cause major headaches, so you must find an alternative.

Subtly shaped driver

Having the know-how and ability to shape shots is a wonderful asset to your game. Though most golfers only try to shape their irons – particularly on approaches – there is huge scope to maneuver your driver as well.

Usually amateurs who do try to shape their drivers only attempt it on a dog-leg – to hug the contours of the hole. But a faint draw or fade from the tee is useful for far more than just that.

Safe shots, finding extra distance and playing for position are all made easier by a subtle shaping of your driver. On a tightish but long hole – where you need length and accuracy – a gentle fade is the shot to hit. Starting down the left side slightly, the ball drifts back to the center of the fairway and lands softly – thanks to a higher flight with more backspin than normal.

A draw is less controllable but produces greater roll and length than a fade – because of the drawspin. This flight is extremely handy for squeezing that extra bit of yardage out of a drive – perhaps when you think a par 5 may be in range in 2.

Both shapes are well suited for positional play. You can avoid trouble on one side of the hole by moving the ball away from it. And by maneuvering a shot to one half of the fairway or other, you can leave yourself a better line into the flag.

Don't be fooled into thinking that you have to make drastic set-up changes to shape a driver. If you do, your intended faint fade turns into a carve and your draw into a big hook. Subtle shaping needs subtle changes – as the straight face of a driver accentuates any sideways movement and exaggerates its effect.

PLAYING FOR POSITION
Thinking ahead is vital if you're to make scoring easier for yourself. When you stand on a tee, look down the hole and work out where best to place your ball for your approach. If you need to hit the ball down the left side to give yourself a better line into the flag – as at the 1st at Valderrama – shaping your driver could be the answer. If you aim down the center of the hole and play a slight draw, you're almost guaranteed to finish down the left side. At worst you should be in the middle of the fairway if the shot doesn't quite come off.

FRACTIONALLY OPEN FOR GENTLE FADE

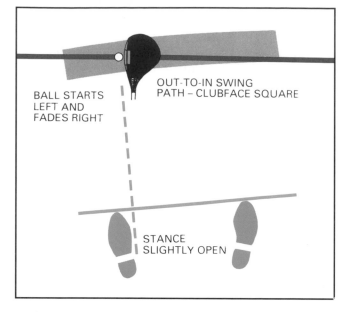

BALL STARTS LEFT AND FADES RIGHT

OUT-TO-IN SWING PATH – CLUBFACE SQUARE

STANCE SLIGHTLY OPEN

ALIGN LEFT, AIM SQUARE
To hit the subtle left to righter you only need to change your normal set-up by the tiniest amount. You must still square up the clubface with the center of the fairway – or the line on which you want the ball to end up – but you must stand a fraction open. It's a matter of an inch or two – any more and the fade can get away from you.

OUTSIDE ATTACK
Forget about your set-up and solely concentrate on swinging as normal – along the line of your feet. You naturally swing slightly outside the target line to the top and then attack the ball from out to in – even though your swing plane in relation to your body is normal.

TELL-TALE THROUGHSWING
As you swing through back on the inside there is a natural tendency to stop your hands releasing as quickly as normal. This is no bad thing as it helps the fading flight, but you must never hold it for too long – or the fade turns into a slice. The high-handed, slight flourish into the finish is a tell-tale sign of the fade.

FAINT DRAWING TECHNIQUE

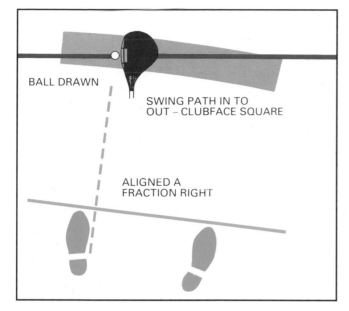

BALL DRAWN

SWING PATH IN TO
OUT – CLUBFACE SQUARE

ALIGNED A
FRACTION RIGHT

ALIGN RIGHT, AIM SQUARE
You probably need to change your set-up less to play
the draw than you do for the fade. If you're not careful
it is easy for the shot to be overdone as the ball flies
lower with drawspin and runs on landing. Align only a
fraction right but keep your blade exactly square.
Position the ball as normal – opposite your left heel.

POINTING RIGHT AT TOP
Swing along your normal plane – resist the temptation
to take the club back too much on the inside in an
attempt to promote the draw. If you move into your
usual top of the backswing position, your driver shaft
should be pointing slightly right of target.

NATURAL INSIDE ATTACK
If you swing down at the ball from slightly on the inside
as usual, the angle of attack is accentuated. Even
though you have dropped the club down into impact in
your normal way, the actual path in relation to the
target line is from in to out due to your alignment. With
the blade square, the ball starts down the right side
and drifts back to the center of the fairway.

Maneuvering Mark

There is such a variety of layouts around the world that you must be able to shape the ball well to become a top flight performer. Not only can it get you out of trouble but it can give you the edge over your fellow competitors.

Mark James has that ability. Although his action is slightly unconventional his understanding of the technique is excellent and he has superb control through the ball. The five time Ryder Cup player is equally at home with hitting a fade or a draw, and has used this prowess to great effect when tackling the courses on the Euro Tour.

The sweeping, tree-lined holes at Woburn – home of the Dunhill British Masters – demand subtly shaped drives if you're to conquer the course. Mark certainly used his maneuvering skills there in 1990 when he won by 2 shots from David Feherty.

Height for flight

Shaping the driver doesn't just mean moving the ball sideways, you can also flight shots at different heights to suit your purposes.

If you want to keep the ball lower than normal – perhaps to combat the wind – try teeing the ball slightly higher than you usually do.

This helps you create a more sweeping action and attack the ball on a shallower angle than normal. Instead of catching the ball on the up, you should strike the ball on a more level plane and drive the ball forward under the wind.

Teeing the ball up also helps you to hit the ball higher if you position the ball forward in your stance – useful to gain distance downwind. Because the ball is forward in the stance the clubhead attacks it more on the up and so sends the shot on a higher flight than normal.

pro tip

Knocking an iron into shape

Although shaping a driver is great for your game, there are times when you should be wary of hitting it. As stressed by all teachers, any change in your driver set-up that isn't only a fraction away from your norm can be dangerous.

Because a driver's face is so straight, it is all too easy to overcook your intended shape. So when you're faced with a curving dog-leg hole – where you need to move the ball quite a lot to keep it on the fairway – it is unwise to hit a driver.

If you try to maneuver the ball too much, just a slight loss of control sends your ball flying away into trouble. Your best option is to hit a long iron. A 1 iron has a shorter shaft and a more lofted face than a driver, making it easier to control. But it still hits the ball a good distance and has a steep enough face to shape the ball markedly.

But beware of hitting a big draw with a 1 iron. The blade – though still square to the target line – is delofted at address, and your draw may become a hook. Go with a 3 or 4 iron instead – they take on the loft of a longer iron.

Driver off the fairway

The driver off the fairway is an extremely effective weapon when used in the correct way. But it should only be played when you can gain a definite advantage.

The shot produces a low-boring trajectory – ideal when hitting into wind, or for a long running ball to a distant target – but it's also difficult to play perfectly. Only advanced players should attempt this shot – it's not for high handicappers.

WEIGH UP THE RISKS

Use the shot to reach a long par 4 into the wind or to get home in 2 on a par 5. Yet if there is only a small chance of success and trouble looms near the green, it's wiser to play a long iron and then

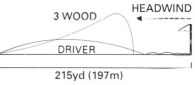

pro tip

Short for control
When confronted by a shot into wind of roughly 3 wood distance, it's sometimes better to go down the grip on your driver and shorten your backswing.

The three-quarter backswing means the ball doesn't go as far as a normal driver but you have more control over the shot. The ball flies low and runs towards the target, while a full 3 wood shot is more affected by the wind as the ball climbs higher than with a driver.

You may be pleasantly surprised how far the ball goes using this method, especially on a firm, dry fairway.

3 WOOD · HEADWIND · DRIVER

215yd (197m)

THOUGHT AND TEMPO
The secret of success is positive and careful thinking, while maintaining good rhythm with a normal swing. With the feet slightly open the ball starts fractionally left and slides back to the right during flight. The ball flies low and can run long distances, perfect for playing into wind.

hit a short iron in.

The lie must be flat or slightly uphill – to act as a launching pad – and the ball must be sitting well, preferably on dry ground. When the ball is lying badly always think hard about hitting the shot even if there is a chance of reaching the green. It's a tricky enough shot to play well without added problems.

Many regard the driver off the fairway as the hardest of all shots, but as long as the lie is good the risks are mainly in the mind. The fact that most good golfers happily hit a 3 wood off the fairway makes their fear all the more unnecessary.

There is only a slight difference in the degree of loft, the center of gravity and length of shaft from a 3 wood to a driver. The driver is just a bit more difficult to play.

THE TECHNIQUE

The basic technique of hitting the driver from the fairway is the same as from a tee peg. At address, position the ball opposite or slightly in front of your left heel and aim the clubface at the target as normal.

Your feet should be fractionally open – this slightly increases the loft on the driver to help get the ball airborne and to guard against the snap hook. Because you are aligning slightly left and your club-face is square, the ball starts left and moves gently to the right in the flight.

Think positively – imagine you are hitting a 3 wood – and swing as normal. Don't overhit the ball – rhythm is far more important when applying power.

The key difference between hitting off the fairway and from a tee peg is timing. It needs to be perfect to achieve good results from the fairway. It's important to strike the ball at the bottom of your swing arc, and to sweep it off the turf.

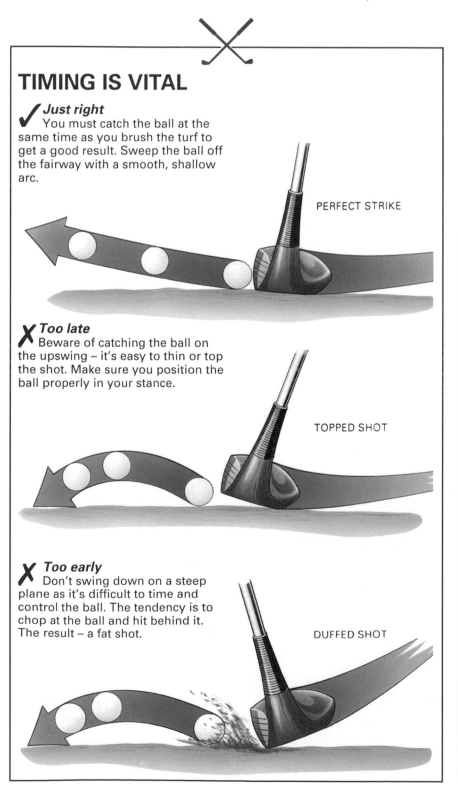

TIMING IS VITAL

✓ Just right
You must catch the ball at the same time as you brush the turf to get a good result. Sweep the ball off the fairway with a smooth, shallow arc.

PERFECT STRIKE

✗ Too late
Beware of catching the ball on the upswing – it's easy to thin or top the shot. Make sure you position the ball properly in your stance.

TOPPED SHOT

✗ Too early
Don't swing down on a steep plane as it's difficult to time and control the ball. The tendency is to chop at the ball and hit behind it. The result – a fat shot.

DUFFED SHOT

masterclass

Ian's killer blow
The driver from the fairway presents Ian Woosnam with few problems because he is such a great timer of the ball. Combined with his power he can reach greens that are out of range for most golfers.

In the 1989 Irish Open at Portmarnock, the little Welshman came to the 514yd par-5 16th neck and neck with Philip Walton. But Woosie struck two drivers one after the other – the second off the fairway – to within 15ft (5m) of the hole to make birdie. He went on to win the title.

Tight drives

Every golfer goes through it – a dreaded fear of driving down narrow fairways. Seeing a tight, tree-lined hole or a hummocked fairway flanked by pot bunkers and heavy rough can be a daunting experience.

A poor mental state is the main culprit for finding trouble down an unforgiving hole, as it badly affects your swing. A nervous disposition tightens the golfing muscles and your action can become abrupt and stiff.

FREE STYLE

Trying to guide the ball off the tee is disastrous. Strive to swing freely with rhythm and make sure you release through the ball – both essential for accurate hitting.

Many players are under the illusion that to find the fairway they must aim smack down the middle and hit a ripper that bisects the hole. But a shaped shot is usually your best asset in finding the short stuff.

By aiming down one side of the fairway and hitting either a fade or draw, you almost double the effective landing area. As a general rule the fade aimed down the left side is the safer stroke of the two, as the ball lands softer than a drawn shot.

Because you must always play away from trouble, be open minded which shape you hit. The severity of the trouble either side of the fairway determines your tee shot.

If there's trouble of equal danger both sides of the hole, play the fade – unless the fairway slopes from left to right. In that case a draw is best to hold the ball on the hill.

DOUBLE TROUBLE

If one side of the fairway is more punishing than the other, play toward the lesser danger – even if it means hitting a draw. It may sound ludicrous, but even if your ball rolls into water on one side it may well be better than the fate on the other side – perhaps out of bounds.

Positioning yourself on the tee correctly also helps you to stay out of trouble. Tee up on the side of the worst trouble so it's easier to hit away from it.

Driving safely down a tight hole isn't just a matter of shaping the ball with a free and easy action – club selection is also vital.

An iron is a safer club than a wood and should be easier to hit the fairway with. Look at the overall yardage of the hole. If you can

CAREFREE DRIVING
Don't be intimidated by a narrow, tree-lined fairway. Try giving your driver a rip to develop a confident, go-getter attitude. Standing up there and letting fly helps you to swing freely and release properly. Finding the fairway with a wood is so satisfying that it boosts your mental state, and should help to cure any timidity.

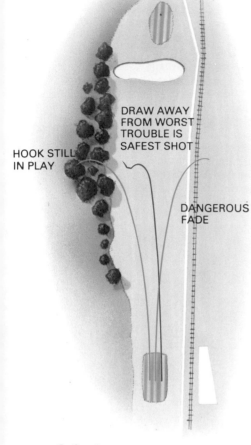

HOOK STILL IN PLAY

DRAW AWAY FROM WORST TROUBLE IS SAFEST SHOT

DANGEROUS FADE

Safe shapes

Hitting down one side of the fairway and moving the ball back toward the middle gives you extra margin for error. Even though a fade is the safest shot, sometimes a draw is the one to play. When an out of bounds fence runs down the right side and trees down the left, play a draw.

The punishment for going OB is worse than overdoing the draw and bounding into the trees. You have to play 3 off the tee for going over the fence but you still have a shot on in the woods. If you're lucky you may have a clear passage to the green, but even settling for a chip out sideways is better than having to reload from the tee.

afford to hit an iron on a par 4 and still reach the green with your next, do so. And if you're certain you can't reach a par 5 in 2, play an iron from the tee to be safe and ensure a good second.

For any tee shot on a tight hole you have to trust your ability and feel as though you can hit a spanker. Sometimes it helps to cure a negative attitude by standing up there and throwing caution to the wind. Let it rip – at least that way you know your swing is free and you release smoothly through the ball.

Think your way around

The width of the fairway needn't be small for the landing area to be tight. Fairway bunkers are sometimes positioned in awkward places around driving distance. Strategy is all important. So when you find a hole with cunning traps that you know you can reach, think carefully.

A driver may leave you a shorter shot than hitting an iron from the tee, but it also flirts with the danger. It takes an exacting strike to thread your ball through the gap. You gain very little by going for the driver – even if you hit a good one – as your approach is tricky. You have to fly a trap and land the ball softly to hold the shallow green.

LAY-UP LEAVES BEST APPROACH

TIGHT DRIVER GAINS NO ADVANTAGE

Hitting an iron or fairway wood short of the trap is much safer and leaves you a better approach. Though your second is longer than from a driver, you have a clear line into the flag and more green to work with.

masterclass

On line Ollie

José-Maria Olazabal blitzed his way to one of the most sensational victories of recent times in the 1990 World Series. Only four players broke par for the week on the 7149yd (6537m) Firestone Country Club course. But, remarkably, the Spaniard was 18 under – 12 strokes ahead of nearest rival Lanny Wadkins.

His record opening 61 followed by three 67s was a superb exhibition of long, straight, controlled hitting on one of the toughest and tightest courses on the US Tour.

José conquered the narrow fairways flanked by thick rough using a combination of sound, powerful technique and clever strategy. He realized that hitting the fairways was more important than length, so opted to play a 1 iron from the tee on many occasions.

Though it often left him a long distance away – perhaps even a wood – he had more chance of making his par or birdie than from 20yd (18m) further up but just off the fairway.

masterclass

Lanny Wadkins: king of the fairway wood

Forget about the armchair pundits, when your fellow pros vote you the best fairway wood player on tour it really means you're the best. That is exactly what the US Tour golfers have said about the seven time Ryder Cup star Lanny Wadkins for years.

Renowned for his no-nonsense approach and magical matchplay abilities, no opponent can ever take Lanny for granted. No one can afford to be complacent after finding the green from long range, if Wadkins is 230yd (210m) away with his 4 wood in hand. He can lay one in there with ease and leave them scrambling for a half.

SWISH HITTER

His fast-hitting, attacking style wins many admirers, but the flurry of wood and steel is not just an aggressive swipe – there is method in his action. The "fastest gun in the west" – a nickname coined because of his speedy approach to the game – is slightly unorthodox, but bases his superb hitting on sound fundamentals.

Lanny's shot visualization and striking are the most impressive parts of his fairway wood play, and every golfer can learn from his method.

By subtly changing his set-up and swing the burly Virginian manufactures exquisite strokes. Whether it's a low, drilling wind cheater or a high, soft-landing floater, Lanny knows the exact technique needed to bring it off.

He takes time to size up the stroke, thinking of the shape of shot he needs and the set-up and swing to produce it. But after careful thought he is quick to get into position and fire the ball away – he never dwells.

GET SET UP, GO

As long as you visualize the shot carefully before you play, there is no need to take time over the stroke. Like Lanny, walk into position, set up and then go for it. If your swing thoughts are correct for the shape of shot you need, only doubts can creep in if you loiter over the ball.

But striking the ball quite quickly after setting up doesn't mean you have to swing fast as well. Though Lanny has a quick tempo, his rhythm is good and he keeps himself under control throughout the swing.

POWER FADE PERFECTION

①SMART SET-UP
Once decided on hitting his stock fairway wood shot – the high power fade – Wadkins moves quickly into position. With the blade square to the target and his feet, hips and shoulders slightly open, Lanny looks relaxed and ready to go.

②POWER EXTENSION
The extension on the takeaway is enormous. His left arm is still perfectly straight, and this creates a very wide swing arc. His legs are active and he has already turned his shoulders a good deal. All of Lanny's backswing moves are designed to produce power.

③TOP MODEL
A powerful action is no good unless your club swings on line. Lanny completes his massive shoulder-turning backswing on perfect plane. There is no hint of an arched or cupped left wrist, which means the clubface is square at the top. If you move into a coiled position like Lanny's, you have a great base to swing down into impact on the correct path.

④ **DYNAMICALLY DOWN**
From the top, Lanny drops his hands down forcefully towards the ball leaving his clubhead trailing way behind. Instead of flailing his arms uncontrollably to the outside – as many amateurs do when they swing aggressively – he controls the slight out-to-in path by keeping his right arm tucked in.

⑤ **EXACTING STRIKE**
Fast hands enable Lanny to return the blade square. Combined with an excellent drive of his legs into and through impact they create a huge amount of power. His balance and clubhead control are so good throughout the swing that he strikes the ball sweetly and true. A full release of the hands through impact is also essential for control.

⑥ **FLOWING AND STABLE**
Lanny stays superbly balanced on his full and flowing throughswing. Staying with the shot – keeping the head behind the ball through impact – ensures that all the good moves on the backswing and downswing aren't wasted by rising off the shot.

⑦ **HIGH HANDS, HIGH BALL**
Because Lanny maintains a good rhythm, strikes fractionally down on the shot and swings on a slightly out-to-in path, the ball starts a fraction left of target and rises high. These traits are all essential to hit a controlled, left-to-right, soft-landing wood.

Hit big with Woosnam

Little Ian Woosnam is renowned for being one of the longest hitters in golf. At just 5ft 4 in (1.65m) in height the Welshman is a prime example of a proven theory – you don't have to be tall to send the ball a long way.

Woosnam drew inspiration from other successful small golfers – for example Gary Player and fellow Welshmen Brian Huggett and Dai Rees. Player has become a legend in the game for winning championships such as the Masters, where the Augusta course favors long hitters.

SWING PLANE

When Woosnam was younger he played a lot of golf with his great friend Sandy Lyle. As he grew older, Lyle developed problems with his swing.

But the swing was not a concern for the stocky Woosnam. His short stature makes it easier for him to swing the club around his body as he is in more of an upright position than a taller player. This advantage has given him one of the simplest and most effective swings today.

SIMPLE APPROACH

Once asked to explain what he thinks before playing a shot, Woosnam said, "I look at the target and hit the ball at it."

This uncomplicated approach is echoed in the way he swings the club – a smooth rhythm which varies little from week to week regardless of pressure. His apparent ease in striking the ball outstanding distances has almost become his trademark.

Before playing the stroke he blocks out all other thoughts by creating a positive image in his mind of how the ball will fly to the target. His concentration and straightforward attitude prevent confusion and let him get on with the game.

Woosnam never overexerts himself when taking a shot and so avoids bad timing and miss-hitting. Although it doesn't appear

DISTANCE HITTING
Although he is not as tall as many of his rivals, Welshman Ian Woosnam is one of the longest hitters in world golf. He achieves good distance because he has perfect rhythm and weight transfer.

WOOSNAM'S SIMPLE STYLE

① **SWEEPING TAKEAWAY**
This is typical of Woosnam's uncomplicated action. With knees flexed, he sweeps the club away, keeping it low to the ground. This creates a wide swing arc, which provides all the power he needs for a long drive.

② **ROTATION AND WEIGHT SHIFT**
As the Welshman swings halfway back his body is beginning to rotate. His weight now starts to move across to his right foot – by the top of the backswing almost all his weight will have transferred.

③ **TAKING HIS TIME**
With ease and comfort, Woosnam finishes his backswing. This relaxed, fluid movement is vital for a powerful swing. Many smaller players mistakenly rush at this point, ready to thrash the ball to achieve distance.

so, he uses only three-quarters of his power when hitting the ball. This method allows his body to synchronize, letting the correct parts work at the right time.

Rhythm is probably Woosnam's greatest asset. Whether he hits a driver, 1 iron or sand wedge, his rhythm remains constant. His quality of movement combined with those famous tree trunk forearms have contributed to his success.

Ian Woosnam has the advantage of being able to play every day. Few can play that regularly, which makes the skill of timing your shots even more important.

Woosie in action
Next time you have the opportunity, go to see Ian Woosnam in action – he is one of the best golfers to learn from. Pay particular attention to the way he swings the long clubs. You can greatly improve your game by imitating his perfect tempo.

④ **SWINGING THROUGH THE BALL**
Woosnam is now in the classic impact position. His left arm is in control of the swing and his right side is passive. The left hip moves easily out of the way, allowing him to swing the club through the ball.

⑤ **PERFECT BALANCE**
As his head turns to watch the ball's flight, the result of Woosnam's calm approach is a perfectly balanced followthrough. He achieves this because of the fluent rhythm he applies to all his shots, from driver to wedge.

A wood from the bunker

It's frustrating when your ball lands in a fairway bunker, particularly if you've notched up a good score. But be positive – all is not lost.

A well negotiated strike could land you in a position to save shots. Most fairway bunkers are shallower than those beside the green – and are often less difficult than they first appear.

Be flexible over your choice of club – an inspired shot is often the result of creative club selection. If the ball is sitting up well a fair distance away from the front of the bunker, it is much easier to get out using a utility wood rather than the more usual iron.

The small head and low center of gravity of the wood allow more weight to pass underneath the ball and so lift it up quickly. And the smooth, rounded shape of the head prevents snagging in the sand which often happens with the long irons.

CLUB CHOICE

One of the keys to success with a fairway bunker shot is choosing the right club. An iron is the obvious choice – but in many situations the wood may give a better combination of lift and distance.

Weigh up the facts carefully – enter the bunker, take your stance to the ball and visualize the shot coming out. You must decide which club is best for getting over the lip of the bunker *and* reaching the green. To work out the lift, consider how far the ball is from the front of the hazard.

The 5 wood lifts the ball higher and sends it further than a 2 iron, because it has more loft and a longer shaft. But if you feel that a wood is not going to clear the bunker, play safe – take a lofted iron instead.

ASSESS THE LIE

It's important to study the lie of the ball carefully. If the ball is sitting down or partly buried in the bunker, choose a lofted iron club and play a safe shot. But if the lie

FAIRWAY BUNKER WOOD
Use a utility wood to good effect to lift the ball up and over the lip from a fairway bunker lie. Grip down the club to compensate for the lower position of your body. A shorter swing and lower grip reduce distance but give greater control. To avoid a 2-stroke penalty remember not to ground the club at address or on the backswing.

MAKE A CLEAN STRIKE

① SET-UP
Take a normal stance – wriggle your feet for a firm footing in sand. To hit cleanly focus your eyes on top of the ball before taking the club away slowly and surely.

② CONTROLLED CONTACT
Make a three-quarter back and throughswing to increase your control. Keep a smooth rhythm to help you swing firmly down and through the ball.

③ BALANCED FINISH
After you've swept the ball cleanly from the sand, aim for a balanced finish. Keep your head still until your right shoulder forces it to turn and watch the ball's flight.

is reasonable and you have a good distance between the ball and the front of the bunker, pick a 5 wood – or even a 7 if you normally carry one.

POSITIVE APPROACH

After you select your club and take your set-up, be single minded in your approach – block out distractions and focus purely on your objective. Set aside thoughts of failure – a positive approach gives a better chance of achieving your target.

Take a firm footing in the sand – to avoid a 2-stroke penalty, remember not to ground the club at address. Grip down the club for extra control and sweep the ball cleanly off the sand with a smooth and purposeful three-quarter swing.

masterclass

Bunker courage
One of the most memorable shots of all time was played at the 1983 Ryder Cup. By the 18th hole the singles match between Seve Ballesteros and Fuzzy Zoeller looked as if it could go either way.

On this final hole, Seve played his drive to the left of the fairway to avoid water – only to find the fairway bunker. He needed to carry the ball some 250yd (230m) over water to reach the green. The risk was high.

Coolly assessing the situation, Seve chose a 3 wood and sent the ball searing over the face of the bunker. As it landed on the green the crowd roared in appreciation. Jack Nicklaus said it was one of the finest shots he'd ever seen.

Off the sand
With its rounded head and low center of gravity, a lofted utility wood lifts the ball quickly and provides the necessary distance for a fairway bunker shot to reach the green.

The long irons have narrow soles which may dig into the sand – the ball is likely to end up at the side of the bunker.

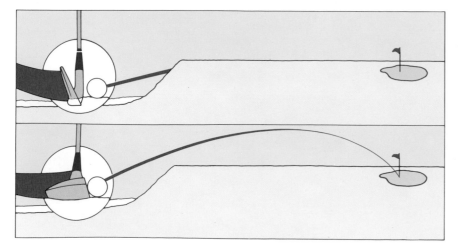

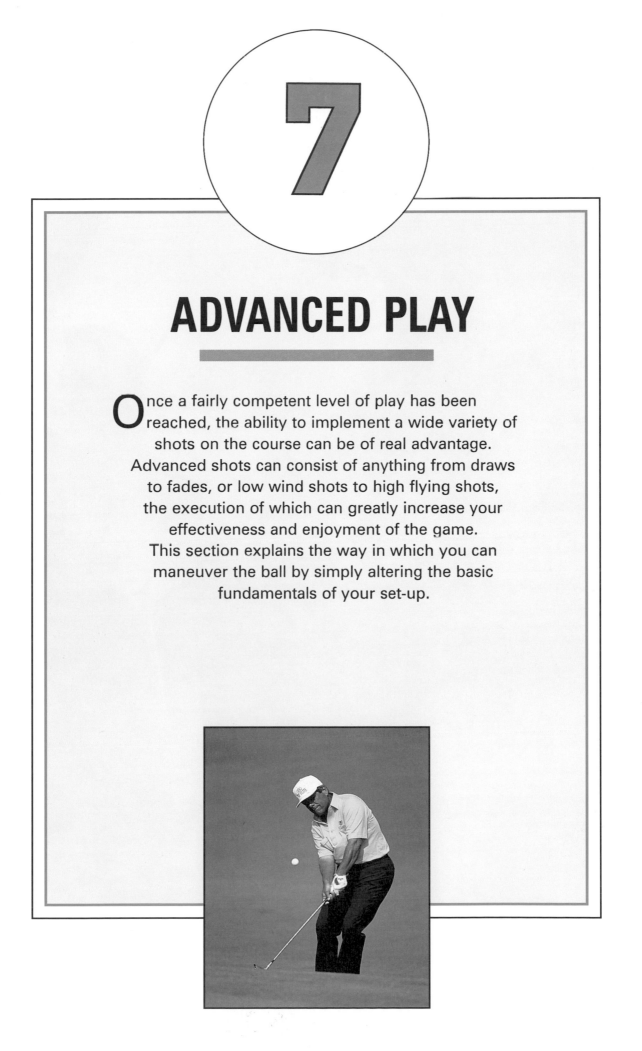

7

ADVANCED PLAY

Once a fairly competent level of play has been
reached, the ability to implement a wide variety of
shots on the course can be of real advantage.
Advanced shots can consist of anything from draws
to fades, or low wind shots to high flying shots,
the execution of which can greatly increase your
effectiveness and enjoyment of the game.
This section explains the way in which you can
maneuver the ball by simply altering the basic
fundamentals of your set-up.

Exploring the fade

Many top players – including Nick Faldo, Lee Trevino and Jack Nicklaus – use the fade as their stock shot. Although you can't hit the ball quite as far with a fade as you can with a draw, you have greater control over the shot – as the ball has a high flight path and lands softly.

Hitting the fade for control and accuracy is not the only way to play this shape of shot. Make full use of the fade to set up birdie chances on awkward holes.

FADING FAVORITES

You can play the fade to counter the effects of both slope and wind. If the fairway slopes from right to left and is hard and running, a straight shot or draw is likely to roll too far left and end up in the rough. But if you hit the fade the ball moves from left to right and runs slightly uphill on landing, which holds the ball on the slope.

Aim the clubface square to a target on the left of the fairway and align left of the ball-to-target line so that when the shot cuts back it has plenty of room to work with. Even if the ball doesn't fade it shouldn't run too far into the left rough.

The fade is also useful to hold the ball in a right to left wind. Instead of aiming right of the target and letting the wind drift the ball back, set it off on a line just left of the flag and cut it back on to the target. The ball lands softly – especially helpful if the green is firm.

Play one or two clubs more than usual – depending on the strength of the wind – as the ball doesn't fly as far when cutting into it.

TARGET RIGHT

Hitting the left to right shot is also very useful for getting at a hidden target on the right.

Some dog-legs right are angled so sharply that you can hit only a long iron to the corner before running out of fairway. But if you hit a driver and move the ball from left to right you can slide a shot around the corner, leaving you with a much shorter second.

CONTROLLED SLICE

Exaggerate the fade – so it becomes a controlled slice – to hit a shot around trouble, usually trees. The technique of the swing is almost the same as normal. The only difference is that your body aligns well left of the target but the clubface is still square to the ball-to-target line. The ball sets off well to the left of the target and cuts back a long way.

▼ **Playing the exaggerated fade is very useful when you haven't a clear shot to the target. By aligning left and aiming your clubface squarely at the flag the ball starts left of the trees and cuts back through the air towards the green.**

Hold the slope

FADE AGAINST SLOPE TO HOLD LINE

DRY SUMMER CONDITIONS

BALL-TO-TARGET LINE

Use the fade to counter the effects of a right to left slope. A straight shot or draw is likely to run off to the left and into the rough. But a fade holds the ball on the slope. Align left with the clubface square to a target on the left of the fairway.

Counter crosswind

FADE TO STOP BALL QUICKLY

WIND

Playing one or two clubs more than usual, hit a fade into a right to left wind to gain control over the shot. Align slightly left and aim your clubface square. The ball cuts back into the wind, lands and stops quickly. A normal shot runs on landing.

Dog-leg driver

1

FADE CUTS DOG-LEG AND GAINS DISTANCE

STRAIGHT LONG IRON

If you hit the ball straight with a wood you run out of fairway on the dog-leg. You must either play a long iron to the corner or a long fade with a wood. Fading left with the wood leaves you with a much shorter second to the green.

masterclass

Faldo's fabulous fade

In the 1989 PGA Championship at Wentworth, Nick Faldo played a magical shot at the 15th hole to secure the title. After driving to the right he found he was blocked out from the green by trees. He had to aim about 60yd (55m) left of the green as he took his stance.

Using a 3 iron he hit a low cut shot some 200yd (183m) to within a few feet of the flag. A possible bogey became a birdie and he went on to win by 2 shots from Ian Woosnam.

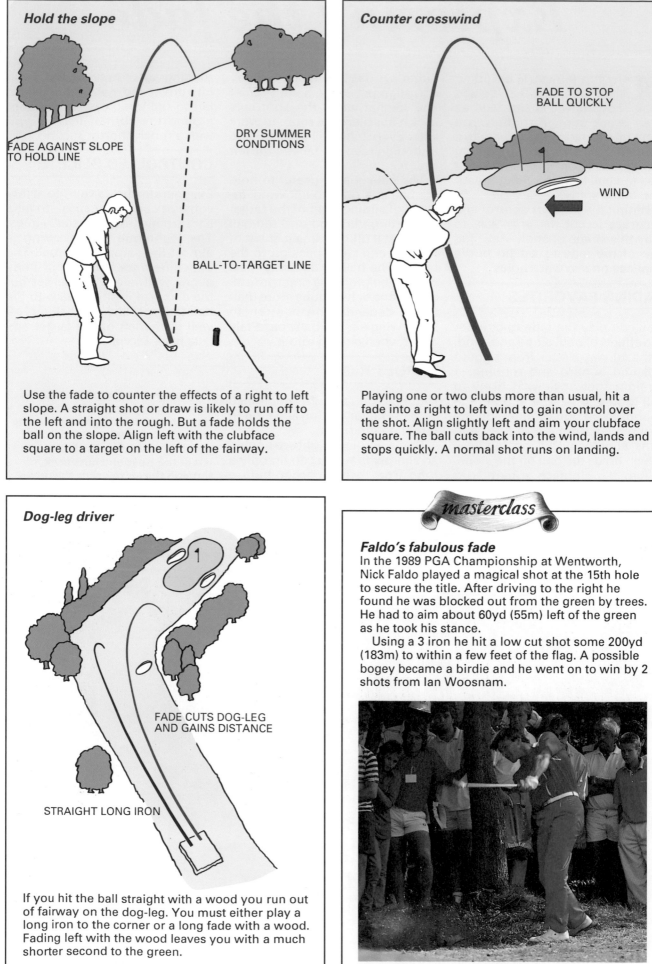

How to fade

When you hit a fade shot, the ball is struck left of the target but travels right during flight. Your most likely use for it is when there is an obstacle such as a large tree between you and your target.

The fade is an advanced, controlled shot – unlike the slice, a poor hit that also moves the ball from left to right during flight.

You achieve the fade by changing your body alignment at address. This alters your swing path – not the swing itself – and puts sidespin on the ball.

The ball flies higher and runs shorter than a normal shot. You may have to take a slightly less lofted club than usual (for instance, a 5 iron instead of a 6 iron).

ALIGN LEFT OF TARGET

Your body should align left of the ball-to-target line, while you keep the clubface aimed square on to it. Slightly open your hips and shoulders by turning them left and swing normally. Your swing follows an out-to-in path: the club-head travels from right to left across the standard swing path, causing it to brush through the ball and giving it sidespin. There is no need to change your grip.

You must have confidence in your set-up and your swing to achieve a successful fade, so rehearse the shot on the practice range. It is a "feel" shot – you must be able to see the shot in your mind if you are to play it well.

Once you have developed a consistent routine, you are ready to attempt the shot on the course.

WHAT HAPPENS WHEN YOU FADE

Fade swing path (out-to-in)
By aligning your body left of the ball-to-target line, in an open position, you automatically shift your swing path. Compared with a normal swing path, the fade produces a path that travels outside the normal line on the backswing and downswing, but moves inside that same line on the throughswing. You alter only your address position to achieve a fade. You do not change your swing to change your swing path.

Clock golf
To help you see your fade swing path in your mind, imagine you are teed up on the center of a clockface, facing 3 o'clock. When you hit a straight shot, you hit along a ball-to-target line stretching from 6 o'clock to 12 o'clock. When you fade correctly, that ball-to-target line remains the same – but you in fact hit along a line from 5 o'clock to 11 o'clock.

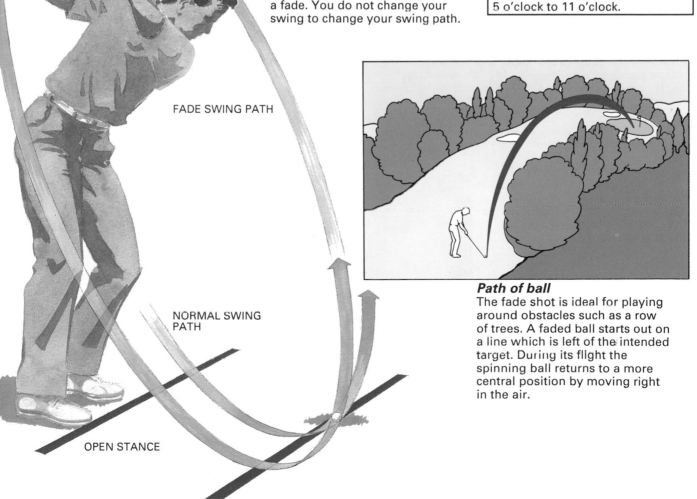

FADE SWING PATH

NORMAL SWING PATH

OPEN STANCE

BALL-TO-TARGET LINE

Path of ball
The fade shot is ideal for playing around obstacles such as a row of trees. A faded ball starts out on a line which is left of the intended target. During its flight the spinning ball returns to a more central position by moving right in the air.

CHANGING YOUR SWING PATH

NORMAL TAKEAWAY

FADE TAKEAWAY

NORMAL SET-UP
In normal set-up, your feet, hips and shoulders are parallel to the imaginary ball-to-target line. During normal takeaway and backswing, the club travels on a straight path inside and parallel to the ball-to-target line. Throughout the swing, the club remains inside this line.

FADE SET-UP
Move your left foot about 6in (15cm) away from the club closest to your feet. This aligns you left of target. Keep the clubface square to the ball-to-target line, even if this imaginary line passes through the obstacle. Although you swing normally, adjustment at address produces an out-to-in swing path, which gives sidespin.

masterclass

Nicklaus' percentage fade
At the 18th tee at Augusta, Nicklaus fades the ball around the right-hand dog-leg, avoiding the bunker on the left. The ball is shown in mid-air, just about to drop.

Nicklaus also uses the fade to reduce his margin for error in a straight shot. Imagine you are 160yd (145m) from the green with a centrally positioned flag and 30ft (9m) either side. If you aim straight at the flag but slice it 20ft (6m) wide, you have a long putt.

Nicklaus' tactic is to aim the shot 10ft (3m) left of the pin and fade the ball. Should he over-fade it by 20ft (6m), he is only 10ft (3m) right of the pin. Should he hit it straight by mistake he is still only 10ft (3m) from the hole, this time on the left. If he hits well he is closer still.

The intentional slice

The word slice is usually associated with a bad shot – one that curves wildly right into trouble. But if you know how to hit the slice deliberately, you can use it to your advantage.

The violent left to right slider comes from a pronounced out-to-in swing path with either a square or open clubface. The effect of cutting sharply across the ball imparts the massive sidespin needed to move the ball right. If you understand that this action produces the slice, it's easy to set yourself up to copy it.

MULTI-PURPOSE

The classic situation for an intentional slice is when your ball is in trees down the right side of a hole and you are blocked out from firing straight at the target with your

A CUT ABOVE THE REST
Being bold and going for your shots is half the fun of golf, especially when they come off. One of the more satisfying is a deliberate cut around trouble. Even if you have to fire towards danger it's possible to hit a big left to righter that curls around to the green.

SLICING SWING

① OPEN ADDRESS
Lay the blade square to the target and align well left of target. Be sure that you align far enough left so the initial path of the ball steers clear of the trouble. Position the ball as normal – forward for a long iron.

② CLUB POINTS LEFT
Swinging back as normal automatically takes the club outside the target line. The club should point well left of the target at the top of the backswing.

③ OUTSIDE ATTACK
You have to attack the ball on an out-to-in path to curve the ball right. The action of cutting across the ball with an opened up blade creates the huge amount of sidespin needed to hit a slice.

④ FULL EXTENSION
Swing through on the natural path and extend fully. Don't try to guide the ball around the trouble – the combination of the swing path and clubface naturally bends the ball well right.

next. You could play the ball out sideways but it leaves you a long approach. Use all your shotmaking abilities and a little imagination to conjure up a saving slice.

You should be able to start the ball well left of target and clear of the trouble, and then bend the ball around towards the target. Although you can't guarantee a perfect result – as you must trust to luck a little with the amount of slice and run – you should be able to play quite a precise shot.

TROUBLE SHOOTER

But the slice isn't limited to playing from the right side around trouble. Sometimes, if you've missed the fairway to the left, a chip back to the fairway or a hook aren't recommended – you may be blocked out by trees. But you may have a chance to aim further down the left – possibly over more trouble – and cut the ball back towards the target.

Though this sounds risky, if you set-up and swing properly and your strike is good, a slice is a certainty. But one problem that can affect the shot is your lie. Controlling the clubface in thick rough is difficult. The blade has a habit of closing at impact as the grass wraps around the hosel and shaft, and this can ruin your deliberate slice.

POSITIVE, SHOT SAVING SLICE

WOOD CARVING
If you have driven the ball left into trees you may have very limited options for your recovery. The direct line to the flag is not on because you can't clear the trees. The chip out sideways between the gap in the trees is a possibility, but leaves a long third to the green.

Try hitting a big left to right carve. Even though you have to hit the ball towards more trouble, you can be confident that it flies over the trees further up the hole and bends right – provided you set up properly. It is possible to play the stroke accurately, but don't be disappointed if you just miss the green – luck plays a big part in the success of the sliced shot.

SAFE CHIP OUT SIDEWAYS

Weigh up the wind
The intentional slice is always easier to hit with the help of a left to right wind – it accentuates the sidespin. Trying to cut a ball into a right to left wind is difficult as the ball is held up on the air.

Think hard whether the slice is appropriate when you're playing in a wind. On a still day the shot around the shelter is a definite possibility, but in a strong right to left wind danger looms. The bunker and the shrubbery come into play if you try to hit the slice as the ball doesn't move as much as usual. The safest option is a chip out sideways and hope to pitch and putt.

There is even scope to play the slider from a fairway. On a severe left to right dog-leg it's important to reach the corner if you're to have a clear sight of the flag. But a drive short of the elbow poses a tricky problem.

Do you nudge the ball further up and just bite a little more off the dog-leg, or do you go for the long intentional slice to the green? Weigh up the situation carefully – a big left to righter may save you shots.

SLICERS SET-UP

Whatever position you're in, you must take plenty of time to set-up correctly, and choose the right club – both critical to slicing success.

Don't forget that the swing path of the club through impact dictates the ball's initial flight path. So align well left of the target to be absolutely sure that the ball starts on a line clear of the obstacle you're trying to avoid.

Aim the clubface at your target – but never lay the blade too open as you can easily hit a shank. If you can't aim the blade at your target without it being too open, settle for a less pronounced slice shot.

The more you have to bend the ball, the longer the iron should be.

Straight-faced clubs impart more sidespin than lofted irons so are perfect for the job. And because the blade is opened up it naturally becomes more lofted. So even if you have only 160yd (145m) to go, a 1 iron could be the best club to play.

Though the deliberate slice is often indicated, you should think hard about the risks. It may be that a safer option – perhaps a chip out sideways or even a drop – is the sensible way to save shots. Never take on the slice unless you are totally confident.

masterclass

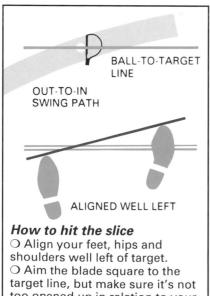

BALL-TO-TARGET LINE

OUT-TO-IN SWING PATH

ALIGNED WELL LEFT

How to hit the slice
○ Align your feet, hips and shoulders well left of target.
○ Aim the blade square to the target line, but make sure it's not too opened up in relation to your feet.
○ Position the ball between your left heel and the center of stance for long irons.
○ Swing as normal – your alignment naturally produces an out-to-in swing path.

Sam's slider
The 18th at the Riviera Country Club in Los Angeles is a long left to right dog-leg par 4, and is one of the great finishing holes in golf. At over 450yd (410m), it needs two big and accurate blows to find the target.

But in the 1950 Los Angeles Open, Sam Snead showed how to play it after a drive that finished down the right side. Needing a birdie to tie with Ben

Hogan, he found himself blocked out from going straight at the green by tall eucalyptus trees. His only option was to play a big left to right slider.

From 195yd (178m), Slammin' Sam cut a majestic 3 iron round the trouble. It pitched just short of the green and ran up to 15ft (4.5m). He holed it for a 66 and the tie, and went on to beat Hogan in the playoff.

Play the draw

The draw is a shot which starts to the right of the target and moves left in flight back towards the target. It's a useful shot for playing around a hazard. It also increases the distance of your shot because the ball rolls on landing more than it does for a straight shot or a fade. This makes it an effective shot to play with woods and long irons.

The draw is a feel shot so it's not easy. Persevere with it and it will give great flexibility to your game.

When playing the draw, the first principle to understand is precisely how the ball spins from right to left in the air.

If you have a ping pong paddle handy, try spinning a ping pong ball from right to left across a table. You soon realize that you need to brush the bat across the ball from *left* to *right* to achieve the spin you want.

Playing a draw in golf is exactly

THE ADVANTAGES OF A DRAW

The draw shot is a great asset when you want to hit the ball around a hazard or a tree. Also play a draw to increase your distance – the ball rolls further on landing.

Aim and align right

IN-TO-OUT SWING PATH

RIGHT FOOT BACK – STANCE SLIGHTLY CLOSED

Aim the club right of the target to allow for the draw spin and to help you visualize an in-to-out swing path. Align your body right of the ball-to-target line, by bringing your right foot back slightly.

FEEL THE SHOT

The draw is a feel shot. To improve your feeling for the in-to-out swing path required imagine you're standing in the center of a clockface. The ball is positioned exactly in the middle and your ball-to-target line stretches from 6 o'clock to 12 o'clock. Now feel as if you're swinging to 7 o'clock on your backswing and to 1 o'clock on your throughswing.

When you hit the draw shot your swing automatically becomes slightly flatter on the backswing. This is because your club is swinging more to the inside. On the throughswing, your left arm is more extended than normal as the club swings outside the ball-to-target line. The ball-to-target line remains the same as usual.

the same. You produce an in-to-out swing path, which takes the clubhead inside the ball-to-target line and then outside it after impact. The clubhead brushes left to right through the ball, like the ping pong paddle.

AIM AND ALIGNMENT

Aim the clubface slightly to the right of the ball-to-target line. This helps you to visualize the in-to-out swing path and also allows for the draw spin. Now align your body parallel to the clubface, by bringing your right foot back a little.

Your body should now be aligned just to the right of target. Correct aim and alignment are essential if you are to start the ball to the right.

Because the draw is a feel shot, first try it with a club you're comfortable with – a 6 or 7 iron. As your confidence grows, move on to the more difficult longer clubs.

masterclass

Tom Watson's winning draw
Many of the world's top players use the draw to give them extra control. Tom Watson, who dominated world golf in the late 70s and early 80s, plays a draw as an important part of his game.

Watson has won the US Masters on two occasions, 1977 and 1981. He can thank his draw for these successes, because Augusta is laid out to suit players who have mastered the draw. It's no coincidence that Lee Trevino, the greatest player of the fade, has never triumphed at Augusta.

A well-played draw is a penetrating shot. This makes it a handy shot for windy courses, where you can fight or use a strong wind to your advantage. Watson's record on the windy, links courses of the Open Championship proves the point. He has won five times.

Punch draw

To cope with a left-to-right crosswind you need a relatively low shot which travels right to left through the air. The punch draw does just that – the word punch describes the necessary firm swing while the draw is the flight path of the shot.

When the wind blows from left to right the draw prevents the ball from drifting to the right of the target and so helps hold the shot on line.

You can also use the punch draw to combat a head wind. When the wind is directly in your face, the spin produced with the draw helps you reach maximum distance. This draw spin is extremely useful and is easy to create with alterations in your set-up.

CHANGES IN TECHNIQUE

For a 150yd (137m) shot from the green you normally use a full swing with a 6 iron. For the punch draw choose one more club and make a three-quarter swing. For

BEAT THE CROSSWIND
For a left-to-right crosswind you need to use the punch draw. The ball stays quite low and swerves from right to left to counteract the direction of the wind.

CONTROL IN THE WIND

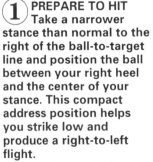

①PREPARE TO HIT
Take a narrower stance than normal to the right of the ball-to-target line and position the ball between your right heel and the center of your stance. This compact address position helps you strike low and produce a right-to-left flight.
For greater control and awareness of the clubhead, hold midway down the grip. Keep the clubface square to the ball-to-target line.

②START THE SWING
Swing the club back naturally inside the ball-to-target line. The clubface feels slightly closed throughout this movement. Make sure you don't rush the shot.

③THREE-QUARTER BACKSWING
The combination of narrow stance and gripping down the club lets you swing to a powerful three-quarter position. Turn your shoulders about 90° – keep the movement smooth.

4 **ATTACK FROM INSIDE**
Your hands must lead the clubface for as long as possible. A draw results when you swing from in-to-out as you strike the ball.

5 **THROUGH IMPACT**
Your club is swung naturally from the inside as you make contact with the ball. Your left arm is more extended than usual through impact. Let your body weight transfer fully to your left side so you maintain a correct balanced position.

6 **MOVE WITH THE SHOT**
Allow your natural body turn to pull your head up as you swing through the ball. The ball starts right of the target and moves to the left in flight.

PUNCH DRAW SWING

For the punch draw adopt a narrow stance with a lower grip and make a three-quarter backswing – a shorter swing enables you to control your shot. The altered set-up and short swing lead to a draw, unlike the full swing used for a standard shot (inset).

Pack a punch Parkin

Some players have a natural punch draw movement, while others must strive to perfect the technique. A natural ability to draw the ball is a skill that's served Welshman Philip Parkin well. In 1984 he earned his ticket to the European Tour and later joined the US circuit. Skill at the punch draw ensures that he plays well in the wind.

longer distances and stronger winds you may need to go up two or even three more clubs.

Adopt a slightly narrow stance. Bring your right foot back a little to align yourself just to the right of the ball-to-target line. Position the ball further back than normal, midway between the center of your stance and the right heel. Square the clubface at address and grip 1in (2.5cm) lower than normal.

This compact address position encourages you to swing in to out of the ball-to-target line. Your swing automatically becomes flatter on the backswing as your club is swinging more from the inside.

With a square clubface and in-to-out swing path the ball flies off to the right of the target when you strike. The altered ball placement keeps the ball low throughout.

You may find it difficult to produce the shot successfully at first – a common problem is that the ball flies right and stays there. This happens because you fail to return a square clubface to impact – the face of the club remains open. You also shoot the ball too far right if you lift your head too soon in the swing.

RHYTHM AND BALANCE

This is a feel shot, so your tempo and speed of swing are important. Apart from the set-up changes at address, treat the punch draw as any other shot.

Although you reduce the length of your swing, your shoulders still turn 90° during the backswing. Your body weight transfers instinctively as you hit, leaving you in a balanced followthrough.

The deliberate hook

Though a hook is one of the more destructive shots in golf if it's unintentional, the pronounced right-to-left shape can be helpful for escaping trouble.

The deliberate hook is especially useful to escape trees down the left side of a hole. A hook can attack the green even if it's blocked from view, and can prove much more productive than a chip out sideways.

As long as you understand how a hook is produced, it isn't difficult to hit. But because the flight of the ball is quite low and at times violently right to left, you mustn't try anything too risky. This shape is the hardest of all flights to control as the ball bounds and rolls a long way on landing.

Accuracy can't be guaranteed – luck plays a major part – but the fortune factor can be lessened by a careful visualization and execution of the shot.

TURN RIGHT TO GO LEFT

The two most critical parts of the stroke are set-up and club selection – your swing is basically normal. You have to align *right* of target with a square blade to play

CURLING IRONS
Any golfer should relish a challenge and escaping trouble is so satisfying it's sometimes worth a risk. Playing a curling right-to-left shot – even if it means aiming out over worse trouble – may be your most productive option to skirt trees and find a distant, tucked away target.

HITTING THE HOOK

1 CRUCIAL SET-UP
Align your feet, hips and shoulders right of target. Square your blade. The further you align right the more the ball hooks and lower it stays. Position the ball as normal in your stance.

2 POINTING RIGHT
Swing as normal – along the line of your feet. This naturally leads you into a top of the backswing position with the club pointing right of target.

3 INSIDE ATTACK
Swing down smoothly on the normal plane. Because you're aligned right your attack is effectively well from the inside. The combination of an in-to-out path and a square blade creates the hookspin.

4 THROUGH AS NORMAL
Let your set-up and clubface do the work – resist any temptation to guide the ball or use your wrists too much to hit the hook. Swing through into a balanced finish position – the hook comes naturally.

ESCAPE ARTIST

SHOT UP ADJOINING FAIRWAY
LEAVES BLIND APPROACH

CONTROLLED HOOK REACHES GREEN

CHIP OUT SIDEWAYS LEAVES
LONG SHOT TO GREEN

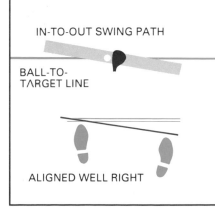

How to hit the hook
○ Align your feet, hips and
shoulders well right of target.
○ Aim the blade square to the
target line, but make sure it's not
too closed in relation to your feet.
○ Position the ball as normal.
○ Swing as normal – your
alignment naturally produces an
in-to-out swing path.

IN-TO-OUT SWING PATH

BALL-TO-
TARGET LINE

ALIGNED WELL RIGHT

Often your options are limited when
you've driven into trouble and
sometimes you only have one. But
when a few different shots are
possible, weigh up the risks and
advantages of each before you
decide what to play.

Even though the deliberate hook
is more often played from the left
side of the fairway, there is scope to
hit it from the trees down the right.

Instead of chipping out sideways
– which leaves you a long way from
the green – or knocking the ball
further up the adjoining fairway
leaving a blind approach, play a
hook. It is the only way you can
reach the green.

You can't gain enough height

and distance by going directly at
the green, so align right, down the
next fairway. If you keep the blade
aiming square or just a fraction to
the right of target and swing
normally, the ball starts down the
line of the trees and curls back over
them and bounds on toward the
green.

Make sure you choose the
correct club – one that you can hit
high enough to clear the trees but
straight faced enough to hook the
proper amount. Bear in mind the
ball runs a good distance on
landing. Beware of this shot if your
lie is bad – one of the other options
is probably best.

a hook.

The combination of your alignment, aim and shape of swing – in to out because your feet, hips and shoulders are aligned right – produces the huge drawspin needed for the hook.

To pull off a deliberate hook you not only have to picture the shot and set up properly for it, but you must also choose the correct club for the intended flight.

When choosing your club, consider two important points:
○ Squaring the blade to the target after aligning right naturally

delofts the clubface – so a 6 iron can easily take on the loft of a 3 if you align well right.
○ The more lofted an iron is, the less it hooks. Take this into account – because even though an 8 iron, for example, may be enough for the distance it may not be able to bend the ball as much as you need it to.

OVERCLUBBING

Correct clubbing is also critical if you have to fly over trouble as well as around it. Don't be fooled

into thinking that just because you're hitting an 8 iron it flies high as usual. Allow for the fact that the blade is delofted, and so the ball flies lower than normal. Visualize the likely flight.

But wherever you play the hook – whether it's around a dog-leg or from the trees – remember to swing within yourself and let the club do the work. One thing is certain – if you set up properly and swing well the ball hooks. It's then just a matter of controlling the shot to take advantage of the right-to-left shape.

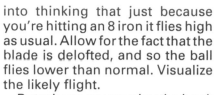

Bending Ballesteros
Seve seems to find more trouble than most top pros, but is probably the greatest exponent of recovery. His visualization and manipulation of shots are superb and he's willing to try anything to gain an advantage – even if it's slightly risky.

When he overcooked a draw from the tee down the dog-leg 10th at Augusta he thought hard about which shot to hit. After rejecting the chip out sideways – because it left him too far to go for his third – he opted to play the low raking hook out and around the trees.

He set up correctly and chose a club that could keep the ball low enough to stay under the trees but fly and bend far enough to reach the green. The shot played with an easy rhythm drew cheers of admiration and amazement from the gallery, and set him up for another birdie.

Langer's strong grip

Bernhard Langer is famous for his unorthodox putting grip, but few players realize that he also grips his woods and irons unconventionally. He has a very strong left hand grip while his right remains in a more normal position.

Most good golfers show two knuckles of their left hand at address, but Langer shifts his hand further over the grip and shows four. Usually the V formed by the forefinger and thumb of the left hand points at the player's right eye. Bernhard's V points towards the outside of his right shoulder.

Langer favors this style because it helps him to rotate his hands, arms and upper body into their correct positions on the backswing.

It also helps him to take the club away on the correct path in a smooth, wide arc. It isn't natural to take the club back outside the ball-to-target line using a strong grip.

The strong grip may help some players to move into the correct positions on the backswing more

STRONG AND CONTROLLED
The powerful German uses his strong left hand grip to great effect – he shows four knuckles rather than the normal two. In the wrong hands this can lead to hooking, but Langer has such good control that he hits the ball long and straight. He has become one of the best iron players in the world.

easily than with the conventional grip.

HOOKING AND SLICING

Although a strong grip is usually associated with hooking the ball, Bernhard has excellent left hand control through impact, and returns his hands to their address position. He avoids letting the back of his left hand face the target at impact, which would close the clubface during the strike.

This type of grip can improve the game of some players who are fighting a slice. If your slice results from an open clubface at impact, strengthening your left hand grip helps the clubhead return square.

But the strong grip doesn't help you if your slice comes from hitting across the line on an out-to-in path with a square clubface. Changing to a strong grip closes the face at impact and you hit the ball straight left.

Players who struggle for distance can also benefit from this change. You get a firmer hold on the club by strengthening your left hand grip and can create a little more power. You can also produce draw spin which makes the ball go further.

TRY YOUR HAND

Make sure you experiment on the practice green before you decide to change to a strong grip – it's a useful variation of standard technique but it doesn't work for everyone.

Never recommend this strong left hand grip to juniors and beginners who are struggling for distance and want a technique for gaining extra length. It's important that they learn the orthodox techniques first – the distance comes gradually with age and experience, and from understanding how a swing works.

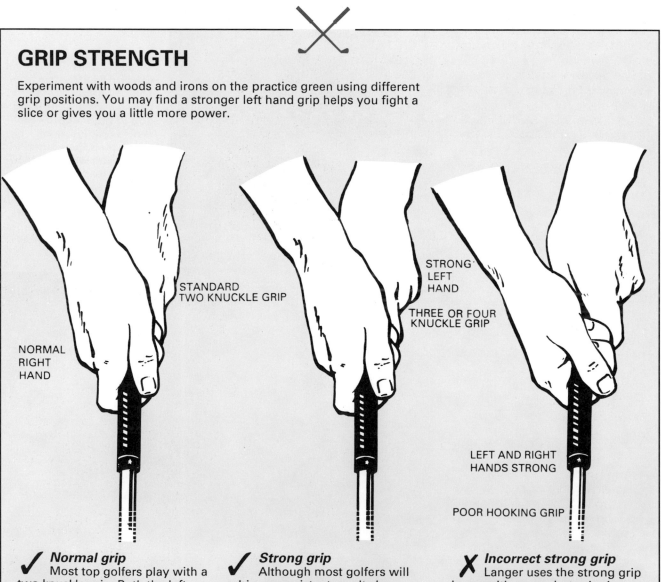

GRIP STRENGTH

Experiment with woods and irons on the practice green using different grip positions. You may find a stronger left hand grip helps you fight a slice or gives you a little more power.

STANDARD TWO KNUCKLE GRIP

NORMAL RIGHT HAND

STRONG LEFT HAND

THREE OR FOUR KNUCKLE GRIP

LEFT AND RIGHT HANDS STRONG

POOR HOOKING GRIP

✓ **Normal grip**
Most top golfers play with a two knuckle grip. Both the left and right hands are in a neutral position, with the right palm and the back of the left hand facing the target. But it is better to have a slightly strong grip than a weak one if you do stray from the normal position.

✓ **Strong grip**
Although most golfers will achieve consistent results by allowing one and a half to two knuckles to show on the left hand, some golfers prefer to adopt a strong grip, allowing three or four knuckes to show on the left hand.

✗ **Incorrect strong grip**
Langer uses the strong grip in a positive way, but gripping the club strongly with both hands is disastrous. On the downswing your hands return to a square position, closing the clubface at impact. It is almost impossible to hit a straight shot using this incorrect strong grip.

Hit high, hit long

A large tree in a golfer's path is an unwelcome sight. When you are blocked out by a tree, it's often difficult to gain enough height and distance to reach the green. If you play a lofted club to fly over the tree the ball may not make the green – but play the club that's right for the distance and the ball crashes into branches.

SHOT MANUFACTURE

You must learn how to manufacture a shot that achieves both height and distance. This isn't difficult as long as you change your basic set-up, swing plane and path.

If the distance requires a 6 iron but you need 7 iron height to clear the tree, you must play a 5 iron and open up your clubface for extra loft. Using the 5 iron like a 7 iron produces both the necessary height and length to reach the green.

To compensate for opening up the clubface align your feet, hips and shoulders left of the target and position the ball forward in your stance. The changes in alignment make you take the club slightly outside the ball-to-target line on your backswing.

STEEP AND FIRMLY DOWN

Your downswing should be slightly steeper than usual which helps the ball to climb higher. Attack the ball firmly. The resulting shot should be an extra high fade. Don't try to lift the ball off the turf by coming up on the shot – it's easy to thin it.

Avoid swinging too fast and take care not to let the right hand overpower the left through impact, or the clubface loft is reduced and the ball doesn't gain enough height to clear the tree.

Visualize the shot before you play. Make sure that the stroke is possible and you're not taking too much of a risk. It may be better to play a shot over the tree and not attempt to reach the green. If you're close to the tree it's often best to play a low shot under the branches.

HIGH RISE
It's a real asset to be able to play a shot over a tree but still achieve the distance needed to reach the green. You can avoid clattering into branches or falling short of the green by playing an extra high long fade. But the shot needs to be struck precisely – weigh up the risks first.

HIGH FADE OVER TROUBLE

① OPEN ADDRESS
Aim the clubface square to the ball-to-target line. Position the ball forward in your stance and align your feet, hips and shoulders left of target. The two balls (inset) show the relative positions for the normal shot and the high fade.

② STRIKING
Using a steeper than normal downswing, you achieve height by striking down on the ball with a square clubface that's opened up for extra loft. Don't try to lift the ball up off the turf – you may thin it.

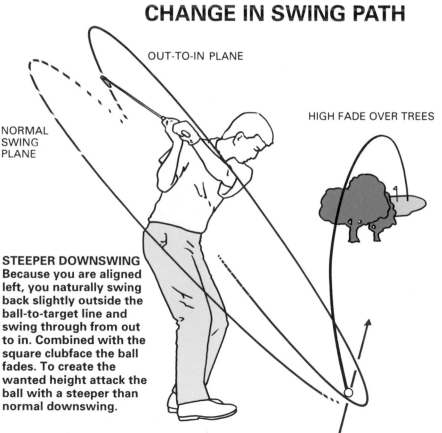

③ LEAD WITH THE LEFT
Control the followthrough with your left hand so that the clubface continues to aim at the target for longer than normal. This helps the ball to fade. Don't let the right hand cross over the left – this reduces loft.

masterclass

High powered Greg Norman
Norman is known for his immense power and an ability to manufacture shots. Because he is a tall, strong man with quite a steep arc he hits the ball with a forceful downward blow, sending it high. With a slight change in his set-up, Greg plays the extra high fade over trouble perfectly.

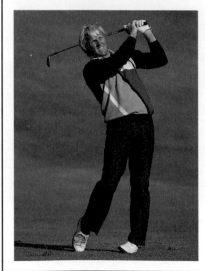

CHANGE IN SWING PATH

OUT-TO-IN PLANE

HIGH FADE OVER TREES

NORMAL SWING PLANE

STEEPER DOWNSWING
Because you are aligned left, you naturally swing back slightly outside the ball-to-target line and swing through from out to in. Combined with the square clubface the ball fades. To create the wanted height attack the ball with a steeper than normal downswing.

Gain more air time

There are occasions when it's good to hit the ball low – when there's a strong wind in your face for instance. But when every shot that leaves the clubface flies lower than it should, you're bound to encounter problems every time you set foot on the course.

A bunker guarding the front of the green presents a daunting challenge at the best of times. And when you're struggling to gain height, water stretching out in front of the tee seems to pose an almost unassailable threat.

For most golfers the difficulty occurs with the driver and long irons. While they are the least lofted clubs in the bag, there's no reason why you should struggle to hit them the correct height.

GOLDEN RULE

The secret lies in letting the loft of a club do the work for you. To put this theory into practice you need first to overcome the mental obstacle often associated with the straighter faced clubs.

STRAIGHT DOWN THE LINE
One of the most impressive features of the professional game is the ease with which top players generate height on their long iron shots. There's no thrash at the ball – they know that if the clubface returns to its original position at impact there's more than enough loft to produce the desired flight. Combined with a downward blow from slightly inside the line the result is an arrow-straight long iron shot with just the right trajectory. Mirror these moves and you're never likely to struggle for height again.

LONG RANGE LONG IRON

①SET YOUR SIGHTS
It's important to align correctly for every shot. When you're standing with a long iron in your hands and the target is some 200yd (180m) away you need to be even more precise – the further you are from the hole the more alignment faults are exaggerated. Set your eyes on the target and block out everything else.

②CLUBHEAD FEEL
Concentrate on making a smooth one piece takeaway to set the club on a wide arc away from the ball – this should pull a little more than half of your body weight on to the right side. Try to feel the precise position of the club at the top – your left wrist should be firm and supporting the club to prevent overswing.

There may not appear to be much loft on a driver, but there's really more than enough – anything between 7° and 12°. Sweep the ball off the tee to evade serious height problems. Efforts to scoop or lift the ball into the air succeed only in producing the result you wanted to avoid most – a low flight.

With every iron club in the bag you must strike down into the bottom of the ball to gain the necessary height on the shot. Make sure your weight is mostly on the left side at impact – this helps encourage a downward blow and the correct ball to turf contact.

UPWARDLY MOBILE

One of the major reasons for hitting the ball too low is toppling backwards as you strike. Golfers who swing in this way probably dream of taking divots after impact. But it simply isn't possible because the clubhead is on the way up at the precise moment it strikes the ball – contact is usually too clean.

At best you don't utilize the proper loft on the club. The trajec-

tory of the shot is weak and lacking penetration. At worst the leading edge of the club thumps into the middle of the ball – either way you'll be struggling for both height and distance.

Remember that weight on the

left side doesn't mean a violent lunge toward the target with your whole body. This sort of technique is bound to cause problems and striking the ball correctly becomes a bit hit or miss.

Try to ensure that your head

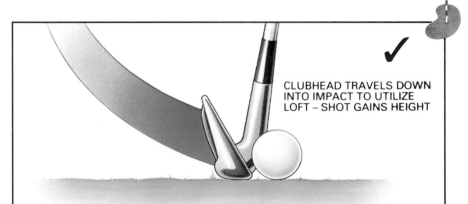

CLUBHEAD TRAVELS DOWN INTO IMPACT TO UTILIZE LOFT – SHOT GAINS HEIGHT

Down the correct path
Most club players understand the principle that you need to hit down on the ball to gain height on a shot. Carrying this through on the course often proves much harder to achieve.

From the moment you start the downswing make sure your

hands lead the clubhead into the ball. This guarantees you make ball to turf contact.

As soon as you allow the clubhead to get ahead of your hands you're in trouble. From this position it's physically impossible to put the club on a downward path into impact.

3) DOWNWARD PATH
The clubhead clearly travels towards the ball on a downward path – even though there is not a great deal of loft on the club. Your body weight moves on to the left foot to promote a downward blow. The right elbow should be tucked in close to your side to ensure the club approaches the ball from inside the line.

4) SOLID THROUGH THE BALL
Always make sure your head is behind the point of impact as you strike – known as staying behind the ball. Note the good extension through the ball – the arms and clubhead are driving low toward the target.

5) SMOOTH FOLLOWTHROUGH
The freedom of movement through the ball is brought about by a combination of correct technique and complete lack of tension. There's a good release of the hands and clubhead and almost all body weight is supported by the left side.

6) EYE ON THE BALL
The followthrough position often tells the story of the shot that's gone before. Perfect balance with the upper body facing the target is an excellent sign. But if your balance is slightly off, there's every chance that you've done something wrong earlier in the swing.

remains very still and behind the ball at the point of impact. This prevents you getting ahead of the ball, a fault which causes a low carve out to the right.

BASIC EXAMINATION

If you're striking the ball well but the trajectory of your shots is still too low, go straight back to the basics and check your address position. A slight fault may have gradually drifted into your game over a long period – these flaws are often the hardest ones to identify.

Make sure the clubface is aligned square to the ball-to-target line. If you hood the clubface at address there's every chance it will return to the same position at impact – this causes the ball to fly not only too low but also left of target.

BALL CHECK

Study ball position and remember the fundamentals – opposite your left heel for the driver and progressively further back until it's central for the lofted irons.

When the ball is too far back in your stance you're in danger of hitting low shots with every club in the bag. It's hard to avoid an impact position where your hands are too far in front of the ball. This severely delofts the club and results in a low, penetrating flight which is hard to control at the best of times.

pro tip

Different club – same swing
Very few golfers fear the prospect of hitting a 9 iron, so why worry about striking a full blooded long iron? The club is longer and there's less loft, but if you make exactly the same swing with each club you can achieve consistent results.

If you're struggling with your long irons, a simple practice drill can restore your lost confidence. Take your 3 iron and 9 iron on to the practice green and hit alternate shots.

Always start with the more lofted club, which is easier to hit. After a good shot with the 9 iron switch to the 3 iron – hitting a long iron immediately after a successful shot should give you the confidence to conquer the club you fear most. Work at making the same swing and try to maintain the same rhythm for every shot.

Note how the position at the start of the downswing is identical for both the long iron and the short iron – the left hand pulls the butt of the club down toward the ball helping to ensure the clubhead travels down into impact.

This is a classic example of the late hit and is crucial to generate clubhead speed. It's not a position you should attempt to put yourself in – rather one you achieve through making the correct moves from the top of the backswing.

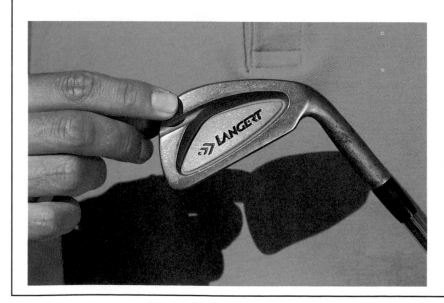

Helping hand
You should always try to cure a fault by first looking to improve your swing, but there are certain clubs on the market that can help you along the way.

By the nature of their design the longer clubs are harder to strike consistently well – if miss-hits do creep into your game then it tends to be with one of the long irons.

A peripherally weighted clubhead has a larger sweet spot than a conventional blade to allow for the occasional shot struck off center. Most manufacturers now produce sets of clubs with the long irons peripherally designed to take this factor into account.

Drive low in the wind

Hitting a drive low is an important aspect of your game when playing directly into the teeth of a strong wind. The wind affects the distance of the traveling ball, particularly if you catch fiercer currents by playing your usual flighted tee shot.

Most golfers instinctively swing faster in the wind and find producing a low drive extremely difficult – but with practice a low shot from the tee gives greater control and distance.

A low drive also gives you the benefit of maximum roll in hot, dry weather when the fairways are rock hard. Tee height is the first consideration when you attempt a low shot but teeing low doesn't always produce a low flight path. Experiment with high and low tee pegs to find what suits different conditions.

LOW TEE

Tee the ball lower so that you can barely see the tee peg. Use a driver and take your usual stance and set-up. Keep your normal swing plane – if you don't, the plane may be too steep. You'll hit sharply downward and make a fat shot.

There's enough loft on the driver to lift the ball provided you hit the shot cleanly off the top of the peg. After you play the ball check the tee peg – an upright peg is proof that you have maintained the correct swing plane and attacked from the right angle.

HIGH TEE

By teeing the ball higher you create a flatter swing plane which tends to produce a lower flighted

CONTROLLED SWING
When playing into a strong wind off a low tee, keep composed and swing the club with an even tempo. The wind exaggerates a miss-hit so concentrate on a solid contact.

Raised club for high tee
One way of hitting a low drive is to tee your ball much higher than normal so that it rests above the top edge of your driver. Assume your normal set-up with the club off the ground at address. Try to pick the ball cleanly off the tee peg as you swing through.

NORMAL TEE HEIGHT

ball with draw. The ball runs on landing and so gains the length that may be lost in the wind.

Take your normal stance, set-up and swing, making sure your club is raised off the ground at address. It's vital that you catch the ball below the sweet spot of the driver – the bottom part of the clubface has the least loft, which helps you to strike a low, pene-trating drive.

TIMING AND BALANCE

Watch your swing speed and tempo. Don't swing too fast – the combination of playing into wind and trying to strike low can make you thrash at the ball. For better control, grip lower down the club – but bear in mind that you lose length by shortening your grip.

Concentrate on transferring your body weight to the left side as you swing. Be loose and com-fortable and move with the shot to avoid leaning back as you strike the ball – any tilting backwards sends the ball up instead of driv-ing it low.

masterclass

Swing low with Woosnam
Ian Woosnam's short stature is perfect for hitting shots low. He has a flat swing plane, letting him sweep through the ball instead of chopping at it.

He performed this clean low strike off the tee at the 1989 Ryder Cup at The Belfry, and went on to secure 2 points for Europe. His team went on to retain the trophy.

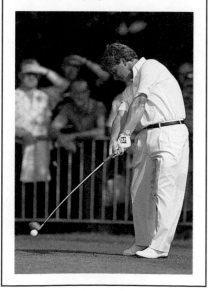

SMOOTH THROUGHSWING
Keep your eyes on the clubhead as it strikes the ball. After impact your hands and arms turn your head to face the target as you swing through fully – maintain your balance in this position. For better control of the clubhead, grip 1in (2.5cm) down from the butt of the club (inset). When visualizing the shot allow for the fact that you're lowering the flight path and reducing the distance.

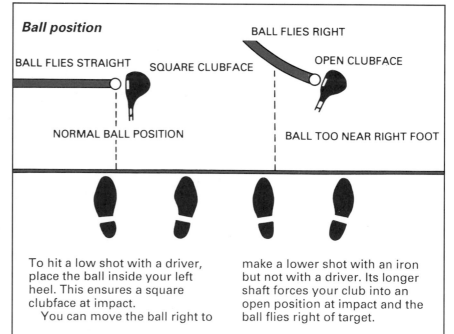

Ball position

BALL FLIES RIGHT

BALL FLIES STRAIGHT   SQUARE CLUBFACE   OPEN CLUBFACE

NORMAL BALL POSITION   BALL TOO NEAR RIGHT FOOT

To hit a low shot with a driver, place the ball inside your left heel. This ensures a square clubface at impact.

You can move the ball right to make a lower shot with an iron but not with a driver. Its longer shaft forces your club into an open position at impact and the ball flies right of target.

masterclass

Lyle's 1 iron play

Sandy Lyle has a reputation as one of the game's longest hitters. Using his awesome power he has consistently destroyed course records throughout his career. Lyle's game has had its ups – and downs, of late – but that's golf. No one doubts his prodigious power and talent.

Although Lyle is capable of regularly hitting 300yd (272m) drives, he often settles for the safety of his 1 iron. Because of his power – he hits the 1 iron about 260yd (237m) – he may reach even par 5 holes in 2 using just his irons. He sees little point in taking a risk with a driver from the tee as a miss-hit flies further into trouble.

CLUB CONTROL

Lyle uses the club even for playing into the wind because he can keep the shot low and controlled. Using just his irons from the tee in the third round at the 1987 Open at Muirfield he shot a level par 71 through horrendous weather, while others struggled with their drivers.

Sandy performs brilliantly with the 1 iron, though his swing is not best suited to hitting long clubs.

1 MODEL OF EXCELLENCE
Sandy Lyle takes up a relaxed position over the ball with a classic set-up. He is well balanced and his posture is superb. Notice how he keeps his chin up clear of his chest to allow the free passage of the left shoulder.

ACCURACY AND POWER

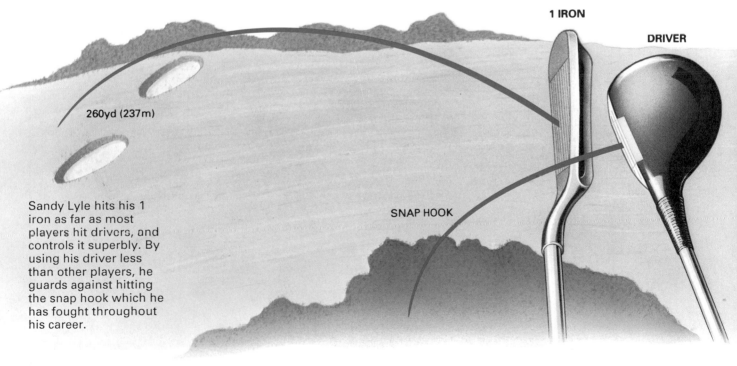

260yd (237m)

Sandy Lyle hits his 1 iron as far as most players hit drivers, and controls it superbly. By using his driver less than other players, he guards against hitting the snap hook which he has fought throughout his career.

SNAP HOOK

1 IRON

DRIVER

②**STYLE OF HIS OWN**
At the halfway stage of his backswing the clubhead is slightly more to the inside of the ball-to-target line than normal. This is a legacy of his younger days when he was shorter and he swung flat, and it can lead to a snap hook.

Because he started playing golf at an early age he developed a flattish swing plane more often used by a short person.

In his teens he shot up to 6ft 2in (1.88m) but kept a swing better suited to a golfer around 5ft 6in (1.68m). Sandy still suffers from the backswing he had when he was younger – it can cause a violent snap hook which easily puts him in trouble.

③**SHORT AND CONTROLLED**
The top of the backswing position is also far from conventional. He swings well short of the parallel and the clubhead is laid off, but it is controlled. Although his club does not reach the classic position his shoulder turn is excellent.

COMFORTING CONTROL

Sandy prefers the 1 iron to a 3 wood or driver because the shaft is shorter. The shorter shaft gives Lyle a comforting sense of control over the clubhead. He feels less likely to hit a poor shot – the iron doesn't produce the extremely flat swing plane that he sometimes has with a wood.

④**CORRECT SWING PATH**
As with all great players, any flaws on the backswing are corrected on the downswing. Lyle is very impressive through the ball, and he displays excellent left side control. Notice the extension through the stroke.

With confidence and a sound technique the 1 iron shot isn't that hard to play, but some players still prefer using a 3 wood for safety play. The main reason is the difference in appearance. There's more loft on a 1 iron than a 3 wood but the thinness of the blade is disconcerting. The lower center of mass and the shape of the wood make it look easier to hit than the iron.

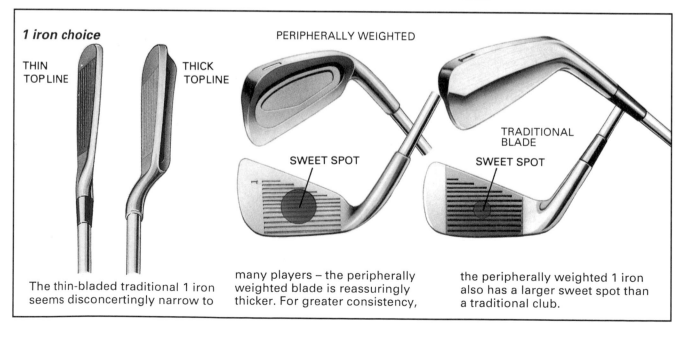

1 iron choice

THIN TOP LINE

THICK TOPLINE

PERIPHERALLY WEIGHTED

SWEET SPOT

TRADITIONAL BLADE

SWEET SPOT

The thin-bladed traditional 1 iron seems disconcertingly narrow to

many players – the peripherally weighted blade is reassuringly thicker. For greater consistency,

the peripherally weighted 1 iron also has a larger sweet spot than a traditional club.

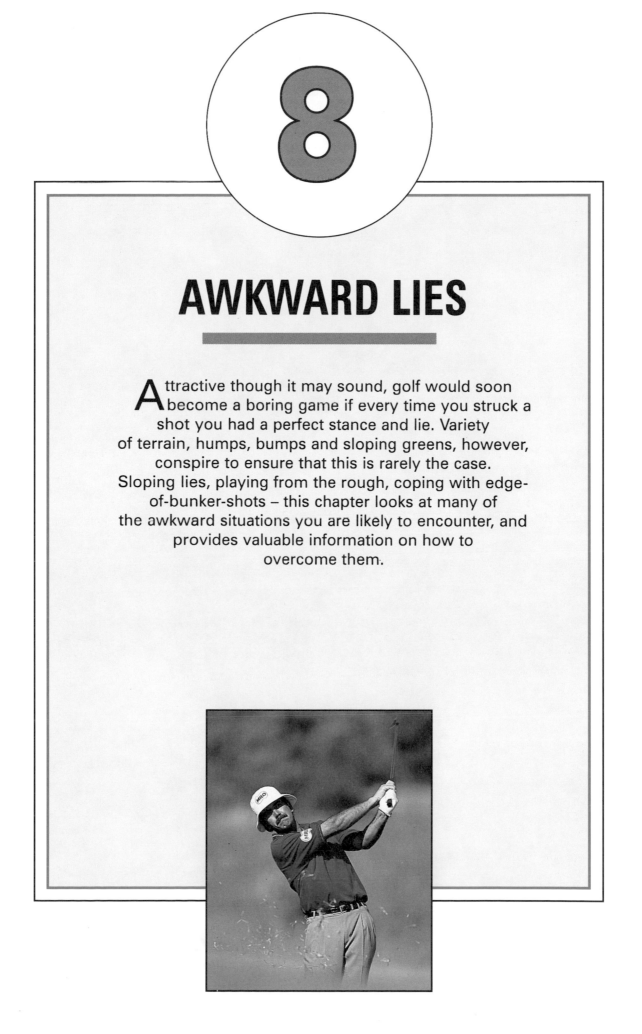

8

AWKWARD LIES

Attractive though it may sound, golf would soon become a boring game if every time you struck a shot you had a perfect stance and lie. Variety of terrain, humps, bumps and sloping greens, however, conspire to ensure that this is rarely the case. Sloping lies, playing from the rough, coping with edge-of-bunker-shots – this chapter looks at many of the awkward situations you are likely to encounter, and provides valuable information on how to overcome them.

Sidehill lies

While developing your golf swing you tend to practice from a flat lie. It won't be long, however, before your ball lands on a hill and you have to adjust your shot. On a sidehill lie your feet are on the same level, but the ball is higher or lower.

You need to practice hitting from these lies to find out just what effect different slopes have on the shape of the shot as it flies through the air. Often with a sidehill lie your ball curves quite dramatically to the right or the left.

Once familiar with the shot from a sidehill lie you'll be able to judge just how far left or right you must aim to compensate for this curve.

BALL ABOVE YOUR FEET

Before setting up the shot you need to choose the correct club for the distance. For better control, grip down the club. This also compensates for the ball lying higher than your feet.

The higher a ball is above your feet the further left it flies. Once

PLAYING THE SHOT
Hitting from a sidehill lie is difficult – only a small part of the sole of the clubhead touches the ground at impact. You must adjust your posture and change your aim to achieve a balanced set-up. You may also need to shorten your swing for a sharper strike.

BALL BELOW LEVEL OF FEET

①SET-UP
To compensate for the left-to-right flight of the ball, aim the clubface and align your body left of the target. Let your weight rest on your heels for a firm balance.

②BACKSWING
As your back is more bent you take the club away sharply, which leads to a steep swing plane. Make a three-quarter backswing. At the top the club points left of target.

③STAY DOWN
Keep your head down through impact for as long as possible. If you don't you fall off the stroke, topping the ball or sending it flying to the right.

STOOP TO CONQUER

The further below your feet the ball is, the more bent your back becomes and the steeper the swing plane is. At address your hands are lower than normal and most of your weight is on your heels. It is one of the hardest shots in golf.

NORMAL SET-UP

BALL BELOW FEET

④REDUCED BODY TURN
The followthrough is more restricted than usual because your bent posture limits body rotation. Your weight finishes on your left side.

BALL ABOVE LEVEL OF FEET

1 ADDRESSING THE BALL
Aim and align right of target to compensate for the right-to-left flight. Grip down the club. Your posture is more upright than on level ground.

2 BACKSWING
Make as full a swing as you can control – a three-quarter one is comfortable. Keep your balance for a crisp strike. At the top the club points right of target.

3 SMOOTH TEMPO
Keep a smooth tempo on the downswing. Your swing is slightly flatter than normal with the clubhead traveling across your body from out to in at impact.

STAND UP TO THE BALL

4 BALANCED FOLLOWTHROUGH
The followthrough should be the same length as the backswing. Your hands finish lower than usual because the flatter swing plane pulls them around your body.

The higher above your feet the ball is, the more upright your back and the flatter your swing plane becomes. Your hands are also higher than normal. It's easier to strike a ball above your feet than below them.

FEET BELOW BALL

NORMAL SET-UP

you have chosen a club, visualize how far left your shot will go and draw an imaginary line right of the target to compensate.

Aim the clubhead along this line and align your body parallel to it. Take special care to check that you are not automatically aligning your body parallel to the ball-to-target line.

THE SWING

Your posture is affected by the slope. With the ball above your feet your back is more upright than normal which causes a flatter swing plane.

Make as full a swing as you can control, and concentrate on timing the strike correctly – your set-up changes should take care of the rest. Confidence is essential for a successful swing. Assume that the ball will come back straight even though you are aiming to the right.

When you play the shot correctly, the ball begins its flight to the right and slowly curves around to your target. The ball will draw (spin in a counterclockwise direction) so allow for it to roll after landing.

BALL BELOW YOUR FEET

Many golfers find it difficult to hit a ball lying below their feet – they tend to lose their balance or swing on top of the ball. Perfect your

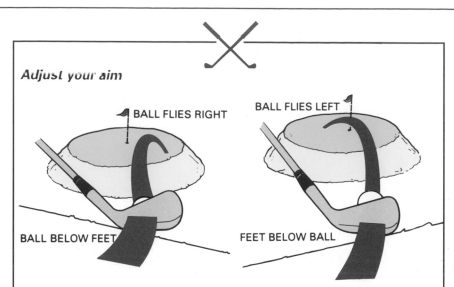

Adjust your aim

BALL FLIES RIGHT

BALL FLIES LEFT

BALL BELOW FEET

FEET BELOW BALL

The ball doesn't fly straight from a sidehill lie because the slope influences the path of the clubhead. The steeper the slope the further off line your ball travels.

When the ball is below your feet the clubhead is pulled across the slope from right to left (out-to-in), causing a slight fade. The ball curves to the right. Aim the clubface and align your body left of the target to compensate.

When the ball is higher than your feet, the clubhead sweeps along the slope from left to right (in-to-out) producing a slight draw. The ball curves to the left. To compensate aim the clubface and align your body right of the target.

Note how only a small part of the clubhead sole touches the ground at impact – near the heel (ball below feet) and near the toe (feet below ball).

address position to help you make a balanced swing.

Because the ball is low you stoop over it, causing a more up-right swing plane. The ball curves from left to right. You may lose distance with this shot, so for a balanced, easy swing it's essential that you use a less lofted club.

ADDRESSING THE BALL

Decide how much the ball will move from left to right and set the club accordingly. Align your body parallel to your chosen line. Adopt your normal posture but place slightly more weight back on your heels. This stops you losing your balance as you swing. Your knees are more flexed than usual.

You have to bend over more – how much depends on the steepness of the slope – and grip down the club slightly if you need more control. If you feel unstable place more weight back on your heels or increase the width of your stance.

SLOW TEMPO

Concentrate on keeping a slow tempo and swing the club only three-quarters of the way back and through. Remember you are using a less lofted club so distance shouldn't be a problem if you make a clean strike.

As with all awkward shots, assume a confident attitude and stay with the shot – don't pull away on your downswing. If you do, you will certainly top the ball from this type of sidehill lie.

pro tip

Grip down for sharp strike

If the ball is on a different level from your feet grip down the shaft for greater control. Because just a tiny area of the sole of the clubface touches the ground at impact, there is only a small margin for error.

To increase your chances of a solid strike slide your hands about 2in (5cm) further down the shaft than normal. The closer your hands are to the ball the more control and better clubhead feel you have.

Sloping lies

Although you develop a technique for playing from level ground there are times in most rounds when you must play off an uphill or downhill lie. For right-handers, an uphill lie is when the left foot is above the right while on a downslope the left foot is below the right. The opposite applies to left-handers.

To play well from a slope you must understand how the angle affects clubface loft – the slope either adds or reduces loft as you strike the ball. You also need to adjust your set-up to compensate for the slope.

KEYS TO SUCCESS

Whatever the direction of the slope, two key principles apply to every shot. The first is that you must tilt your shoulders and set

HITTING OFF A SLOPE
To hit a good shot from a sloping lie, try to take up a posture similar to the one you use on flat ground. You must also alter the ball position and adjust your alignment to compensate for the slope. Practice hitting from uphill and downhill slopes to develop a feel for these lies.

PLAYING FROM AN UPSLOPE

1) ADDRESS POSITION
Position the ball slightly nearer your left heel than usual and tilt your shoulders in the direction of the slope. Aim and align right of the flag.

2) THE BACKSWING
Make no more than a three-quarter stroke or you lose your balance. The slope lets your weight move easily on to your right foot during the backswing.

3) START OF DOWNSWING
To ensure good tempo make a smooth start to the downswing. Your swing plane becomes a little flatter, so that you strike from in to out.

4) INTO IMPACT
The upslope makes it difficult for you to use your lower body correctly. Concentrate on sweeping the clubhead smoothly through the ball – don't try to force the stroke.

5) THE FOLLOWTHROUGH
Your throughswing should be the same length as your backswing but, if the slope is severe, your weight will hardly shift at all. The ball travels from right to left in flight.

PLAYING FROM A DOWNSLOPE

①ADDRESS POSITION
Tilt your upper body in the same direction as the slope. Align your body and aim the clubface left of the target, with the ball slightly nearer your right foot than normal.

②THE BACKSWING
Keep your backswing as smooth as possible and shorter than usual – the slope stops you making a full swing. Don't try to force the stroke. Your body weight does not transfer easily to your right side.

③DOWNSWING
As the upper body leads the clubhead more than during a stroke from a level lie, you must consciously swing down the slope.

④IMPACT
To strike cleanly concentrate on the back of the ball. Your hands pull the clubhead across your body from out to in and the ball moves slightly left to right in the air.

⑤THE THROUGHSWING
Move smoothly into a three-quarter followthrough position – don't try to swing to a full followthrough or you may overbalance.

HOW SLOPES AFFECT LOFT

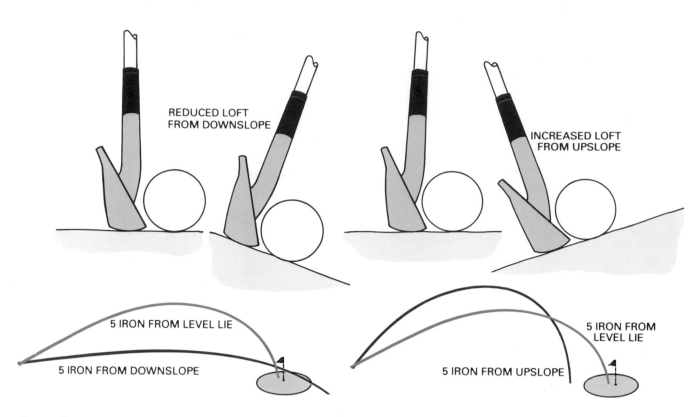

REDUCED LOFT
FROM DOWNSLOPE

INCREASED LOFT
FROM UPSLOPE

5 IRON FROM LEVEL LIE

5 IRON FROM DOWNSLOPE

5 IRON FROM
LEVEL LIE

5 IRON FROM UPSLOPE

Downslope

Take less club than usual from a downhill lie as it reduces loft. At impact a 5 iron may have a loft similar to a 4 or 3 iron, depending on the slope. The ball flies lower and longer than normal so take care not to overshoot the target.

Upslope

Take more club than normal on an upslope as it increases clubface loft. At impact a 5 iron can have the loft of a 6 or 7 iron – the steeper the slope the greater the loft. The ball travels higher than usual and may land short of the target.

your upper body on the same angle as the slope – you can then take up an address position similar to the one you use on a level lie.

The second basic adjustment is to reduce the length of your swing so you are able to maintain good tempo and rhythm. If you try to make a full swing on a severe slope you lose your balance.

Your swing length should vary from about three-quarters on a gentle slope to half on a steep slope.

UPHILL SLOPE

From an uphill lie take more club than usual or your ball ends up short of the target. An upslope increases loft so that you hit higher and shorter than normal. The steeper the slope the higher your ball travels, so choose your club wisely.

For example, on an upslope a 7 iron may have the loft of an 8 or 9 iron, depending on the severity of

the slope.

Tilt your upper body so that you are positioned at the same angle as the slope. Place the ball a little nearer your left heel than usual – this helps you sweep it smoothly off the slope.

Transferring your body weight is extremely difficult if the slope is severe – you hardly shift your weight at all. This leads to a flatter in-to-out swing, so you must adjust your alignment accordingly.

Aim the clubface and align your body right of the target to compensate for the right-to-left flight of the ball. Use a three-quarter swing for extra control – try to avoid forcing the shot.

DOWNHILL LIE

The downhill lie is by far the most difficult slope to play from. Obtaining height is tricky as your body naturally leads the clubhead through impact. This makes your angle of attack steeper than normal, which delofts the clubface.

You also make an out-to-in swing. Allow for these changes when you consider your club selection and body alignment.

Always take less club from a downhill lie to avoid overhitting the target – the reduced clubface loft caused by the downslope means that you hit the ball lower and further than usual.

For example, a 7 iron loft can be the same as a 5 or 6 iron on level ground. Because of this delofting beware of using anything lower than a 4 iron or 4 wood – the smaller the loft the more difficult the club is to use.

Position the ball slightly closer to your right heel than usual to increase your chance of a clean strike. The nearer the ball is to your right heel, the steeper your swing plane. Align and aim left of the target to offset the left-to-right flight of the ball. The greater the slope the steeper your swing plane is and the more your ball flies from left to right. Make no more than a three-quarter swing.

Playing from loose lies

During a round of golf your ball often finishes on, or among, loose debris such as leaves, stones or twigs. This problem is particularly common on parkland and heathland courses in autumn.

Hitting from this type of lie is tricky. The ball is often delicately perched and the slightest nudge might make it topple over. It's natural to worry about accidentally moving the ball at address – which means a 1-stroke penalty. Expecting the worst leads to a hesitant swing.

KNOW THE RULES

To play well from loose debris you must understand the rules, use

Sharp practice

To help you hit the ball cleanly, practice playing off a piece of wood. Because there's no give in a hard, solid surface you can't take a divot – you must pinch the ball cleanly off the top. If you don't, the wood slows down the clubhead speed considerably and you fluff the shot.

Practice frequently to improve technique and increase your confidence from loose and unstable lies.

TAKE BALL CLEANLY
To strike solidly from a loose lie, take the ball cleanly. Hitting loose debris before you strike the ball loses you power and control.

HITTING THE BALL FROM LOOSE DEBRIS

① ADDRESS POSITION
Remove as much loose debris as you can without moving the ball. Keep the sole of the clubhead just above and behind the ball.

② THREE-QUARTER BACKSWING
For a controlled strike, make a smooth three-quarter backswing with your normal tempo. Your upper body should still rotate fully – make about a 90° turn.

PREFERRED LIES

To stop you digging deep divots in winter fairways most clubs apply the "preferred lies" rule. This lets you lift your ball from a depressed lie and place it within 6in (15cm) of where it finished – but you must not move it nearer the hole.

Mark your ball by sticking a tee peg, or a special marker, into the ground just behind the ball. Lift the ball, clean it carefully to remove water, grass and mud and replace it within 6in (15cm) of the marker.

③ THE DOWNSWING
To help you take the ball cleanly, maintain a smooth, relaxed tempo on the downswing and focus on the back of the ball.

them to your advantage and swing confidently and positively.

The rules describe leaves, stones and twigs as loose debris – objects that aren't fixed to, or grow out of, the ground. You can move them out of the way as long as your ball stays where it is.

Make sure you know what counts as fixed to, or growing out of, the ground and what doesn't: you can clear a dead branch or twig that has fallen to earth, but not one still growing from a tree. If you're in doubt about what makes up loose debris, refer to the relevant section of the rules.

ASSESS THE LIE

Before rushing to clear away loose material, carefully assess how much you can safely touch with-

④ IMPACT POSITION
Concentrate on hitting the back of the ball, keeping your wrists firm through impact. If you don't strike the ball cleanly, loose debris cushions your power and the ball doesn't travel as far. There's little margin for error.

⑤ THE THROUGHSWING
The followthrough is the same three-quarter length as the backswing. Your weight finishes on your left side, leaving you in a relaxed, balanced position.

REMOVING LOOSE DEBRIS

LEAVES
Most leaves can be moved without affecting your ball. Pick them up with your hands – don't scoop them away with the club. Never touch those trapped by the ball.

STONES
Assess which stones are held in place by others – don't disturb those touching the ball. Remove any stones which might hamper the clubhead at takeaway and impact.

TWIGS
When clearing twigs, be careful not to disturb any that are stopping your ball from rolling. Moving one twig may also mean that more fall on to your ball, making matters worse.

out disturbing your ball in any way.

Clear loose material with your hands. Don't try to scoop it away with the clubface – you're likely to knock and move the ball.

At address the ball should sit in as stable a position as possible. By removing too much loose material you might leave it teetering on the edge of a stone, so that a sudden gust of wind would blow it over.

Try not to be put off by the ball's unstable position. Instead, concentrate fully on making a solid, purposeful swing. You must be free of all distractions when making the stroke.

AVOID DEBRIS

Grip the club about 2in (5cm) further down the shaft than normal for greater control. Don't ground the clubhead at address if the ball appears in any way unstable – the slightest vibration might move the ball.

Keep the sole of the clubhead just above the ground and behind the ball. Make sure you aim the clubface square to the target and align your stance, knees, hips, chest and shoulders parallel to the ball-to-target line. The ball position is normal.

For a clean strike concentrate on hitting the back of the ball. You must avoid taking debris first – it cushions the power of the stroke and slows down clubhead speed.

The more debris you take the more power you lose, which affects your control and the distance you hit the ball.

THREE-QUARTER SWING

To help achieve a clean strike, make no more than a three-quarter swing with your normal tempo. Don't increase the length or speed of your swing to make up for any loss of distance.

Hitting off small hard stones is more difficult than playing from soft leaves because there is less give at impact.

Unless you're confident you can reach the green, just try to knock the ball down the fairway with no more than a medium iron. Even top professionals rarely use a wood or a long iron from an unstable lie. Your aim is to achieve a firm, controlled strike.

Rough recovery play

On every course you can find different types of rough – dense and sparse, long and short, fairway and greenside. Alas, so can your ball.

If you're lucky, rough is no more difficult than playing from the fairway. But introduce a hazard or two, add a more challenging lie, and a recovery shot from rough is a demanding test.

Common sense is often more important than being a master magician at shot making. Know what you can do and resist the temptation to try any more. Don't risk turning a minor mistake into a potential disaster – landing in even the most severe rough need never cause you to run up a high score.

Even Seve Ballesteros – a genius at recovery play – confesses he'd have more trophies on display in his living room if he'd known when to exercise a little self control earlier in his career.

OUT OF THE ROUGH STUFF
It's impossible to rehearse every recovery shot out of rough, because now and then you come across a totally unfamiliar lie. Your main thought must always be to find a safe route back to the closer mown grass – this is the first step away from disaster. By applying common sense to every situation, you can achieve a satisfactory result the first time – and perhaps an even better outcome when you're next faced with a similar shot.

LIE MATTERS

Study the lie carefully – this has a tremendous bearing on how ambitious you can afford to be with your recovery. A vital point is that it's harder to control the ball from rough. Backspin is almost impossible to achieve and shaping the ball through the air is difficult.

Look at which direction the grass is growing around your ball. If the grass is with you (leaning towards the target) it's easier to strike the ball cleanly without making adjustments to your swing.

If the grass is against you a more precise strike is required. The clubhead must come down at a steep angle to prevent too much grass coming between the clubface and ball at impact.

Don't rule out the possibility of a flyer, particularly if the rough is wet. This can add yards to the flight of your shots.

A ROUGH RIDE

When you hit a tee shot into **rough lining the fairway**, survey the entire hole as you approach your ball. You then have a clearer picture of the situation when you come to prepare for the shot.

If the ball is sitting down, you may have to accept that the green is out of reach. Decide on a club you're confident with – one that guarantees a comfortable escape from the rough and puts you in a good position for your next shot.

If the green is in range, don't forget it's hard to apply spin from

Keeping watch
Make sure you keep an eye on your ball when it's heading for the rough. Don't turn away in disgust even though bad shots can be upsetting – your ball may prove very difficult to find in thick rough if you fail to watch it all the way.

Try to pick out a mark where the ball eventually comes to rest – perhaps a lighter patch of grass, a small tree or a different colored bush. You can then walk straight to it and avoid holding up play.

FIRING THROUGH THE GAP

DECIDE ON THE SHOT
There's not much green to work with here, so concentrate on finding the putting surface rather than trying to place the ball close. When you size up the shot there are two points to consider – you must keep the ball low to avoid the overhanging branches but have enough height to carry the rough in front of you. Be careful – it's usually better to flight your ball too low than too high. If there's one stray branch jutting down lower than the others, a ball often has an uncanny knack of hitting it. You may then finish in an even worse spot.

① SET UP TO HIT LOW
Choose a 9 iron for this shot and position the ball back in your stance opposite the right heel. With your hands pressed forward in front of the ball and the clubface aiming at the flag, you effectively decrease the loft of the club (above). This address position and the poor lie mean the ball comes out lower than normal.

rough, so pitch the ball short and allow for a little run on the shot. From a good lie you can almost afford to play your normal game, but you must still allow for less backspin. Don't expect to stop the ball quickly, even if it's lying cleanly.

SALVAGING SHOTS

In **greenside rough** the first concern is the lie. You should have a fair idea long before you reach the green – if you can see your ball from a distance you can expect a reasonable lie.

You immediately have a greater choice of shots open to you. Hazards shouldn't present you with a problem – you can safely negotiate your way around every form of obstacle.

If you can't see your ball as you approach it, prepare for the worst. A bad lie limits your options, so resign yourself to salvaging what you can without taking a big gamble.

② SMOOTH PICK UP
Swing back smoothly along the ball-to-target line and allow your wrists to hinge (above). Don't take the club back outside the line – there's no need to cut across the ball with this shot. Stop the backswing when your hands are about waist high (below) – this is the perfect length to enable you to accelerate down into impact.

ONTO THE GREEN

③ **STEEP ATTACK**
You need to be extra firm from this lie or you risk moving the ball no distance at all. Strike down with your hands ahead of the clubhead (above). Even though you're using a lofted club, the slight variation in your technique ensures the ball flies fairly low. From behind, your impact position looks almost identical to address (below).

Check how much green you have to work with – if you're not sure of the exact distance, try standing to the side of your ball for a better view.

FLYING HIGH OR LOW

If there are bunkers to carry, a **high float shot** with a soft landing is called for, particularly if there's not much green to work with. Treat the shot much as you would if you were in the bunker – the same techniques in a different situation serve you well.

Adopt an open stance with the ball central, or slightly towards your back foot if the rough is very thick. Swing back steeply by breaking the wrists early and strike down firmly into the bottom of the ball. The clubhead cuts through the grass from out to in and the ball pops up high in the air.

You may have to play a **low trajectory shot** at any time – perhaps to avoid overhanging branches. Depending on the lie,

④ **COMFORTABLE FINISH**
Your left hand dominates before impact and it should continue to do so after the ball is on its way. Make sure the back of your left hand faces the target for as long as possible (above). This serves a double purpose – it prevents the clubface closing and guards against you scooping at the ball.

your club selection may vary from a long iron down to as little as an 8.

Judge the height and the amount of run you want on the ball and match the club best suited to the shot. Play the ball back in your stance and grip down the club for extra control. Strike down crisply, leading the clubhead into impact with your hands.

CALCULATED RISK

Much depends on the situation when you decide how ambitious you are with your recovery. If you're on a good score in a competition it usually pays to play cautiously. You can then limit the damage and move on to the next hole with your card intact.

In a relaxed game there's less at stake so you can afford to be more adventurous when you make your decision. You learn a valuable lesson whichever option you decide to take, and whether it's a success or not.

pro tip

On closer inspection
Identifying your ball in long or dense rough is sometimes a bit of a problem – thick grass easily conceals the manufacturer's name or number. If you're at all uncertain the rules allow you to lift the ball, check if it's yours and carefully replace it.

You must first announce your intention to someone in your playing group. This gives the player an opportunity to observe the correct lifting and replacement of the ball. If you fail to do so you incur a one stroke penalty.

CLEAN THROUGH
As you look up you're greeted with the sight of your ball flying low towards the target – safely avoiding the overhanging branches. You're likely to take no more than 3 shots from an awkward predicament.

Occasionally you take one less – it's then you start to notice how the ability to recover makes a difference to your score. It's also a tremendous boost to your confidence.

THRASHING AWAY TO SAFETY

1 ◄OPEN UP
You can find some pretty wild rough on most courses. It's difficult to escape from but you can do better than hit and hope. Stand open with your shoulders, hips and feet aligning left of target. Aim the clubface at the flag. Grip firmly and further down than normal – hover the club above the ground to prevent the ball moving.

2 ► LEFT AT THE TOP
Make a full backswing along the line of your body to create an out-to-in swing path. Make sure your right elbow points down at the ground to help keep the backswing compact at the top. The club should point well left of target. Maintain a firm grip – particularly with the left hand – to prevent the club twisting when you swing down through the grass.

3 ◄CUTTING EDGE
Generate plenty of clubhead speed coming down – you want to remove as much grass around the ball as possible. The out-to-in swing path combined with the cushion effect of the grass means the ball is unlikely to travel very far.

4 ▼ WRAP AROUND
Concentrate on completing your followthrough, even though you may feel some resistance from the wiry grass. Some of the dense rough is still tangled around the hosel of the club – this emphasizes the need to grip tightly throughout the swing.

Unpredictable lies

An unpredictable lie around the green is a cruel slice of luck. The ball may be lying down or sitting up, on unforgiving bare ground or in a divot.

If you're extremely unlucky you may be faced with a combination of more than one problem, with an awkward stance or perhaps a bunker in front of you to add to your troubles.

But unpredictable lies happen to every golfer – from the experienced professional to the raw beginner – and on all types of course. While no one can expect to get up and down in 2 shots every time, it's important you learn how to handle each situation so you can limit the damage to your score.

LIE DETECTOR

The lie of your ball is the main reason the shot is made difficult, so think about this first. Depending on how you see the shot, the lie determines the club you use.

From a bare lie on hard ground a pitching wedge is the ideal club – particularly if you need a little height on the shot. The leading edge is fairly straight and most suited to nipping the ball cleanly from unforgiving surfaces. If there are no hazards to carry, a less lofted iron is an effective and safe club to use.

A thin sends the ball shooting across the green and is the most common fault off hard ground. Avoid using the sand wedge – it has a wide, rounded flange and the clubhead easily bounces into the middle of the ball at impact. A sand wedge is also unsuitable from a bare lie on soft ground. The rounded sole of the clubhead

SHORT GAME SHARPNESS
Each shot from an unpredictable lie is demanding in its own way – you need to judge which club is best suited for the job and predict how the ball behaves. Basic techniques help you escape from most situations, but occasionally you have to be inventive in your approach. By combining the fundamentals of the short game with a lively imagination, no situation should hold any fear.

CLOSE TO THE EDGE

① OPEN STANCE
Loose sand around the edge of bunkers presents you with a testing lie, but it's more predictable than it looks. Align your feet, hips and shoulders left of target and aim the clubface at the flag. Feel free to ground the club behind the ball.

② PICK UP
Swing the club back steeply outside the line. Let your wrists hinge so that the shaft of the club and your left arm form a right angle. The club points almost straight up – don't allow it to travel any further or you risk losing control.

③ SPLASH DOWN
Concentrate on splashing the clubhead down on a mark about 1in (2.5cm) behind edge ball. Generate lots of clubhead speed into impact – the ball is unlikely to travel too far, but if you do miss the green it's better to be long than in the bunker.

④ HIGH FLOATER
Stay down long after the ball pops up in the air for its soft landing on the green. The back of the left hand stays ahead of the clubhead to prevent the face closing – never let your right hand roll over the left through impact.

digs in behind the ball – the result is a frustrating duffed chip.

From clinging rough the emphasis is on striking down steeply into impact. From short range use a sand wedge. Keep your hands forward at address with the ball central in your stance. Break your wrists quickly on the backswing and strike down crisply into the bottom of the ball.

Loose sand outside the bunker under your ball can act as a cushion at impact if you play the shot correctly. Treat it as you would a normal bunker shot and hit down with a sand wedge into the sand behind the ball. Accelerate on the downswing and you can be confident of a satisfactory result – the ball floats high on to the green and lands softly.

Unless the sand is very compact don't try to strike the ball cleanly. Your margin for error is tiny and even the slightest miss-hit results in disaster. The chances are you play your next shot from sand, too, but from the bunker in front of you this time.

TAKING A STANCE

When you have an awkward stance as well as an unpredictable lie, sound technique helps you cope with every shot. Remember, the ball reacts according to the slope of the ground.

On an uphill lie the ball flies higher than normal – downhill the reverse is true – so make allowances when you judge the roll of the ball on landing. With the ball below your feet the shot flies to the right – when it's above your feet the ball drifts to the left.

The basic chipping stroke stands you in good stead in unpredictable lies, but you may also

Once is enough
Finding your ball lying in a divot mark is very frustrating and the result of someone else's thoughtlessness. One such experience alone should encourage you to replace your own divots every time. If replaced immediately the turf makes a quick and full recovery – it's also one less divot mark on the course for your ball to land in.

Predict the unpredictable
Divot marks wouldn't be on a golf course in a perfect world, but alas this isn't the case. There is very little margin for error from this lie – the clubhead may dig into the ground causing a duff. A thinned shot also happens all too easily if your technique is incorrect. You must keep your hands ahead of the ball and strike down steeply into the bottom of the ball.

Hard ground tests your technique in the hot summer months when the fairways become parched. The danger is of the clubhead bouncing off the hard, unforgiving surface into the middle of the ball – a thinned shot is the depressing result. Avoid using the sand wedge from a bare lie – the wide flange bounces more than any other club. Use a straighter faced iron and nip the ball cleanly off the surface.

High on a tuft of grass your ball is precariously placed – the outcome can be disastrous if you don't play the shot correctly. Your normal swing with an iron sends the clubhead on a downward path into impact, but you must guard against chopping clean underneath the ball and causing a dreaded air shot. Grip further down the club than normal and hover the clubhead above the ground at address to promote a clean strike. It's important to accelerate into the ball – don't quit on the shot or you risk a double hit.

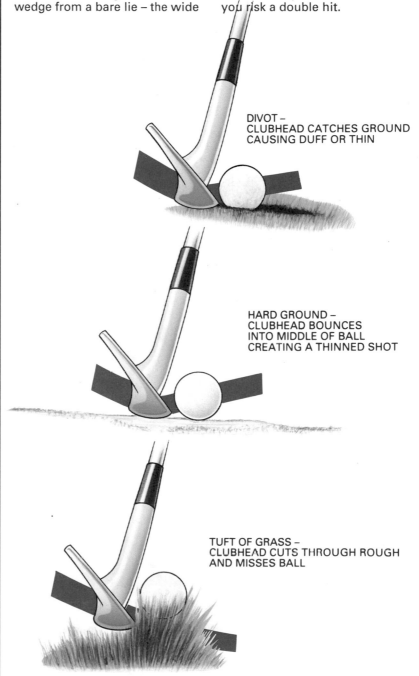

DIVOT –
CLUBHEAD CATCHES GROUND
CAUSING DUFF OR THIN

HARD GROUND –
CLUBHEAD BOUNCES
INTO MIDDLE OF BALL
CREATING A THINNED SHOT

TUFT OF GRASS –
CLUBHEAD CUTS THROUGH ROUGH
AND MISSES BALL

BALL PERCHED IN THE AIR

1 STURDY STANCE

While it doesn't happen too often, the sight of a ball perched high up on a tuft of grass fills many golfers with dread. But for a shot of 80yd (73m) you can hit the green every time. Your stance is awkward, so make sure you're balanced at address.

2 TAKING BACK

Your main thought is to strike the ball cleanly, so grip down the club. Hover the clubhead above the ground to help you take the club smoothly away from the ball. Make a normal backswing and break your wrists halfway back.

5 OUT ON RELEASE

Most of your weight is now on the left side to put you in a strong position in the hitting area. Let your hands release through impact and stay down on the shot until you feel your arms pull your body up naturally.

6 BALL FLIES HIGH

As always, a good controlled swing results in a perfectly balanced followthrough – there's no toppling back from this position. The clubhead throws the ball – and plenty of grass – high into the air.

3 TOP OF BACKSWING
Concentrate on turning your shoulders fully and stop short of horizontal to stay in control of the club. Keep your legs flexed and head very still to prevent your body coming up off the ball.

4 LEFT IN CHARGE
Focus your eyes on the back of the ball and pull the club down with your left hand dominating the swing. Drive your right knee towards the target to help you transfer your weight on to the left side.

need to improvise a little to play a shot precisely.

Treat every situation as a challenge and take time to compose yourself. Be creative and use your imagination – there's an effective way to play a shot from every lie. All good shots are enjoyable – but a successful escape from an unpredictable lie is extremely satisfying and a tremendous boost to your confidence.

There are no short cuts to mastering escapes from difficult situations, so don't expect a shot to come off first time. Every golfer knows the difficulties of those awkward shots near the green. If you don't know what to do, you're in for a frustrating time as you helplessly watch good scores deteriorate through sloppy short shots.

Try to find time in your practice sessions to experiment with shots from different lies – you learn to remove some of the element of chance and judge how the ball reacts. You can then create the shot in your mind and be confident of playing it correctly.

pro tip

Deep in trouble
If your ball comes to rest in a deep divot mark, or one that points way off line, you're faced with a serious problem. It's hard to judge how the ball reacts, so look to play the shot with the greatest margin for error.

Playing along the line of the divot is usually the best option. You must strike down sharply into the bottom of the ball – expect a very low flight on the shot and plenty of run.

DIVOT SHOT

① MAKING A STANCE
A ball in a divot mark is one of the most daunting lies you find on a golf course. Providing the divot points at the target and isn't too deep, the shot is not nearly as fearsome as it looks. Stand open to the ball-to-target line with the clubface aiming at the flag.

② SHORT AND STEEP
Pick the club up steeply by hinging your wrists as you swing your arms back. Keep your body very still and your weight towards the left side – if you sway away from the ball you're likely to thin the shot through the green or move the ball no distance at all.

③ BALL TO TURF CONTACT
Accelerate the club down into the bottom of the ball making sure you keep your tempo smooth. It's very much a hands and arms shot, so avoid body movement. The clubhead strikes the ball first and then the ground.

④ FIRM WRISTS
Keep your left wrist firm and ahead of the clubhead through impact. The ball often flies lower than from a normal lie and may overshoot the target, but that's better than a heavy duff which moves the ball no distance at all.

Perched on the edge

Awkward stances are among the most unfair scenarios in golf, and there are few more upsetting than a precarious lie on the edge of – though not inside – a bunker.

You're faced with a testing recovery, having hit an acceptable previous shot. In these situations it's easy to dwell on your hard luck. But it's essential you learn to accept your fate when things go against you, then tune your mind to the task at hand.

LIE AND DISTANCE

The lie is a crucial factor when you're considering which shot to play. If your ball is sitting well then

▼ **WEIGHT ALLOWANCE**
Maintaining your balance is the hardest part about this shot because the lip of the bunker pulls you toward the sand. Make allowances by keeping your head directly over the ball at address and throughout the swing – resist any swaying as this usually leads to a complete miss-hit.

CLOSE TO THE EDGE

① BUILDING THE FOUNDATIONS
As soon as you find your ball in this position you should start thinking about how you intend taking your stance. One foot in the bunker is an option, but it lowers your right side a good deal. A far more secure stance is standing with your right foot as close to the bunker as possible. A little more than half your weight should naturally be supported by your right foot.

② WEIGHT CENTRAL
Unlike any other full shot in golf, you must avoid transferring your weight away from the ball. If you do, you risk losing your balance altogether on the backswing. Apart from this one-off change in technique, your backswing should be the same as any other full shot.

count yourself lucky – this at least allows you a selection of clubs to choose from.

However, if the lie is bad any difficulties are worsened because you cannot stand normally to the ball. This restricts you in your choice of shots and you may have to accept that an ambitious recovery isn't on the cards.

Club selection also takes on a new perspective when you have an awkward stance. The distances you usually hit the ball have absolutely no bearing on the matter. You may hit a 6 iron from about

150yd (137m) on a flat lie, but if one foot is planted below the other you can probably afford to take two or three more clubs.

Your next concern should be how you intend keeping your balance. It's never easy, but there's usually a way of taking a fairly secure stance, and at the same time aiming in the general direction of the flag.

Experiment with a few different stances to find out which is most comfortable. Shuffle your feet around, try one foot in the bunker and one out, or perhaps vary the

width of your stance if it helps.

Simulate the backswing you intend making to see if you can maintain your balance. It's best to restrict yourself to a three-quarter backswing. This is certain to improve your chances of remaining steady over the ball.

Very occasionally it's too risky to take a direct line at the flag. Your stance may be so awkward and your ball so precariously placed that you're in grave danger of hitting an air shot.

BAIL OUT

Only when these situations arise can you know when it's best to bail out sideways. Use your common sense and decide how much there is to gain by being adventurous. More important, how much do you stand to lose if the shot goes wrong?

There aren't many occasions when you have to resort to taking a drop. Even when your ball is so close to the edge that it seems to defy the laws of gravity, you can usually nudge it out sideways.

pro tip

Message from the master
Playing in a charity match with Sean Connery on the Old Course at St. Andrews, Jack Nicklaus was once asked what he considered to be the most important factor to overcome in golf. "It is an unfair game," came the reply from the master.

If anything in golf is certain, it's that you are bound to have your

share of bad luck. Perched on the edge of a bunker is one example – a cruel bounce is another.

Instead of cursing your misfortune, you'd do well to remember these wise words from Nicklaus. Because the golfer who brushes off bad luck is the one most likely to string together a good score.

③ PERFECT CONTROL
Restrict your backswing to three-quarter length to help you keep your balance. Notice how the left knee is more flexed than usual – this helps compensate for the fact that your right foot is below the level of your left. If you didn't make this adjustment you would almost certainly come up off the ball on the backswing.

④ STAYING DOWN
Your key thought at the start of the downswing is to prevent any sideways movement of your head – this is a little more difficult than normal because of the upslope which almost forces you backward. Try to think of your head being positioned directly over the ball throughout the stroke.

⑤ NATURAL PROGRESSION
A good impact position and extension through the ball are the benefits of making the correct move from the top of the backswing. At this stage you should be able to draw a straight line from your eyes down to the point of impact.

⑥ EFFECTIVE STROKE
The followthrough may look ungainly, but at least you're not floundering in the sand. This is an indication that you've successfully kept your balance throughout the swing – in a very awkward position this is more than half the battle.

TOPPLING BACKWARDS

BALANCING ACT

A host of disasters are waiting to befall every golfer who sets foot on a course. Awkward stances increase the number and also make mistakes more likely to happen, so be mindful of the difficulties.

When you're perched on the edge of a bunker the most important factor is balance. If this deserts you, you're almost certain to make a mess of the shot – perhaps even miss the ball altogether. You need to make a conscious effort to stop yourself falling backwards into the bunker. It's not at all easy, so you

need to work hard at building a solid stance at address, with a little more than half your weight on the right foot. Make a controlled three-quarter swing to enable you to keep your balance for as long as possible.

Don't be afraid to play safe from this position. If you have doubts whether you can successfully play a shot at the flag, knock the ball out sideways. The entire problem then disappears because you can stand normally to the ball and swing without risking a loss of balance.

TRYING TO HIT THE BALL TOO
HARD CAN ONLY END IN DISASTER

AWKWARD STANCE – HARD
TO KEEP YOUR BALANCE

Hover to be safe

When your ball is perilously close to the edge of a bunker, think twice before you ground your club behind it. There's every chance your ball is resting on a slope – if you disturb the grass around it, your ball may trickle back into the sand.

If you're in any doubt, hover the club at a safe distance above and behind the ball. This should guarantee you don't do anything silly before you've had a chance even to start the swing.

Ball perched up in rough

The perched lie is one of the most misunderstood shots in golf because you don't come across it often. It can be just as demanding as dislodging your ball from a half buried lie in rough.

Ignore your usual rules concerning rough play. It's essential you sweep the ball away like a wood shot from a tee peg. Don't strike down into impact, as you do with a normal shot from long grass.

One of the most reliable methods for clipping the ball sweetly off a perched lie is to grip down the club slightly and make a three-quarter swing. Try to quiet down the movement of your wrists on the backswing. Also position the ball a fraction further forward in your stance than you would normally.

SITTING PRETTY
At first glance your ball may look as though it's resting invitingly on a tee peg, but a perched lie in the rough is no time to be complacent. It's one of those rare occasions in golf where the lie looks better than it actually is. You must sweep the ball away for best results. Don't strike down steeply like a normal rough recovery shot.

SUCCEED FROM A PERCHED LIE

① NEW ADDRESS
There are two changes you can make to your address when the ball rests on a perched lie – either hover the clubhead or choke down on the grip. Each helps you strike correctly, so choose the one you feel most comfortable with. Also, position the ball a little further forward than you normally would to encourage the sweeping action through impact.

② SHALLOW START
You must create a shallow swing arc from the start because this is the key to sweeping the ball away on the downswing. Concentrate on drawing the club back wide and low to the ground. Reducing the amount of wrist break helps you achieve this, and at the same time ensures the club doesn't travel too steeply on the backswing. Stop the club just short of horizontal to increase your clubhead control – vital from an unusual lie.

Rough rider
Aiming straight at the target is unwise if the ball is perched a long way above the level of your feet. It's the same as playing from a sloping lie, so you're almost certain to drag the ball left of the flag.

Align right of target – how far depends on the severity of the perched lie – and allow for the ball to draw back on line with the flag. Your swing plane becomes more rounded with the ball above your feet, so this change in flight path should happen naturally.

All of these factors help ensure that the clubhead reaches the bottom of its arc at the precise moment of impact, thus giving you the shallow angle of attack that you need. Less grass is taken in comparison to a normal shot from rough, and the clubhead sweeps the ball away.

STROKE WITH DISTANCE

One very positive aspect of the perched lie is that it doesn't prevent you from gaining as much height and distance as you require. You're not restricted in your club selection.

Because of the shallow angle at which the clubhead meets the ball, this shot doesn't generate a great deal of backspin. So don't expect the ball to stop quickly, unless you're firing into a sponge-like green in the distance.

The ball travels at least one club further, possibly two, from a perched lie, so choke down on the grip to compensate. This small adjustment in technique reduces the width of your swing arc. Taking this into account you can probably hit the same club as you would from a normal lie.

Make sure you allow for a little more run on the ball. Backspin is hard to generate because you're not hitting down on the ball. So if

(3) **KNEE DRIVE**
Make sure your head stays behind the ball on the downswing to ensure that your angle of attack doesn't get too steep. Drive your knees towards the target to encourage good weight transfer. Note how the hips are already square – an early indication of the left side clearing.

(4) **SWEPT AWAY**
A combination of good moves help you sweep the ball away. By the nature of the strike less grass is taken at impact – this is a positive sign because it means you haven't chopped down too steeply on the ball. Note the impressive firm left side, providing solid resistance against which you can release the clubhead through square towards the target.

the ground is hard, or there's a strong wind at your back, your ball can easily run out of control on landing.

If you create an angle of attack that is just too steep, the clubhead can easily cut underneath the ball. A miss-hit from the top part of the blade is likely to happen depressingly often. This results in a shot that flies very little distance through the air.

PERCHED PITCHING

The rules for playing a short shot from a perched lie are the same as from long range. The ball sits up nicely for you, so the critical move is sweeping it away cleanly rather than striking down.

Grip down the club and hover the blade at the same level to the ball. This simple, and very important, change in address promotes a clean strike.

WRIST REMINDER

Also reduce the amount of wrist break on the backswing because this is the most effective way to promote a shallow angle of attack on the downswing.

If you have any doubts about the use of your wrists, remember one very constructive rule of thumb – the more you hinge your wrists on the way back, the steeper the arc at which the clubhead approaches the ball. On the other hand, no wrist break produces a very shallow angle of attack – more of a sweeping action in fact.

WISE CHOICE

Allow for more run on the ball when you chip off a perched lie. You're likely to find a mid iron more reliable than your sand wedge from the same position.

Provided you target a flat landing area – preferably on the putting surface – it's easier to predict the progress of your ball on the ground than it is through the air.

pro tip

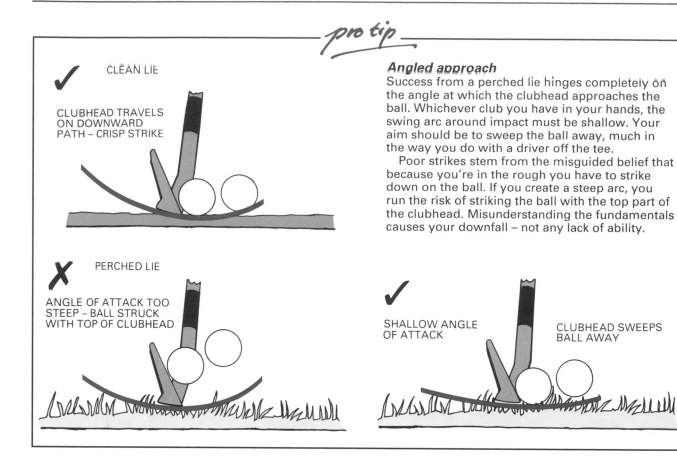

CLEAN LIE

CLUBHEAD TRAVELS
ON DOWNWARD
PATH – CRISP STRIKE

PERCHED LIE

ANGLE OF ATTACK TOO
STEEP – BALL STRUCK
WITH TOP OF CLUBHEAD

SHALLOW ANGLE
OF ATTACK

CLUBHEAD SWEEPS
BALL AWAY

Angled approach

Success from a perched lie hinges completely on the angle at which the clubhead approaches the ball. Whichever club you have in your hands, the swing arc around impact must be shallow. Your aim should be to sweep the ball away, much in the way you do with a driver off the tee.

Poor strikes stem from the misguided belief that because you're in the rough you have to strike down on the ball. If you create a steep arc, you run the risk of striking the ball with the top part of the clubhead. Misunderstanding the fundamentals causes your downfall – not any lack of ability.

On the bright side

A perched lie usually means you have to work extra hard at producing the right result. However, if you need to play a lob shot over a bunker, having your ball sitting up is a definite advantage.

Concentrate on your set-up. Align your shoulders, hips and feet left of target. Aim the clubface straight at the flag and make a full swing, keeping your wrists out of the swing as much as possible.

There's a certain security about this shot, because it's almost impossible for your ball to fly wildly out of control. If you play it correctly, the ball flies high and lands softly.

Awkward stances

Escaping from trouble on a golf course doesn't just mean playing the run of the mill shots – such as a straightforward splash shot from sand. You're often faced with a shot that needs imagination and an improvised swing.

When your ball finds a tricky spot, be ready and willing to adapt both your body position and technique for a safe and sometimes attacking getaway.

BALANCING ACT

The key to playing from an awkward lie when your stance is hampered is to stay balanced throughout the stroke. Concentrate on your posture, and then try to swing as normally as possible.

Experiment with your stance before you play. Shift and fiddle around until you feel comfortable and stable. However, you must realize that finding the most secure posture doesn't necessarily mean you can play the most productive shot.

Try to find a stance that gives you the freedom of movement to play a meaningful recovery – even if it means you have to stand in a slightly unfamiliar and compromising way.

SEE THE SHOT

Take time to choose your club and go through the stroke in your mind several times before you play. Decide which shape of swing you want. Then practice the backswing and the start of your downswing to see if either are impeded and if your balance holds true.

Also check the throughswing path to find out whether you need

to modify it – perhaps having to stop it short so that the club doesn't crash into a tree.

Always swing smoothly – a jerky, forced action often fails to free the ball – and stay as steady as possible throughout the stroke.

Too much movement during the

swing makes it hard to return the blade precisely to the ball.

Never try to overhit the shot – be content to knock the ball back onto the fairway if firing for the green is likely to go wrong. This cautious approach should save you shots in the long run.

STRADDLE-LEGGED
Often it's not possible to adopt a normal stance to play a shot. Imagination and a clever modification of your set-up mean you can turn a near disaster into a positive result. With the ball well below your feet, standing wide-legged astride the ball helps you to reach it, and if you stay balanced and steady you can play a powerful and accurate stroke.

BACK TO BARK

① UPRIGHT STANCE
To cope with a ball that's landed close to an obstruction, it may still be possible to squeeze between ball and obstacle and play a positive shot. Adapt your stance and swing so that you can still move the club freely without hitting the tree.

② HIGH BACKLIFT
Standing upright means you have to pick up the club sharply to avoid the tree. It's better to swing it up almost over your head than try for a near normal action if it means you lessen the risk of hitting the obstruction. This shot is nearly all hands and arms, so you must swing smoothly with control if you're to strike the ball properly.

③ EASY TEMPO
Since your action is unfamiliar, concentrate on swinging down with an easy tempo and rhythm so that the clubhead meets the ball squarely. Look at the back of the ball – this improves your eye, hand coordination and increases the chance of the shot coming off. Don't dip down into impact – stay upright – otherwise you can easily stab behind the ball.

④ CONTROLLED FINISH
Swing through keeping the blade going straight at the target so that the club doesn't crash into the tree. Stop the throughswing shorter than normal to help avoid a collision. If you're firm and controlled through the ball there is no reason why your shot can't fly powerfully straight.

HEAD START

1 BEND AT THE WAIST
Finding a balanced and stable stance is crucial to the success of any awkward shot. To cope with a ball on a steep downward slope, adopt a straddle-legged position – where your feet are set at well over shoulder width apart. Bend over from the waist more than usual to help you reach the ball. Once you have found a comfortable stance, feel how your body is positioned, as it's vital to keep it the same throughout the swing to be sure of making good contact with the ball.

2 NO LIFTING
Make your backswing while keeping the head perfectly still. Note that its position at the top of the backswing is the same as at address. Resist the temptation to rise up into your usual body position – this is bound to lead to a miss-hit, as you must dip back down to have a chance of connecting at all with the ball. Even though your swing is hampered and likely to be more arms than lower body, strive for a full shoulder turn, but not at the expense of overbalancing.

3 LEVEL ATTACK
Swing smoothly down into impact. Don't force the shot – this helps you stay balanced and gives you a greater chance of hitting a crisp stroke. Notice how the head has stayed in the same position throughout the back and downswing. Though you can't swing as powerfully or fluently as normal, it's still possible to attack the ball with vigor.

4 POISE AT THE FINISH
The only time you should rise up and into a more normal swing position is after impact. Trying to stay in the bent posture throughout the swing means you can't release the club properly. You probably overbalance and fall forward – in this case with dire consequences. Moving through into this upright finish also helps you to hit the ball powerfully.

Up a tree

When you're in difficulties close to an obstacle, it's vital to practice your swing several times to find a clear path. Once you have found a route along which you can swing freely, make sure your action is controlled.

If you try to force the shot you swing on a slightly different path than you intended, and the results are disastrous. There is a good chance of your club tangling with the obstacle on either the back or downswing.

The worst possible scene is when you start down towards impact and you clip a tree. This throws your rhythm and balance well out and it's easy to hit an air shot.

Temper your desire to hit a forceful shot with a sense of safety – never take on too much.

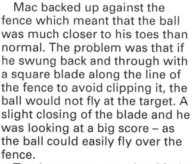

masterclass

Mac's predicament

It isn't just amateurs who find themselves in a jam now and then – top pros land in trouble too.

In the final of the 1990 World Matchplay Championship at Wentworth, Mark McNulty put himself in a tricky spot on the 12th. His second to the par 5 finished dangerously close to the out of bounds fence. He had to improvise.

Mac backed up against the fence which meant that the ball was much closer to his toes than normal. The problem was that if he swung back and through with a square blade along the line of the fence to avoid clipping it, the ball would not fly at the target. A slight closing of the blade and he was looking at a big score – as the ball could easily fly over the fence.

To play an accurate shot Mark

made his downswing while holding the back of his left hand – and hence his blade – open in relation to his feet but square to the target. The ball came out well but landed just short of the green.

Unfortunately for Mac, Ian Woosnam took 2 putts and made his birdie. Even though the Zimbabwean had made a good recovery it couldn't prevent Woosie walking off with the title.

Divots in detail

Taking turf just after you hit the ball is essential for crisp striking. Some grass should be taken with every fairway shot – the amount varies depending on the steepness of swing and which club you use.

It's important you strike the ball before you take a divot – hitting turf first leads to a fat or heavy shot. Not taking any grass means you hit the ball too clean – often resulting in a thin.

Balance the amount of divot you take with the sort of shot you need, what club you use and the type of course. The shorter the iron the bigger a divot you take since you play from further back in the stance and your downswing is steeper than with a long iron. With a 1 or 2 iron the turf taken can be a few blades of grass – the divot mark is as small as a coin.

A steep downswing makes the ball rise – to hit a club higher than normal you must attack from a steeper angle and take more divot. But the size of divot also depends on the type of grass and how firm the ground is. Divots are smaller on a dry, firm links course than on a lush one because the links ground doesn't give as much.

CRISP CONTACT
Taking a clean divot after hitting the ball shows you have struck it crisply with a firm downward blow. Good contact means the shot flies its full distance with the maximum amount of backspin helping the ball stop on the green.

With a quality strike the natural loft of the clubface throws the ball high even though you have hit down on it. At this early stage the spin is clearly visible – the red stripe on the ball has already moved well off its original vertical position.

PRECISE STRIKING

✓

1 BALL BEFORE TURF
At impact the blade of the wedge – as with all clubs – should strike the ball fractionally before the ground. This ensures that no grass gets between the clubface and ball, which would deaden the strike. But be sure not to hit the ball too cleanly and skim the grass well after the strike as you are bound to thin the shot. The red stripe is vertical at the start, so that the amount of spin can be gauged.

2 FIRMLY THROUGH
Continue to swing through firmly after contact.
Your club cuts the turf and the ball pops into the air
with backspin – because the clubface is square the red
stripe starts to rotate backward with no hint of
sidespin. Don't decelerate after impact and quit on the
shot – if you do, the ground stops the club from
swinging through fully and the ball doesn't fly as far as
usual. The sign of a good square strike is if your divot
mark points at the target.

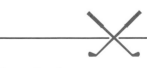

Don't go digging
Though taking a divot is important for crisp
striking, trying deliberately to dig up the turf is
dangerous. Don't force yourself to dig down –
taking a divot should be a natural part of your
swing. Stabbing down hard at the ball stops the
club from sliding through the turf and you lose
distance. A digging action can also damage your
wrists – and the course.

HEAVY HITTING

X

(1) BEHIND THE BALL
Make sure you don't take a divot before you contact the ball. Even though a firm attack still cuts through the turf, grass gets between the ball and clubface and striking is dramatically impaired. The result – a fat or heavy shot that doesn't fly the full distance.

X

② SHORT AND NO BACKSPIN
Because the club has collected the divot on its face before the strike, the ball can't make good contact. The shot still climbs, but not as high as with a crisp strike and there isn't the same power. As the ball doesn't contact the blade, no backspin is produced – the red stripe is in almost the same position as at impact. The result is a much shorter shot than normal that runs slightly on landing.

pro tip

Exact sand trapping
The ideal shot off a fairway arises when you trap the ball between the club and the ground. One good way of perfecting this strike is to practice hitting medium irons out of a fairway bunker. You soon learn to avoid catching the ball fat. If you catch the ball first and then take a shallow slice of sand the shot flies a good distance. Hit the sand before the ball and the shot is fluffed.

Woosnam leaves his mark

Ian Woosnam is one of the finest strikers of the golf ball of all time. His easy rhythm and stocky build combine perfectly to crack the ball away with exquisite timing and power. He is convinced that a player must hit the ball before taking turf to gain the best strike possible.

Huge, scorecard-sized divots fly into the air when Ian hits a short iron, but they shrink as he plays the longer irons. With a short iron his attack is steep and the club naturally tears through the turf. When Ian hits a long iron his angle of attack is shallower and he takes much less turf – but he always takes some to ensure a good strike.

The only time you might see Woosie taking quite a bit of turf with a long iron is if he hits a low punched shot from back in his stance.

► **Woosie takes huge chunks of turf with a short iron.**

Divot reminders

It's important to go and practice your striking, but treat the practice green with care. When you start hitting your irons, work in a small area to limit the damage to the range.

Roll your balls onto the grass just in front or to the side of another divot. By the time you finish practicing you'll have worn a small patch of bare ground. Don't replace your divots – a patch is easy for the greens-keeper to reseed.

The opposite applies on the course. You must always replace divots unless you're told otherwise by the club. Some courses provide a mixture of seed and sand to fill in your divots – especially in America or in Europe – as the type of grass doesn't take root when replaced. Or they ask you to leave divot marks alone so that the greens staff can repair them.

Remember not to take a divot if you make a practice swing out on the course. A practice swing is an aid for finding rhythm, visualizing the shot and relieving tension, not an exact copy of your stroke.

▲ **Sweeping long iron leaves only a small divot mark.**

Restricted backswing escape

S eeing golfers struggle to free their ball profitably from trees is common all over the world. Too much ambition and the wrong escape technique are both causes for a duffed recovery.

Upper body coordination is vital to the success of any stroke where your backswing is restricted. Playing a decently flighted and forceful shot out of trouble needs good hand and arm control. Poor use of your wrists and arms, and a snatched action can leave you humiliated as the ball hardly moves.

Problems start when you try to gain too much distance out of the shot by being forceful. Your backswing becomes too long in an attempt to gain power, often causing your club to crash into the obstruction. If it does, it can be so rhythm destroying that a fresh air shot can't be ruled out.

IMPROVISED SWINGS

You need to change your normal technique to avoid such mishaps. Remember that power can still be produced by an unconventional action. Instead of swinging back with the normal wrist break for a pitch shot, you have to alter your takeaway to cope with different types of obstacle.

If your backswing is hindered by a wall, fence or large tree trunk, you may have to pick up the club very steeply with plenty of wrist break to avoid a collision. This should automatically make your downswing steeper than normal – if it isn't, the clubhead snags and you fluff the shot.

When you can't make a full backswing – because of overhanging branches – you must make as wide a takeaway arc as possible with little wrist break. This puts the clubhead a long way from the ball but not too high off the ground and gives scope to create power.

But whatever the shape of your backswing, you must repeat its swing path back to the ball to be able to strike the shot properly. If you combine this action with the smoothest rhythm you can – don't snatch the stroke – you should produce a crisp, positive recovery.

BRANCHING OUT
Overhanging trees can play havoc with your shotmaking if you use your normal action. Escaping awkward positions needs imagination and a careful rehearsal of your technique. Just because your backswing is short, it doesn't mean you can't hit the ball powerfully. All it takes is a shallow, no wrist attack to keep the club away from the branches and deliver the blade firmly into the ball. The flight of the shot should be near normal.

BEAT THE RESTRICTION

①USUAL ADDRESS
Try to address the ball normally. If you have to compromise, make your stance as comfortable as possible. It often helps to grip down for better clubhead control – vital for crisp striking. However your body is positioned, try to aim your blade square.

②SIDEWAYS PUSH
There is no hint of wrist break – a normal pitching hand action sees the blade rise up and strike the branches. Instead of picking up the hands, it's best to push them back laterally to create as wide an arc as possible.

③SHORT AND FIRM
Retain the angle between your left arm and shaft throughout the backswing. Swing to the highest point you can without hitting the branches. If you do clatter the branches, stop your swing and start again, as this or any pause at the top destroys your rhythm.

④ A HINT OF WRIST
You can use your wrists slightly on the downswing to create power and to ensure the blade attacks the ball on a steeper angle than the takeaway. Pulling your hands back along a horizontal line and keeping your shaft parallel to the ground for a short distance creates a lag effect of the blade.

⑤ SMOOTH STRIKE
Be content to make decent contact with the ball. Don't force the downswing with too much hand action or by getting ahead of the ball – you tend to stab the shot. The lag you have created and a little working of the wrists are enough to power the ball away.

⑥ CONTROL AT THE FINISH
Your followthrough should be naturally firm wristed like your back and downswings. A tendency to break your wrists through the ball leads to a flicking action and a loss of power. Don't be worried about using this shallow-pathed, firm and punchy style stroke with a wedge – the angle of the clubface is enough to loft the ball out.

pro tip

Angled approach

Your swing path and angle of clubface dictate how the ball flies. In most cases the ball starts off on line with your swing path then moves sideways in the air – how much and in which direction depends on where your blade is aiming. But when the angle between your swing path and clubface is severe – perhaps when your blade is well hooded – the ball flies off on a line square to your blade.

This information is very useful when you're stymied by a fence and have a restricted backswing. If you can't align and aim straight at your target because the ball is too close to the fence and a full backswing is not possible, turn sideways slightly. Turn until you have a clear swing path along the line of the fence.

Aim your blade square to the target then make a normal swing along the line of your feet. The ball flies behind you towards the target. Remember to choose your club carefully – you need to select a more lofted one than normal because the face is hooded. Also make sure the blade is not too shut in relation to your swing path or a miss-hit is the result.

masterclass

The hands of José

All the top pros have good hands. Their clubhead control is the key to their success. Knowing how your body and hand positions relate to the clubhead is essential for hitting the ball as you want to – even out of trouble. But only a few possess brilliant clubhead control which separates them from the also rans.

Spain's José-Maria Olazabal is one of the lucky ones. His touch and feel are legendary, whether it is from long range or a delicate chip. He understands how much wrist action is needed for any given shot, and how it affects the path of his clubhead. This visualization and excellent reading of a shot help José out of tight spots.

Even near the thickest of undergrowth, the Spanish whizzkid can conjure up a purposeful stroke despite having almost no room for a backswing.

Although he has natural talent, Olazabal's escape techniques have been honed by trial and error and by hard practice. Anyone hoping to emulate him must also be prepared to put in the practice and not just rely on luck when they find themselves in trouble out on the course.

Playing from a divot

To play golf to a consistently high standard you have to be able to cope with the unexpected setbacks that occur on the course.

If you've played a superb drive down the middle of the fairway, it's always hard to contain your feelings when you find your ball lying in someone's divot mark. Your second shot is that much harder to cope with. Having teed off so effectively, you think you're in a great position – then you have to manufacture a shot you're not confident of playing.

A CLEAN STRIKE

Etiquette demands that golfers replace their divots. Although some players may forget, birds are often the culprits, removing the divots when they look for food. Your ball always carries the risk of running into a divot mark – it's vital you know how to play the stroke as if the mark wasn't there.

Your priority is to strike down and through the ball – concentrate on taking an even larger divot. Assess the depth of the hole because it affects the length of your shot. If the hole is shallow it's possible to strike a reasonable distance – if it's deep, you have to try just to move the ball as far as you can.

Performing the shot well means changing your set-up and reducing your swing, as your energies are geared solely into delivering the club through the back of the ball.

PLAYING THE SHOT

Narrow your stance, dropping your left foot back a little as if about to play a pitch. Grip slightly further down the shaft than usual. This reduces your swing arc and lets you pick the club up more steeply than usual, so that you can approach the ball at a more acute angle.

Stay smooth, because rhythm rather than brute force is the key to playing from a divot mark. Good upper body movement is essential.

TRANSFER YOUR WEIGHT
To play successfully from a divot mark, your weight must transfer fully – good upper body turn towards the target is essential.

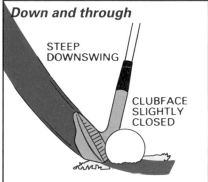

Down and through

STEEP DOWNSWING

CLUBFACE SLIGHTLY CLOSED

When you have to play out of a divot mark, concentrate on striking down and through the ball, making a bigger mark. This helps you blast the ball out. If the mark is shallow, you can hit a long way. From a deep mark concentrate on a clean strike.

SET-UP AND SWING

①SET-UP AND STANCE
At address, place the ball between the center of your stance and your right foot. Slightly close the clubface to help dig the ball out. This delofts the clubface – take a heavily lofted club to compensate.

②BACKSWING
Although you only need a three-quarter backswing, make sure that you complete your wrist break and turn your shoulders a full 90° to obtain maximum leverage and power at impact.

③DOWNSWING
Let your left hand and arm pull the club back down toward the ball. The strike feels a lot later than when you play a normal shot because your hands are ahead of the clubface from address to impact.

④IMPACT AND THROUGHSWING
You must stay solid through impact. Keep your left wrist and forearm firm when you strike as it's easy to let your right hand overpower your left.

masterclass

Stadler's Master stroke

Every golfer must be able to play confidently from divot marks because they can appear at any time – even at a crucial moment of a championship.

During the final round of the 1982 Masters, Craig Stadler came to the 12th hole with a 5-shot lead. Then the tough holes of Augusta began to take their toll. His lead looked brittle as he dropped strokes at the 12th, 14th and 16th, and others began to catch up with him.

He needed a good drive at the 17th to steady his confidence. Although he did just that, he must have thought his luck had run out when he found his ball lying in a divot mark. But Stadler played a perfect shot to the green and made his par.

Saving that possible lost stroke was enough to take him into a playoff – which he won at the first extra hole.

Playing out of water

There are few sights more discouraging than a ball sitting in a water hazard. But don't be immediately put off – the shot may well be playable, especially if half or more of the ball is clear of the water.

Sometimes it's wise *not* to attempt the shot. This forces a 1-stroke penalty which allows you to drop the ball back on dry ground.

Know your capabilities and practice playing from different water hazards so you learn to judge when to play the shot and when to take a penalty. While the high handicapper may panic and be best off dropping the ball, the advanced golfer can often save strokes by playing the shot.

ANALYZE THE SITUATION

Weigh up the advantages and disadvantages of hitting a par-

THINK POSITIVELY
For the advanced player, hitting out of water is often a better option than taking a penalty. If the ball lands in shallow water and you feel capable of clearing the bank, play the shot – you may save yourself a valuable stroke.

THE WATER SHOT

(1) CAREFUL PREPARATION
Take a firm footing, as if in a bunker. Keep the clubhead just above the water, taking care not to let the club touch anything inside the hazard. If the lie of the ball is good, aim for the green.

(2) STEEP ANGLE OF ATTACK
Take the club back with your arms and hands. An early wrist break helps produce the necessary lift to get the ball over the bank. Don't lose confidence – it's important to keep an even rhythm throughout.

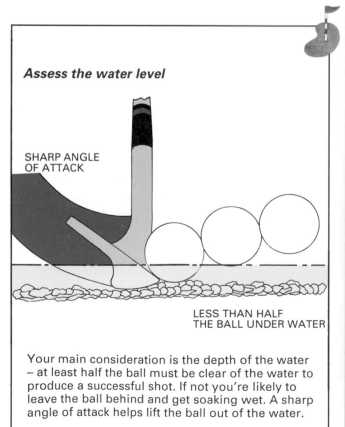

Assess the water level

SHARP ANGLE
OF ATTACK

LESS THAN HALF
THE BALL UNDER WATER

Your main consideration is the depth of the water – at least half the ball must be clear of the water to produce a successful shot. If not you're likely to leave the ball behind and get soaking wet. A sharp angle of attack helps lift the ball out of the water.

ticular shot from water. If the green is not in range it's best to accept a penalty and drop the ball. But if you are near the green or you can appreciably shorten the distance along the fairway, you may well be saving the vital shot in a close game.

When playing the ball from a ditch or stream you probably have to clear a bank. If you feel that the shot is too difficult even with your most lofted club, it is best not to play it – your lack of confidence could well lead to disaster. Play safe. Take the penalty instead.

The ball must be at least half clear of the water and sitting on a firm surface for you to lift it out. The club may sink into a soft surface, making the shot extremely risky.

It is very difficult to assess the exact striking point when part of the ball is beneath the water. The effect of light through water makes the ball appear bigger and further away.

PREPARATION FOR THE SHOT

Once you decide to play the shot your next consideration is keeping yourself dry. A water shot is rather like an explosion shot from a bunker – a great deal of water splashes as you strike the ball. For complete protection wear waterproof gear.

Another sensible measure when the ball lands in deep water is to remove your shoes and socks. Have a towel ready for when you come out of the water and remember to dry the club as well.

PLAY WITH CONFIDENCE

Generally for water shots the best club to use is the sand wedge. Because of its high angle of loft it really lifts the ball, especially over a bank. The sand wedge is also the heaviest club so it travels through the water smoothly.

Before you enter the water visualize the precise path that the ball will take towards your chosen target. This helps you to develop confidence in the shot, preventing the most common cause of disaster – anxiety.

The rules concerning water shots are very similar to the ones for bunker play. You incur a 2-stroke penalty if your club makes

3 MAKING CONTACT
You usually need to strike the water just before the ball. How far behind the ball you strike depends on how much of it is submerged, but ½in (1.5cm) is a good guide to follow.

4 SMOOTH THROUGHSWING
It is vital to maintain a smooth, even tempo as you follow through – the water slows down the path of the club considerably. Don't hesitate with the shot – even if water is flying in your face.

contact with anything inside the hazard before your downswing. This rule applies even in summer when the hazards may be dry.

Take a couple of practice swings above the water to get the feel of your shot. If about half of the ball is submerged in the water, you need to focus on a point about ½in (1.5cm) behind the ball.

The ball should be on the inside of your left heel – near the green use a slightly open stance. If you need to lift the ball sharply out of the hazard, open the clubface and aim an appropriate amount to the left to compensate.

An early break of the wrists on the backswing also helps to produce a steep angle of attack.

Above all, make sure that you maintain confidence in the shot and keep your eyes on the club-head as it strikes the ball.

Beware the stiff penalty
When playing from water your club must not touch anything within the confines of the hazard *before* your downswing begins. If it does, you are penalized 2 strokes.

The area is marked by colored posts or lines – don't forget that in most cases the grass on the bank is also part of the hazard.

To avoid the penalty don't ground the club at address. Make sure that you create a steep angle of attack as this limits the risk of contact with the hazard.

masterclass

Marsh in the wet
Australian Graham Marsh came across trouble at the 8th hole in the 1985 Lawrence Batley International at The Belfry. He hit his second shot on this par-4 hole into a water hazard near the green.

He recovered successfully by chipping the ball out onto the green and finished off with a 12ft (3.7m) putt. His confidence in tackling the shot under pressure saved his par – he went on to win the competition.

9

CORRECTING YOUR FAULTS

All golfers, even top professionals, play badly on
occasions. Good players, however, have
the ability to identify their bad shots, and by
understanding how and why they
happen are able to correct them. This section deals
with a catalog of hooked, topped, thinned
and pulled shots, all frequently encountered, and
explains the causes so that these problems can
more easily be cured and avoided.

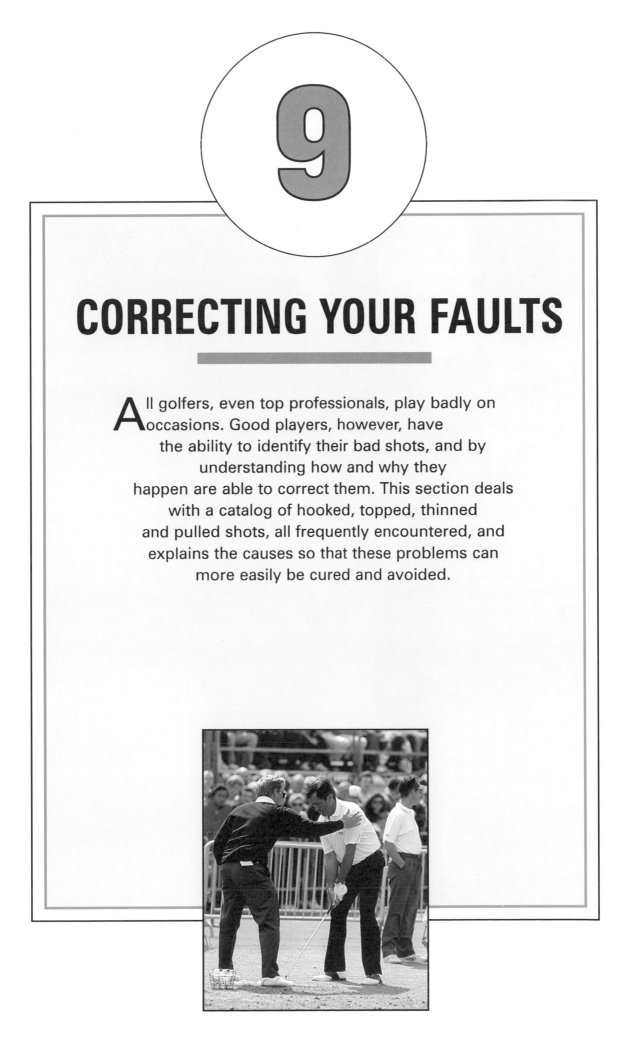

Curing the slice 1

INCORRECT ADDRESS
A slice may arise from several different errors. It can be a fault in your grip, body alignment, ball position and angle of clubface.

You slice if you grip the club too tightly or wrongly, align your body left or right of the target, place the ball too far forward in your stance or open the clubface at address.

At address you must have a relaxed grip, be aligned parallel to the ball-to-target line and aim the clubface squarely.

CORRECT ADDRESS

The destructive slice
A slice is an uncontrolled shot that curves to the right. It is very destructive, especially if there are hazards or out of bounds on that same side. You lose distance, direction and strokes so it's important to correct this common fault.

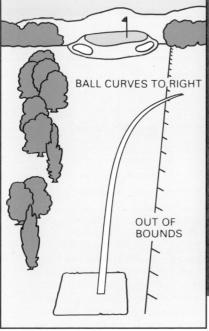

BALL CURVES TO RIGHT

OUT OF BOUNDS

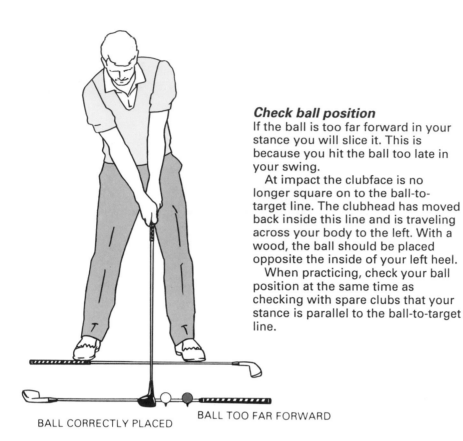

BALL CORRECTLY PLACED   BALL TOO FAR FORWARD

Check ball position
If the ball is too far forward in your stance you will slice it. This is because you hit the ball too late in your swing.

At impact the clubface is no longer square on to the ball-to-target line. The clubhead has moved back inside this line and is traveling across your body to the left. With a wood, the ball should be placed opposite the inside of your left heel.

When practicing, check your ball position at the same time as checking with spare clubs that your stance is parallel to the ball-to-target line.

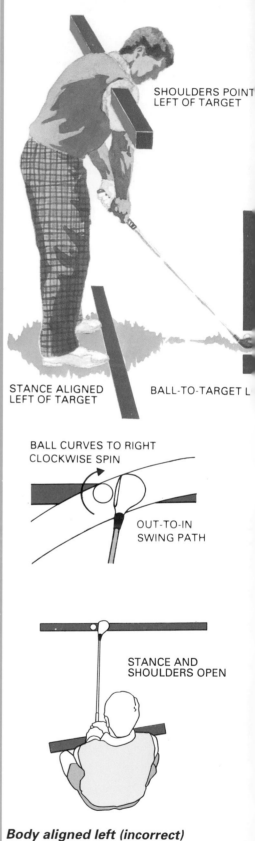

ALIGNMENT PROBLEM

SHOULDERS POINT LEFT OF TARGET

STANCE ALIGNED LEFT OF TARGET   BALL-TO-TARGET L

BALL CURVES TO RIGHT CLOCKWISE SPIN

OUT-TO-IN SWING PATH

STANCE AND SHOULDERS OPEN

Body aligned left (incorrect)
If your body is aligned left of the target you take the clubhead away outside the ball-to-target line. From here it is difficult to return it squarely and the downswing usually follows the same path as the backswing.

The slice is the most common fault in golf. It is an uncontrolled shot in which the ball curves to the right of the ball-to-target line, causing you to lose direction and distance.

Most slices are the result of an unintentional out-to-in swing path, though other faults may also produce slicing. Whatever the swing path, the clubface always moves across the ball from far right to near left. This causes the ball to spin in a clockwise direction, which moves the ball from left to right as it flies through the air.

Faults that lead to a slice occur at either the address position or during the swing itself. This chapter deals with errors at address which can be caused by a bad grip, an open clubface, wrong body alignment or an incorrect ball position.

GRIP PRESSURE

A slice can result from gripping the club too tightly. This creates tension in your upper body, which restricts movement and prevents you from turning correctly. Your upper body, arms and hands pull the clubhead around your body and across the ball from right to left – on an out-to-in swing path.

It is vital to check grip pressure regularly. When you grip a club, imagine you're holding a bird in your hand. If you hold it too loosely it can flap its wings or even escape, while gripping it too tightly squashes it. Ideally, the bird should not be able to move but must not be harmed either.

The correct grip pressure allows your hands, wrists, arms and upper body to swing freely. Your hands, wrists and arms must feel relaxed at address and during the swing.

OPEN CLUBFACE

A tight grip can also lead to an open clubface at impact. If you hold the club too tightly your hands don't turn naturally through the ball and the clubface doesn't return to its position at address. The clubface stays slightly open and the ball flies to the right.

Unintentionally opening the clubface at address is the most obvious fault in an otherwise good stroke.

The clubhead still travels

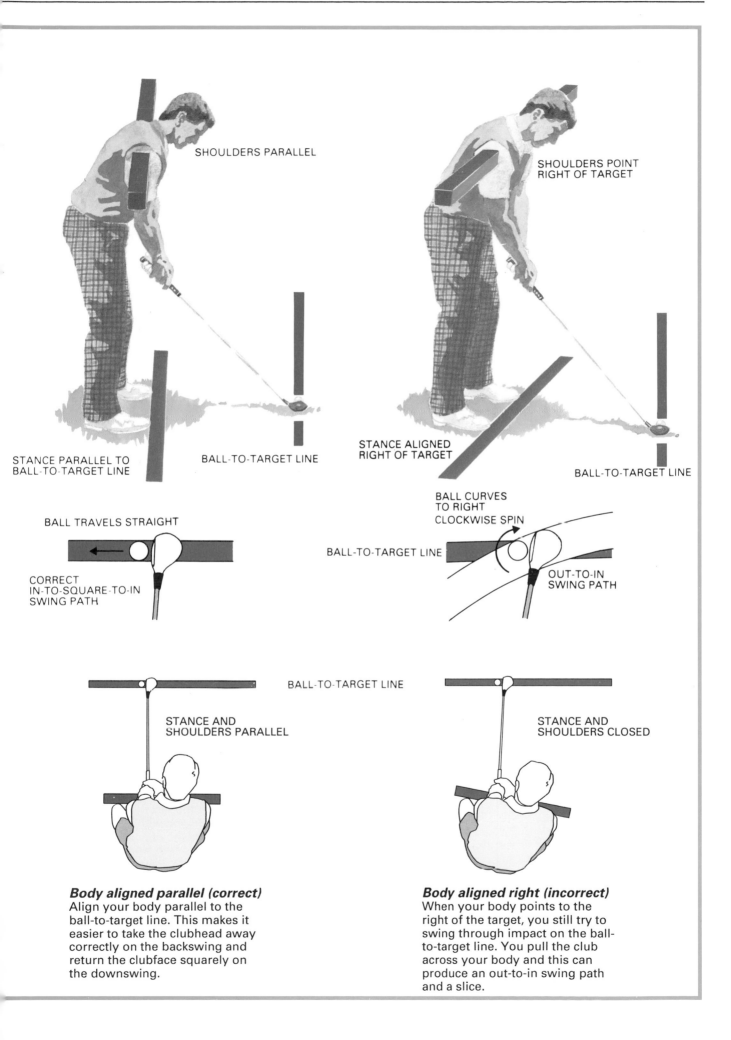

SHOULDERS PARALLEL

SHOULDERS POINT
RIGHT OF TARGET

STANCE PARALLEL TO
BALL-TO-TARGET LINE

BALL-TO-TARGET LINE

STANCE ALIGNED
RIGHT OF TARGET

BALL-TO-TARGET LINE

BALL TRAVELS STRAIGHT

CORRECT
IN-TO-SQUARE-TO-IN
SWING PATH

BALL CURVES
TO RIGHT
CLOCKWISE SPIN

BALL-TO-TARGET LINE

OUT-TO-IN
SWING PATH

BALL-TO-TARGET LINE

STANCE AND
SHOULDERS PARALLEL

STANCE AND
SHOULDERS CLOSED

Body aligned parallel (correct)
Align your body parallel to the
ball-to-target line. This makes it
easier to take the clubhead away
correctly on the backswing and
return the clubface squarely on
the downswing.

Body aligned right (incorrect)
When your body points to the
right of the target, you still try to
swing through impact on the ball-
to-target line. You pull the club
across your body and this can
produce an out-to-in swing path
and a slice.

Check your grip

As well as too tight a grip, a weak – wrongly placed – grip can cause a slice.

You have a weak (slicer's) grip if you can see only one or less than one knuckle on your left hand and you can't see the "V" between the thumb and forefinger on your right hand. With this type of grip it is difficult to control the clubhead because your hands don't turn easily through impact. The clubface stays open and you slice the ball.

With a correct grip you see two to three knuckles of your left hand, and the "V" on your right hand points between your chin and right shoulder.

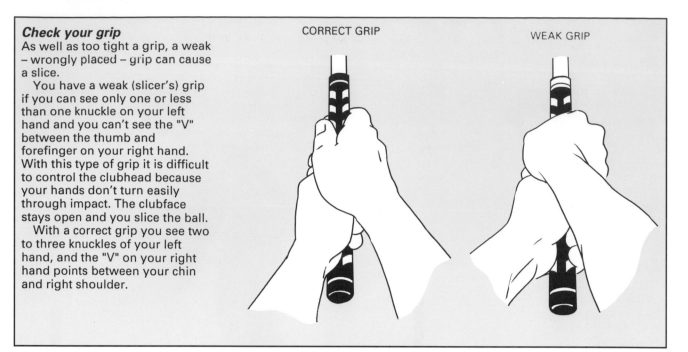

CORRECT GRIP

WEAK GRIP

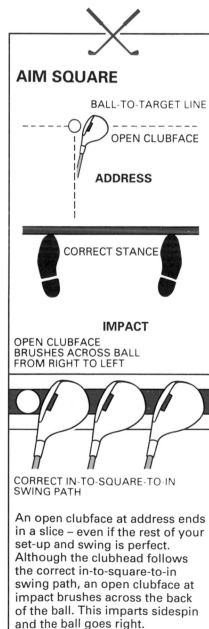

AIM SQUARE

BALL-TO-TARGET LINE

OPEN CLUBFACE

ADDRESS

CORRECT STANCE

IMPACT

OPEN CLUBFACE BRUSHES ACROSS BALL FROM RIGHT TO LEFT

CORRECT IN-TO-SQUARE-TO-IN SWING PATH

An open clubface at address ends in a slice – even if the rest of your set-up and swing is perfect. Although the clubhead follows the correct in-to-square-to-in swing path, an open clubface at impact brushes across the back of the ball. This imparts sidespin and the ball goes right.

through impact on the correct in-to-square-to-in swing path but the clubface doesn't meet the ball square on. It brushes across the back of the ball causing it to start right of the ball-to-target line and then spin further to the right.

Always check that the clubface is aimed correctly. A slightly open clubface can ruin a good set-up and swing.

BODY ALIGNMENT

Misalignment also causes you to slice. At address your shoulders, chest, hips and feet should be aligned parallel to the ball-to-target line.

If your stance, hips, chest and shoulders point right of the ball-to-target line, you try to compensate by swinging the clubhead towards the target. This drags your right shoulder across the ball from right to left (out-to-in).

If you align left of the target it is impossible for your upper body to rotate correctly. You take the clubhead away outside the ball-to-target line on the backswing and the downswing follows the same path. The result is an out-to-in swing through impact, which leaves you struggling to recover from a slice.

INCORRECT BALL POSITION

Always check your ball position carefully. Even if your grip, alignment and swing path are correct,

you can still slice if the ball is placed too far forward in your stance. Impact is delayed and the clubface is no longer square on to the ball-to-target line. The clubhead has moved back inside this line and is traveling to the left. The clubface brushes across the ball from right to left, imparting unwanted sidespin.

Remember that correct ball position differs from club to club. For a wood and a long iron place the ball opposite the inside of your left heel. For a short iron the ball is in the center of your stance, while for a medium iron you need to place the ball midway between the two positions.

Limit your slice

It is risky to try to correct a slice during a round. If you find you are slicing most of your tee shots, compensate for the fault rather than fight it. Instead of looking for an immediate cure, limit its effect for the rest of your round.

Stop driving with a 1 or 2 wood, and move down to a number 3 which won't hit the ball as far – so the distance the ball travels off-line is reduced. The extra loft and shorter shaft of the 3 wood also give more control. When you tee off, aim a little further left than normal.

When the round is complete, analyze your technique to eliminate the slice.

Curing the slice 2

Problems at address may lead to an incorrect swing path and a slice, but you can produce the same poor shot from a faulty swing alone.

Errors that create an unwanted out-to-in swing path can occur on the backswing and throughswing. These faults lead to the clubface brushing across the ball from left to right, giving a slice.

SWING SLICE

A slice is usually the result of a poor swing which produces an untidy and unbalanced finish. Your weight transfers incorrectly and your body finishes up facing the wrong direction. The result – a slice.

POOR HEAD MOVEMENT
If your head fails to move together with your rotating body you can't turn freely.

LACK OF SHOULDER ROTATION
You can't shape your swing correctly if your shoulders don't turn enough.

UPPER BODY TENSION
Faults in your swing can be exaggerated by errors at address. If your grip is too tight, your upper body becomes tense and fails to rotate fully.

POOR WEIGHT TRANSFER
If your body rotates incorrectly, you finish the swing with your weight on the wrong foot.

BODY ROTATION

The most common cause of the slice is lack of body rotation, a flowing movement which shapes the swing. The individual parts of your body must move as one unit.

If your body fails to turn correctly and fully, your arms and hands shape the swing. Working on their own, these take the club away outside the ball-to-target line. From this position it's difficult to return the clubhead on the correct in-to-square-to-in swing path.

The downswing usually follows the same path as the backswing, so the clubhead is pulled incorrectly across your body from far right to near left (out-to-in).

Although the effect is always the

PREVENTING A SLICE

CORRECT – CLUBHEAD INSIDE BALL-TO-TARGET LINE

CORRECT – CLUBHEAD POINTS AT TARGET

① TAKEAWAY FAULTS
The start of the backswing establishes the swing path. To avoid an out-to-in path on the downswing, don't take the clubhead outside the ball-to-target line. Let the clubhead move gradually inside this line on takeaway.

② TOP OF THE BACKSWING
Unless your body has rotated fully on the backswing there isn't any power to unleash on the downswing. If you lift the club outside the ball-to-target line, the shaft doesn't point to the target at the top of the backswing.

CORRECT FOLLOWTHROUGH – FACING TARGET

⑤ UNBALANCED FOLLOWTHROUGH
An out-to-in swing path pulls the club across your body on the followthrough and your weight finishes up awkwardly on the tip of your right foot. Always try to achieve a balanced finish with your weight on the left foot and your body facing the target.

pro tip

Keep your chin up
For your shoulders and chest to rotate properly there must be a clear gap between the tip of your chin and the top of your shoulders. If your chin drops too low it gets in the way of your upper body and prevents it from turning fully.

CORRECT DOWNSWING AND WEIGHT TRANSFER

CORRECT – GOOD IMPACT AND THROUGHSWING

3 TRANSFER OF WEIGHT
If your weight is not on your right foot at the top of the backswing your hands and arms can't follow the correct swing path on the downswing – they usually swing independently across your body. Just over half your weight should transfer on to your left foot by impact.

4 ROTATION THROUGH IMPACT
If upper body movement is restricted through impact, the momentum of your hands and arms pulls the clubhead across the ball from right to left. Your upper body must continue to rotate to the left to pull the clubhead through the ball on the correct in-to-square-to-in path.

same, lack of rotation has many causes. Failing to turn the body on the backswing is a common problem for players who believe that the less body movement you have, the more compact and efficient your swing is.

While a swing needs to be compact, it must also be shaped by the rotation of your body as a unit and not as a mixture of different moving parts – such as your arms and hands. These must remain passive until impact.

HEAD MOVEMENT

Lack of rotation is also caused by poor head movement. Many golfers who obediently keep their eye on the ball follow this rule to the extreme by not moving their heads at all. If your head does not rotate with your upper body, overall movement is restricted.

Even if head movement is correct on the backswing, problems can creep in if your head stays down too long on the throughswing.

The moment that your head stops turning freely it prevents your right shoulder from rotating

One bad turn leads to another
One fault leads to another so it is vital that you practice your backswing until it is correct in every detail.

If your body doesn't rotate fully, you lift the club outside the ball-to-target line and at the top of the backswing your weight has not transferred on to your right foot.

From this point it is difficult to return the clubhead squarely, and you swing it across your body. You are left with an unbalanced finish.

POOR SHOULDER TURN

UNBALANCED FOLLOWTHROUGH

towards the target, and your arms and hands pull the clubhead across your body to the left. You complete the followthrough awkwardly, with your weight on the wrong foot and the clubhead pointing to the left.

THE HALF SWING

Develop correct body rotation and head movement by practicing the half swing. This makes it easier to judge how your body is moving, and to gauge the passage of the clubhead. You are also more relaxed than during a full swing.

Concentrate on letting your shoulders rotate freely through impact so your body faces the target at completion of the swing.

This automatically brings your head up to face the same direction. Allow your upper body to rotate as one. By rotating on the downswing and followthrough, your arms and hands swing smoothly through the ball.

Shape body rotation
To develop the correct body rotation on the throughswing, follow this simple practice routine. Take a club in your left hand and hold your left wrist in your right hand. Then make a normal swing keeping your right elbow tucked into your side.

As you swing through impact your right arm prevents your right side from swinging across the ball. This shapes the swing correctly – the clubhead moves inside the ball-to-target line.

Checklist
If you keep slicing the ball, run through this checklist to see where the problem is – it can be caused at address or during the swing. It's important to cure any bad habits before they become ingrained.

Grip pressure: are you gripping the club too tightly?

Ball position: are you teeing the ball too far forward in your stance?

Alignment: is your body incorrectly aligned left or right of the target?

Clubface: is an open clubface at address causing you to slice?

Grip position: can you see two to three knuckles on your left hand, with the "V" between the thumb and forefinger of your right hand pointing between your right shoulder and chin? If not you are gripping incorrectly.

Body rotation: are you failing to rotate your body enough?

Head movement: are you keeping your head down too long?

Umbrella tip
You can eliminate a swing problem by placing an umbrella against the tip of your left foot. This stops you swinging across your body – from out to in – because your hands hit the umbrella if you do. Practice frequently and you should eliminate the out-to-in swing path.

Throwing your right shoulder

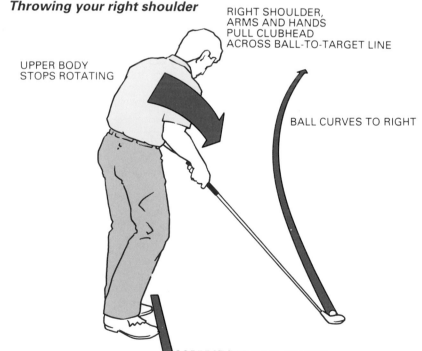

UPPER BODY
STOPS ROTATING

RIGHT SHOULDER,
ARMS AND HANDS
PULL CLUBHEAD
ACROSS BALL-TO-TARGET LINE

BALL CURVES TO RIGHT

CORRECT PARALLEL STANCE

One of the main causes of the slice is the failure of your hands, arms, shoulders, chest and hips to work as a unit. Even if your stance and ball position are correct, this prevents the swing from being shaped properly.

If your upper body doesn't turn fully on the backswing, you tend to throw your right shoulder across the ball-to-target line on the downswing.

Curing the hook

HOOK FAULTS
A hook – when the ball flies left – can ruin a good score. You need persistence to overcome this uncontrolled shot.

The hook is the result of a fault in set-up or swing. You hook if your body is aligned right of the target, the ball is too far back in your stance or the grip is too tight. In each case the clubface makes contact with the ball along an in-to-out swing path.

PREVENTING A HOOK

CORRECT: INSIDE TARGET LINE

CORRECT BACKSWING

①THE TAKEAWAY
The path of your swing is dictated by the takeaway. To prevent moving the clubhead inside the ball-to-target line too early, make as wide an arc as possible.

②MID POINT ON BACKSWING
The clubhead should be level with your right elbow at the mid point of the backswing. With an in-to-out swing the clubhead has moved inside your right elbow.

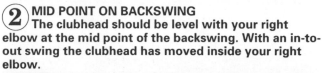
CORRECT: CLUB POINTS AT TARGET

CORRECT DOWNSWING

③TOP OF THE BACKSWING
Check that the club points at the target at the top of the backswing. With an in-to-out swing, the club points right of the target.

④MID POINT ON DOWNSWING
The downswing follows the same path as the backswing. If the clubhead moves inside the ball-to-target line too early, it's difficult to square the clubface at impact.

The hook is an uncontrolled shot in which the ball curves left of the ball-to-target line. It goes off line further than the slice, so make sure you rid your game of this destructive shot.

The hook is usually the result of an error at address or during the swing. But whatever the cause, the clubface usually brushes across the ball along an in-to-out path, causing a counterclockwise spin.

You're likely to hook if your body is aligned right of the target or the ball is too far back in your stance. Both faults force you to strike along an in-to-out path. Too tight a grip or a closed clubface at impact also produce a hook.

ALIGN CORRECTLY

At address your body must align parallel to the ball-to-target line. Check your set-up by laying a club on the ground next to the ball, pointing at the target. Stand parallel to it. Then hold another club across your shoulders, chest, hips and knees, in turn. Is your body aligned parallel to the ball-to-target line?

Remember, you can only hit a straight shot if you are correctly aligned and you swing along an in-to-square-to-in path. The slightest misalignment stops you swinging along the correct path and the ball flies off line.

If your body is aligned right of the target, you hook the ball. Although your upper body turns correctly on the backswing, you are swinging along the wrong path. Instead of a normal in-to-square-to-in swing path, you create an in-to-out path and the shot isn't hit square. The ball flies right of the ball-to-target line before curving left of the target.

Counterclockwise spin
With an in-to-out swing path, the clubface brushes through the ball, giving an counterclockwise spin. The ball then flies left of the target.

With the correct in-to-square-to-in swing path, the ball is hit straight.

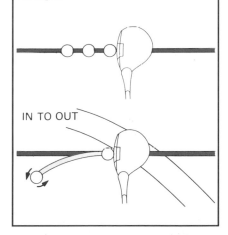

IN TO OUT

CORRECT: CLUBHEAD BACK INSIDE

(5) **THROUGH IMPACT**
For a straight hit the clubface must be square at impact. If you swing from in to out, the clubface brushes across the ball which curves right then left of the target.

(6) **FOLLOWTHROUGH**
By the end of the swing your upper body should face the target. An in-to-out swing prevents this, delaying and reducing upper body turn on the throughswing.

BALL POSITION

You also hook if the ball is too far back in your stance. Impact takes place earlier than normal – before the clubface is square to the ball-to-target line. The clubhead travels across the ball on an in-to-out path. This creates a counter-clockwise spin. The ball flies right of the target before starting to curve to the left.

Check your ball position by placing two clubs on either side of the ball and parallel to the ball-to-target line. Lay a third club between your feet, at right angles to the other two.

The exact position of this third club depends on the shot you are playing. If you're taking a wood or a long iron, place it next to your left heel. For a short iron, position the marker club in the center of your stance. Place the club midway between the two positions for

a medium iron. A correctly placed ball should touch the club between your feet.

CLOSED CLUBFACE

A hook is also caused by a closed clubface at address – which usually leads to a closed clubface at impact. Although the clubhead swings along the correct path, a closed clubface brushes across the ball from in to out. The ball starts left of the target and curves further left.

To ensure that the clubface is square at address, use the same test that checks ball position. Place two clubs parallel to the ball-to-target line and another at right angles to these. For a square aim set the leading edge of your clubface parallel to the marker club between your feet.

Too tight a grip also leads to a closed clubface. If you grip tightly,

your right hand controls the club through impact, turning the clubhead to the left – the ball flies in the same direction. At address your hands, wrists and lower arms must be relaxed. This keeps your hands passive during the stroke.

SWING SQUARE TO IN

Most hooks are caused by an in-to-out swing path. The clubhead moves inside the ball-to-target line too early on the backswing and the downswing follows the same path. The clubface brushes across the ball, giving a counterclockwise spin.

To train yourself out of the in-to-out swing path, try swinging from out to in, across your body. This corrects the in-to-out action and should leave you with a swing that's midway between the two paths, reducing the likelihood of a destructive hook.

HOOK CORRECTION

One way to cure an in-to-out swing is to practice swinging from out to in. By attempting to replace one fault with another, you usually swing midway between the two – reducing the amount you swing from in to out.

Imagine you're standing on a giant clockface so that the ball-to-target line passes through 6 and 12 o'clock. Try to swing on a line through 5 and 11 o'clock (out to in) on the downswing – repeat this practice.

BALL-TO-TARGET LINE

PARALLEL TO BALL-TO-TARGET LINE

Curing the shank

A shank happens when you strike the ball with the heel of the club, causing the ball to fly sharply to the right.

It is the shot many advanced golfers fear most because if you're prone to this type of miss-hit it tends to emerge time after time in your game. This destroys your score and – worse – your confidence.

FORMING THE SHANK

Many players are afraid of shanking simply because they don't understand why it comes about. Realizing why and how you shank is the best way to make sure it's scrapped from your game.

The shank is usually the result of tension. This causes your arms and hands to lock, so that they don't work together with your body.

Your torso takes over the swing. You push the club through with your body instead of making a co-ordinated movement with your arms, hands and shoulders.

Pushing makes your shoulders move ahead of the clubhead – and so the heel of the club is forced towards the ball. The ball then flies off at almost a right angle (90°) to the ball-to-target line.

A common situation which makes a shank more likely than usual is hitting a small chip under pressure. The desire not to over-hit combines with the urgency of the moment, and you slow down the club just before impact.

Address toe of club
If you start to shank during a round, you can take quick action by addressing the ball with the toe of the club.

Although it isn't an effective long-term cure for the shank, it does help you to get through 18 holes. Then you can sort out the shank on the driving range afterwards.

OVERCOMING THE SHANK

CORRECT DOWNSWING

①**NORMAL BACKSWING**
Faults in the backswing rarely cause a shank. But if you're prone to shanking, make sure you start the swing in positive mood. Loosen up any taut muscles first – be careful not to take so long that you slow play.

②**SHOULDER PUSHES AHEAD**
Problems generally creep in at the start of the downswing. The club correctly comes from inside the ball-to-target line, but tension makes the right shoulder push ahead of the clubhead.

CORRECT IMPACT

③ STRIKING WITH THE CLUB HEEL
As the right shoulder pushes ahead, the heel of the club moves toward the ball. This makes the ball fly sharply to the right. When you swing correctly, the right side of your body follows the arms and clubhead in a smooth, coordinated movement.

④ FLAT FINISH
Most shankers end up with a very flat, low followthrough. This is because their right shoulder moves far ahead of the hands, arms and clubhead. Keep your grip on the club light throughout, so that you swing the clubhead through much more freely.

Unfortunately, this lets the shoulder lead the clubhead and a shank is the result.

You need to loosen up and free your arms and hands. Let them swing the club through the ball without too much help from your right shoulder.

Practice with your feet close together. This exercise promotes swinging the clubhead with your arms and hands, and avoids moving your right shoulder ahead of the club on the downswing.

POSITIVE APPROACH

Gripping gently lets you swing the clubhead freely, and releases your arms and hands from your shoulders. Try to feel the weight of the clubhead – the sensation helps you swing ahead of your shoulder.

Be positive with the shot and swing through the ball. Make a conscious effort to stay relaxed – remember that tension is the shanker's greatest enemy.

masterclass

Barber's anti-shank club
The American professional Jerry Barber, 1961 USPGA Champion, once devised an ingenious cure for all shankers.

Aware of the misery which the heel of the club can inflict on a player, Jerry Barber designed an anti-shank club. It is built with the hosel (the last part of the shaft before the head) placed on top of the clubhead. The heel is cut out altogether. Happily, with this heel-less club shanking becomes impossible.

Although this is not a true or permanent cure (the club is not widely available), it certainly restores confidence – and morale is at the heart of the curing process.

Curing topped shots

Topping the ball is a common fault – especially among beginners and high handicappers. The error happens when you strike the ball close to the top, applying topspin so that it pops up and down along the ground.

Every golfer fears the topped shot – as well as adding to your score it looks embarrassing. But once you know why you top, you can rid your game of it for good.

Your purpose with the longer shafted clubs is to make the club strike through the back of the ball. With the shorter clubs, when you

WHAT TOPPING IS
When you strike at or near the top of the ball it scuttles along the surface or is pressed into the ground before jumping into the air a short distance. Fix your mind on making contact with the back of the ball to avoid a topped shot.

CLUB SOLE STRIKES
TOP OF BALL -
APPLIES DAMAGING TOPSPIN

WATCH YOUR WEIGHT SHIFT

1 TOP OF BACKSWING
Your position at the top of the backswing is good, with the weight nicely shifted to the right. The shoulders have coiled to a full turn and your head remains still and in a good position over the ball. You have avoided three possible causes of the topped shot – your ball position is correct for the club, your grip is firm but not tight and your backswing is smooth and controlled.

2 POOR WEIGHT SHIFT
As you start the downswing, your head and body move too quickly, shifting too far to the left. Your hands and arms are left behind as your head moves forward – your weight fails to transfer smoothly. The downswing is no longer under control, the power generated on the backswing has been lost and your timing is poor.

let clubface loft lift the ball for you, the club must strike through the back before traveling underneath the ball.

This means striking down and through the ball. After making contact with the back of the ball, the club travels smoothly down under the bottom of the ball. Taking a large divot – shaped like a bank note – usually proves that you've achieved just that.

Make sure that the club doesn't dig down too much, making the divot too large – this could lead to a loss of distance.

WHY YOU TOP

○ **Poor ball position** is the most obvious cause of topping, so place your ball carefully. If it is too far forward in your stance for the club you're using, you hit on the upswing. You make contact halfway up the ball – causing a thinned shot – or, worse, you top it.
○ **Tension** is another cause of topping, mainly by inexperienced players who are nervous on the

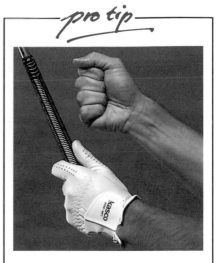

Grip tip
Make sure that you hold the club firmly but lightly. If your knuckles are white, you're gripping the club too tightly. This leads to a loss of timing in your swing because you restrict muscle movement in your arms and shoulders. The clubhead is likely to arrive at the ball at the wrong moment, possibly leading to a topped shot.

(3) TOO LATE
The club arrives too late and crashes into the top of the ball at impact – this is because your hands and arms were behind your lower body movement, resulting in poor coordination. On this shot the weight has shifted too much to the left but take care you don't over correct the fault – leaving too much weight on the right side also leads to a topped or thinned shot.

(4) LACK OF BALANCE
You finish overbalancing to the left. The ball may jump into the air before trickling only a short distance. After the shot, look for the tell-tale indentation in the ground where the ball has pressed into it. If you find that poor weight shift often leads to topped shots when you strike, practice smooth weight transfer with a mid iron and move gradually up to the woods.

Careful when you chip

When facing a gentle chip don't make the mistake of topping or thinning the ball so that it races through the back of the green.

In trying to give the ball a delicate nudge it's tempting to lift up your head and upper body with the stroke because you're anxious to see the result. At the same time you lift the clubhead, giving the face no chance of striking down through the bottom of the ball. Don't quit on the stroke.

USE THE CLUBFACE LOFT

When you want the shot to gain height right away, let the loft of the clubface do it for you – that's what it's designed for. Don't try to lift or scoop the ball (above) as you swing through. Your weight stays incorrectly on the right side throughout and the clubface has begun its upward path when it makes contact with the ball, causing a topped shot. Concentrate on taking a divot and letting your weight transfer naturally – one of golf's oddities is that you must strike *down* to get the ball *up*.

1st tee – especially if there are plenty of onlookers. Learn to blot out everything except the stroke in hand.

○ **A tight grip** makes the muscles in your arms and shoulders lock, severely reducing your chances of a free-flowing swing. Relax as you address the ball and concentrate on sweeping the tee peg away as you swing through.

○ **Poor weight transfer** – either too much or too little – is often the main culprit when you top. Scooping the ball with the club leaves your weight on the right side as you swing through. You're almost certain to top the ball – or catch it thin – because you strike on the upswing. How far up the ball the clubface hits determines if you top or thin the shot.

○ **Chopping** at the ball results when your weight shifts left too quickly on the downswing. If you don't strike fat you top the ball down the fairway.

pro tip

Balancing act

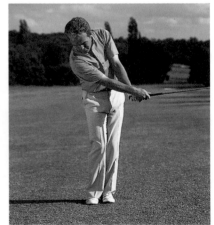

If you're not making a clean strike on the ball, check your head movement – your head may be shifting as you swing because of body sway. Cure the fault by standing with your feet close together and hitting balls with a half swing. Concentrate on the back of the ball as you swing through. If your head moves too much you are likely to lose balance – whichever club you use.

Curing the pull

The pulled shot is destructive – it can ruin a good score. A pull flies immediately left and stays left – unlike the hook, which starts slightly right before curving violently left.

OUT-TO-IN PATH

If you pull the ball, you're unlikely to hook, because each of these shots is the result of opposing swing paths.

The pull is related to the slice – both faults are caused by an out-to-in swing path. The difference is that pulling stems from a closed clubface at impact while for a slice the clubface is open. A hook results from an in-to-out path.

PULL CAUSES

Poor ball position is one cause of this damaging out-to-in path. If the ball is too far forward in your stance, you strike as the clubhead is coming back inside the line. If the clubface is closed at this point, you pull.

Remember the correct ball position: opposite the inside of your left heel for woods and halfway between this and the center of your stance for mid irons. Place the ball in the center of your stance for the short irons.

Aligning too far left makes you swing along an out-to-in path because you're not parallel to the ball-to-target line. Aligning too far right can also cause a pull.

Check your alignment – with one club against your chest and another on the ground – to be sure you're parallel to the ball-to-target line.

Bad posture – when you stand either too straight or stooped over the ball – makes you tilt, rather than turn, your shoulders on the backswing.

A full shoulder turn is impossible, so your weight fails to transfer properly. This leads to an out-to-in swing.

Ensure that you're properly balanced and comfortable in almost a slight bowing position before you swing – though don't take so long doing it that you delay play.

X HITTING LEFT OF TARGET
A pulled shot flies straight left, while a hook starts right and curves left. Cure the pull by making sure your ball position, alignment and posture are correct – you must avoid an out-to-in swing path. The player below sees his ball fly left after a basic alignment fault.

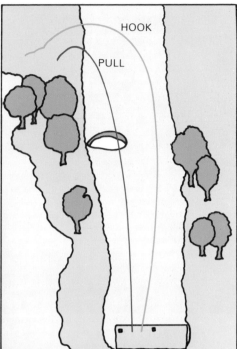

PULLING FROM POOR ALIGNMENT

① FAULTY SET-UP
Your problems begin when you align directly at the target rather than parallel to the ball-to-target line. The takeaway is smooth, but rendered useless by your basic alignment error. A normal swing now would send the ball right of the flag.

② CLUB POINTS INCORRECTLY
You make a correct, full turn with the knees still flexed. Because of your incorrect alignment, the club points right of the target instead of toward it. It's usually at this point that you suspect your alignment is wrong.

③ FAULTY SWING PATH
To compensate for your poor alignment you try to bring the clubhead down along a normal swing path. You do this by sharply moving your right shoulder just ahead of the clubhead. Because it's a hard movement to judge you overdo it so that the clubhead begins traveling on an out-to-in path.

Check your grip size

If you feel confident that your set-up and swing are sound but you still have a tendency to pull the ball, check your grip size with your local pro.

It's possible that your grips are too thin for your hands. This causes too much hand action through the ball, which often closes the clubface. Even with a good swing path, a closed clubface sends the ball left of the target.

Your pro can fit grips that exactly suit the size of your hands and rule out this tendency to pull.

BALL POSITION

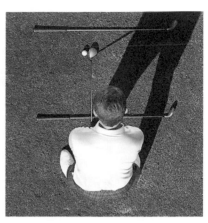

✗ **With the ball just too far forward in your stance, the clubface is closed when it makes contact – the ball goes to the left.**

✓ **With the ball in the proper position – opposite the inside of your left heel with woods – the clubface is square at impact and the ball flies straight.**

④ CLUBFACE CLOSED AT IMPACT
Because your right shoulder stays just ahead of the clubhead throughout the downswing, your out-to-in swing path carries on through impact. The clubface is closed – the ball flies to the left. You started the swing well, so you still make good contact with the ball.

⑤ BALL FINISHES LEFT
The ball keeps left because of the closed clubface – an open clubface would have caused a slice. The irony of the pull is that although the ball flies left your problems can begin because you align too far right. The need to over compensate ruins an otherwise good swing.

SWING PATHS AND CLUBFACE

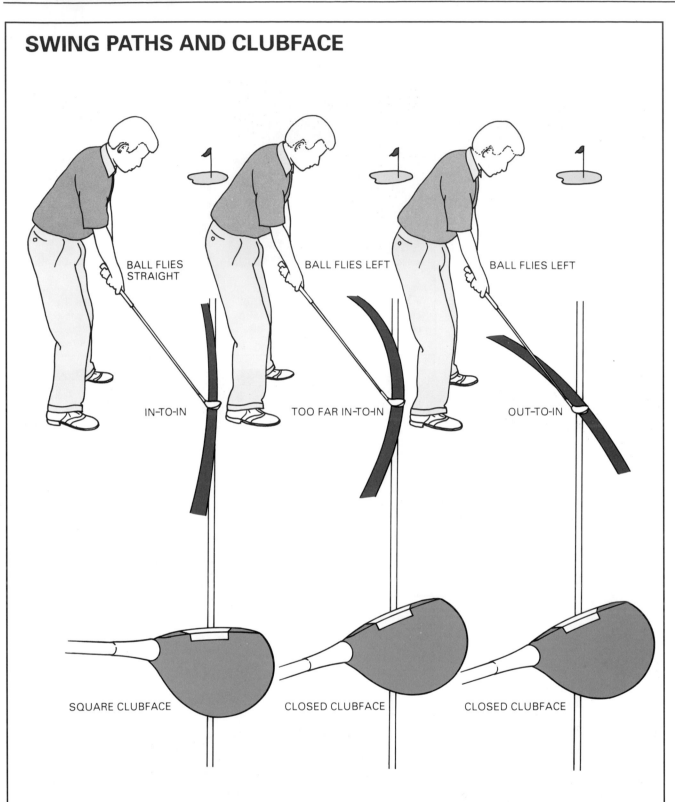

BALL FLIES STRAIGHT

BALL FLIES LEFT

BALL FLIES LEFT

IN-TO-IN

TOO FAR IN-TO-IN

OUT-TO-IN

SQUARE CLUBFACE

CLOSED CLUBFACE

CLOSED CLUBFACE

✔ In-to-in: square
If you swing the clubhead on an in-to-in path and the clubface is square at impact, your shot flies straight. To achieve this, your alignment, posture and ball position must all be correct.

✗ In-to-in: closed
Even if you swing along a good path, you pull the ball left if the clubface is closed at impact. Don't grip so tightly that the clubface closes at address.

Swinging inside too much on the backswing and throughswing may also close the clubface and cause a pull.

✗ Out-to-in: closed
An out-to-in swing path combined with a closed clubface at impact causes a pull. If the clubface is open at impact you slice. Strive to rid your game of the unintentional out-to-in swing path so that you are unlikely to slice or pull.

Curing the push

The push is a shot that flies straight right. More closely related to the hook, the push is the opposite of the pull – the shot that travels straight left.

CHECK SET-UP

Both the hook and the push are caused by in-to-out swing paths. A push happens when the club-face is open at impact. When you hook, the clubface is closed at impact. The ball starts right before sharply curving left.

Pushing the ball can come from a simple error in set-up or ball position or a fault in your swing.

Before you swing, make sure – as always – that you're correctly aligned parallel to the ball-to-target line. If you're aligned slightly right with your feet, hips or shoulders, you unknowingly swing along an in-to-out path. Your swing may be perfect but wayward alignment lets you down and the ball flies right.

Check ball position. If the ball is too far back in your stance for the club you're using the clubface may be open when it meets the ball, making the shot fly right. Impact is too early in the swing – the ball placement has not given the clubface enough time to reach its square position at the bottom of the swing.

BALL FLIES STRAIGHT RIGHT
The push flies right and stays right. A basic set-up error – such as aligning slightly right of target or placing the ball too far back in the stance – can cause a push. If these aren't to blame, a swing fault may be the culprit.

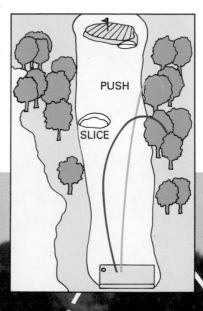

POOR SWING LEADS TO PUSH

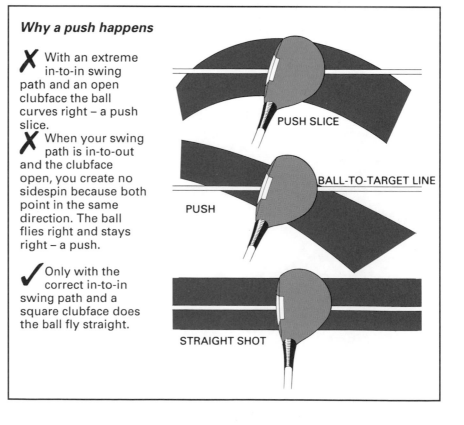

(1) **START OF DOWNSWING**
If a push is not caused by alignment or ball position errors, your swing is to blame. Problems usually begin at the start of the downswing, when your lower body moves too far ahead of your arms.

(2) **TOWARDS IMPACT**
As the clubhead approaches the ball it's traveling on a clear in-to-out path. Because your body has moved left so quickly, it's in the impact position long before the club has arrived. You drag the club through impact.

SWING COMPLAINTS

Technical faults in the swing can lead to a push. You must make sure that your upper body does not shift too far left during the downswing and through impact. You then lose balance and drag the clubhead through so that the face can't return square to the ball. The open face makes the shot travel right.

Proper hand and forearm action through impact is vital. If your forearms rotate correctly and your wrists release the clubhead when they should, the ball cannot fly to the right.

An impeded throughswing is another likely cause of a push. If your left hip does not clear fully to the left, you finish pointing slightly right of the target, instead of facing it directly. This promotes an in-to-out path with an open clubface – and a shot that goes to the right.

Why a push happens

✗ With an extreme in-to-in swing path and an open clubface the ball curves right – a push slice.

✗ When your swing path is in-to-out and the clubface open, you create no sidespin because both point in the same direction. The ball flies right and stays right – a push.

✓ Only with the correct in-to-in swing path and a square clubface does the ball fly straight.

PUSH SLICE

BALL-TO-TARGET LINE

PUSH

STRAIGHT SHOT

③ FOREARMS FAIL TO ROLL
Instead of rolling through the impact area, your forearms leave the blade open as you strike. With the in-to-out path this sends your ball right. A closed clubface with an in-to-out path causes a hook.

④ ARMS OUT OF CONTROL
Although you're now correctly facing the target, your arms are finishing the swing too high up and out of control. The ball keeps speeding right in a straight line. It stays straight as you've applied no sidespin.

pro tip

Good wrist and forearm action
To work on rotating your forearms correctly through the ball, try hitting practice balls with a half swing to gain greater control.

When you release the clubhead properly, your wrists and forearms make a rolling action – similar to what happens when you skim stones across water. This flicking movement ensures the clubface closes after impact, ruling out a push.

Take care you don't tighten up, especially under pressure. Rigid wrists and forearms make you block the shot, with the clubface open at impact.

Grip tip
Make sure you hold the club with your fingers and palms resting comfortably on the grip – don't ever grip with a tightly clenched hand.

Try an exercise to test your grip strength. If you're right handed, take a wood in your left hand with your normal grip and hold the club horizontally, pointing right.

Feel the muscles in your left forearm with your free right hand. Are they tight, or firm but relaxed? If you find that the muscles in your arm are more than comfortably tense you're gripping too tightly.

As well as restricting a flowing swing, too forceful a grip at address can cause you to loosen your hold during the swing. This may open the clubface, which makes a push – or a slice – possible.

LEAD WITH THE LEGS

Your swing is complete only when your body faces the target at the end of the swing. If you fail to clear your left side correctly you encourage an in-to-out swing path, which leads to a push or a hook.

Practice leading with your legs and left hip on the downswing. This encourages your left side to clear fully – once the lower body is cleared, its momentum helps to bring your upper body around.

Clearing the upper body first ruins your balance and gives you no chance of making a proper throughswing.

LEAD WITH YOUR LEGS
TO CLEAR THE LEFT SIDE

Curing the sky

A skyed shot sends the ball almost straight up in the air and is usually hit with a driver. Though you lose distance by hitting a sky, it's one of the few bad shots that travels in the proper direction.

You aren't alone if you sky the ball. Golfers of all abilities are likely to experience the frustration of this poor shot at some time or other.

If you hit a sky don't jump to the conclusion that you are teeing the ball too high. It may be the cause from time to time, but if you often hit a sky it's unlikely to be the main reason – so teeing the ball lower

KNOWING WHY YOU SKY
Understand the reasons why you sky and you can set about trying to eliminate the shot from your game. The large divot taken by this player indicates too steep a downswing – the ball shoots uselessly high.

SKYING THE BALL

(1) GOOD BACKSWING
At the top of the backswing the position is sound, with a full shoulder turn and the weight nicely transferred on to the right side. The feeling to foster at this stage is of a coiled spring about to release.

(2) HIPS AHEAD
Things start to go wrong as you begin the downswing. The hips spin to the left of the target line too early, causing the club to attack the ball at too steep an angle from outside the line.

Don't slouch
Don't hunch yourself up over the ball at address. This restricts the movement in your shoulder and upper body muscles, preventing you from making a wide backswing and full shoulder turn – faults that often lead to a sky.

Dipping left shoulder
A reverse pivot – where you sway towards the ball on the backswing and dip your left shoulder – leaves you in an unbalanced position. Always transfer your weight away from the ball on the backswing.

won't solve the problem. You need to look for a fault somewhere in your swing.

A sky happens when too much of the clubface is below the center of the ball at impact. Though it may result from poor ball positioning, it's usually caused by too steep an angle of descent on the downswing.

The ball should be swept off the tee with the driver. Never feel as though you are chopping down at the ball.

WIDE BACKSWING

Picking the club up too quickly outside the intended line on the backswing is the major cause of a sky. By taking the club back in this way, you are likely to bring the club down steeply toward the ball.

On every shot – but particularly the drive – draw the club back low and inside the line, brushing the turf with the clubhead for 12in (30cm). This helps you transfer your weight correctly onto the

3 WEAK LEFT SIDE
Close to impact your whole left side collapses. The hips have cleared out of the way too early and provide no support in the hitting area. The clubhead is chopping down at the ball.

4 POOR CONTACT
The position just after impact is typical of the skyed tee shot. The clubhead comes down too steeply and digs into the ground, taking a large divot. The ball travels a short distance and straight up in the air.

5 STUNTED FOLLOWTHROUGH
You are left struggling to maintain poise. The followthrough is cut short and there is no extension of the arms through the ball.

6 OFF BALANCE
A combination of earlier mistakes in the swing results in a terrible followthrough position. There is a total lack of balance as the skyed ball falls short of the target.

CHOPPING ACTION

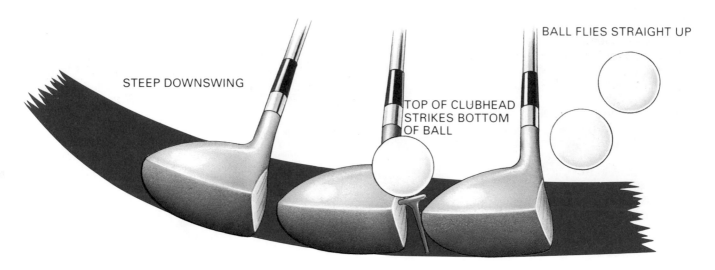

STEEP DOWNSWING

TOP OF CLUBHEAD STRIKES BOTTOM OF BALL

BALL FLIES STRAIGHT UP

✗ A steep angle of descent on the downswing often leads to a skyed shot. The clubhead hits below the center of the ball, sending it upwards almost as far as it travels forwards.

With a wood, sweep the ball off the tee, letting the club loft determine the height of the shot. The head should travel parallel to the ground just before and after impact.

right side and make a full shoulder turn.

Don't try to hit the ball too hard. The only way to apply power on all your shots is by swinging smoothly with a gradual transfer of your weight onto your left leg on the downswing. Keep a steady tempo as you swing through – this stops you from chopping down at the ball.

USE THE LOFT

It's tempting to try and help the ball into the air by scooping in the impact area – this is a common fault with the straighter faced clubs. But the loft of the club is specifically designed to get the ball airborne – so you must trust the club to do just that. Imagine the clubhead traveling parallel to the turf about 12in (30cm) before and after making contact with the ball.

Check the ball is positioned correctly in your stance. Place it opposite your left heel at address with the driver. This encourages you to sweep the ball smoothly off the tee.

This rule applies to the wooden clubs only. An iron shot is hit best when the clubhead strikes the ball with a descending blow. So place the ball further back in your stance when you play a shot with an iron club.

pro tip

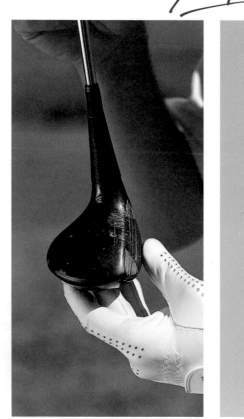

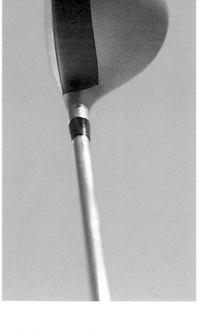

Protect your driver
Frequent skying of the ball is likely to damage your clubhead as well as ruin a good score.

When you hit a sky you fail to strike the ball with the center of the clubface, which is designed to withstand tough treatment. Instead, the ball makes contact with the top of the clubhead, causing ugly scuff marks.

To prevent damage to your driver, stick electrical tape carefully on the surface just above the clubface. Then work on finding a solution to stop you skying the ball.

Curing the thin shot

When the leading edge of the clubhead strikes the middle of the ball, you hit a thin (also called a sculled shot). The ball flies very low, sometimes skimming the ground, and runs a long way.

You can often get away with hitting a thinned shot. In dry conditions the ball can travel as far as a good shot – if not further – and may finish close to the intended target. It's one of those shots in golf known as a good bad one.

THIN EFFECTS

Providing the ground ahead is flat the thinned shot is often no great disaster. But put a hazard in front of you and a thin is a potential card wrecker. You can be frightened into hitting the shot you want to avoid most.

A thin can happen to you at any stage in a round of golf – from the longest iron shot down to the shortest chip.

Thinning a long iron can be upsetting, but if you hit this shot in cold weather you can add pain to your troubles. The impact of clubhead on ball vibrates up the shaft and has a numbing effect on your fingers. Massage your fin-

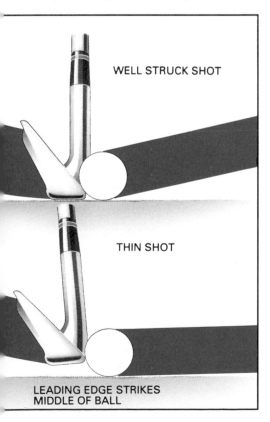

WELL STRUCK SHOT

THIN SHOT

LEADING EDGE STRIKES MIDDLE OF BALL

▲ AVOID THE THIN
When faced with a shot over a hazard the tendency is to hit the ball too hard. Anxiety leads you to swing more quickly than normal – this is a frequent cause of the thinned shot. Always play within yourself. You increase your control over the clubhead and reduce the risk of hitting the thin.

REGAIN LOST TEMPO

1 **RELAX AND GRIP LIGHTLY**
If you're regularly thinning the ball practice some three-quarter shots with a 7 iron to help regain lost rhythm. Stand relaxed in your normal address position and grip the club lightly.

2 **SMOOTH BACKSWING**
Draw the club back on as wide an arc as possible – keep your movements smooth and unhurried. Never snatch the club away quickly as this throws your swing out of plane. Make a full shoulder turn.

gers as much as possible to get the feeling back into them before you hit your next shot. It's important to give yourself every chance of striking cleanly.

Always use a tee peg for your first shot on a par 3 – you give yourself a good lie and stand a better chance of making a reasonable strike on the ball. When you don't use a tee peg it's very easy to hit the ball heavy. Once you start thinking of a heavy shot, there's every chance you'll over compensate and end up thinning the ball.

SHORT SHOTS

In general the closer you are to the flag the more destructive a thin becomes. Few experiences in golf are more frustrating than watching your ball scuttle through the green and into a bunker the other side. It's easy to see how high scores can build up if you thin a lot of short shots in a round.

Number one priority is to eliminate the thinned chip from your game. Place the ball back in your stance at address and take care to

keep your hands ahead of the ball throughout the swing.

Strike down crisply and confidently – at impact it's important to concentrate on making contact with the ball first and then the turf. In golf, you must strike down to make the ball rise into the air.

If you're not comfortable with your wedge, play chip and run shots with a 7 iron to help build up your confidence. Make sure you never slow down into the ball – this is one of the major causes of the thinned shot.

Lucky escape
Never berate yourself when things go badly during a round. Take a mental note of your error; if you can't put the fault right there and then, resolve to work on it later.

You sometimes find you can capitalize on hitting a thin – over flat ground devoid of hazards it

may finish close to the flag, while a well struck shot could bounce through the green into trouble. Accept this good fortune as a bonus rather than pondering over your poor shot – but go on working on ridding your game of the thin. Don't push your luck by relying on happy accidents.

pro tip

A thin cut
Look closely at your ball after you've hit a thin – it may be damaged. The leading edge of the clubhead tends to cut into the cover of a less durable golf ball. You are allowed to change it but show the ball to your playing partner first – he must agree that it is unusable.

3 **THREE-QUARTER STROKE**
Stop the club short of horizontal on the backswing – by this time most of your weight should be on your right side. This is a very controlled position from which to strike the ball precisely.

4 **WEIGHT SHIFT**
Start the downswing with a gradual transfer of weight onto your left side. Resist any temptation to strike the ball too hard – imagine you're hitting a 7 iron the distance of a 9 iron.

5 **SMOOTH STRIKE**
Stay down through impact. Your left side should be firm to provide support in the hitting area. There's no flurry of movement or frantic swiping at the ball – the strike is almost effortless.

6 **PERFECT RESULT**
Maintaining control throughout the swing produces a beautifully relaxed followthrough position. It's a good test of balance if you can stand on your left leg after completing the swing.

SLOPING LIES

The natural slope of the ground on a hanging, downhill lie (ball below feet) makes it very easy to hit a thinned shot.

The ball should be further back in your stance to compensate. This automatically reduces the loft of the club, making the ball fly lower – so remember to take one less club.

Faced with a hanging lie, flex your knees a little more than usual and bend from the waist. It's vital that you keep your head at the same level throughout the swing. If you lift your head your body will follow – and a thinned shot usually results.

Aim slightly left of target because the ball tends to fly right from a hanging lie.

GOOD SHOT

BALL RUNS THROUGH BACK OF GREEN

THIN SHOT

HANGING LIE BALL BELOW FEET

WHY DO YOU THIN?

This is an excellent position at the top of the backswing. Well balanced and poised to swing down into the back of the ball, you have total control. There's nothing hurried about this swing.

Different swing – different story. This action is known as the reverse pivot. Two faults here are typical of the thin – no transfer of weight on to the right side and a sway toward the ball on the backswing. The club is also past horizontal.

The reverse pivot makes you topple back on to your right side on the downswing – it all looks ungainly. The clubhead strikes the ball on an upward path – the club's leading edge strikes mid ball, causing a thin.

Index

Page numbers in **bold** indicate major references

A

accuracy
  approach shots 106
  tight drives 237-8
address 40
  hitting low 272
  moving ball 287
  perched lie 308
  posture 29-32, 66-7
  sidehill lie 280-2
  slice **333-6**
  tension 35, 48, 66, 135, 160
  toe of club 345
  weight distribution 69-71
  windy conditions 74
  woods 216, 218
aids, artificial 43
aim 36
  before aligning 15
  draw shot 255-6
  perched lie 308
  sidehill lie 282
  slice 333
alignment
  checking 16
  faults **13-16**
  for draw 255-6
  for fade 249
  hook 343
  pull 351-3
  push 355
  sidehill lie 282
  slice 334-6
Allen, Michael 155
Alliss, Peter 162, 196
anti-shank club 346
approach shots
  backspin 106
  downhill 114-15
  pitch **113-18**
apron
  chip & run over 86
  putter 94
arched position 48
arms
  flying elbow 44
  forearms 357
  position 31, 46-8
awkward lies
  divots **315-20**, 325-6
  edge of bunker **303-6**
  loose **287-90**
  restricted backswing **321-4**
  rough **291-6, 307-10**
  sidehill **279-82**
  sloping **283-6**
  unpredictable **297-302**
  water, playing out of **327-30**
awkward stance 299,

311-14
edge of bunker shot **303-6**
in-out bunker shot 195, **199-202**, 304

B

back
  injuries 29
  position 30, 32
backspin 74, **105-6**, 118, 126, 315
  in rough 292-3
backswing 51, 64, 67, 80
  hook 342-3
  improving **45-8**
  leg action 65
  mid point 46-7
  putting 159-61
  restricted **321-4**
  sand wedge 108
  shortening in wind 65, 74, 235
  skyed shot 360-2
  slice 338-9
  swing with body 40, 43-4
  top of 45-8, 54, 77, 216, 218, 233, 239, 301, 338, 342, 348
  woods 216, 218
balance **73-8**
  awkward stance 195, 303, 304, 306, 311·
  drive 76-7
  followthrough 61, 63
  & head movement 350
  weight transfer 72
  windy conditions 73-5
ball
  damaged 364
  identifying 295
  ridged 135
  striking player 184
ball placement **21-4**
  chipping drill 122
  driver 22-3, 25
  experimenting with **25-8**
  hitting low 272, 274
  hook 344
  long iron 21-2, 27
  medium iron 21, 27
  pull 351, 353
  push 355
  putting 141
  short iron 21, 24, 27
  slice 334, 336
  topped shots 348
  woods 216, 218
ball-to-target line 15
Ballesteros, Seve 27, 34, 112, 137, 244, 264
banks
  ditch/stream 329
  two-tier green 132, 148-9
Barber, Jerry 346
bare lie 297, 299

chip from 102, 104
low pitch 123
see also hardpan
baseball grip 139
bell ringer drill 222
belt swing exercise 43
bent grass 153
Bermuda grass 153, 210
blind man's putt 157
blindfold exercise 34
board practice drill 211, 287
body position *see* posture
body rotation 31, **49-52**, 66
  backswing 46-8
  downswing 55-6
  followthrough 62, 64
  slice 337-40
borrow 97
  see also slope
bowls game putting practice 155
branches, overhanging 292, 321-3
break, assessing 150
bump & run 102
bunker
  bunker shot from grass **207-10**
  chip over 88
  downhill shot **195-6**
  edge, perched lie **303-6**
  fairway 167-9
    avoiding 238
    cross hazards 168
    long slider **203-6**
    mid-range shot **197-8,** 211
    using woods **243-4**
  greenside 169-70
    escape shot 180-1
    recovery shots **177-82**
    safety shot 182
    up & over shot 178-9, 198
  in-out shot **199-202**
  obstructions 186
  penalty drop 180-1
  Player masterclass **193-4**
  plugged lies **183-6**
  positioning **167-70**
  practice drills 180, **211-12**
  shallow **171-6**
  splash shot 171-6, 180, 212
  close-ups **187-92**
see also sand

C

Canizares, José-Maria 149
casting *see* early hit
chin position 338
chip **85-8**
  downhill 95, **99-100**
  fringe play 89-94
  high chip & stop 122

from fringe 92-3
  up two-tier green 131
low chip & run 122, 364
  from bunker 176
  from fringe 89, 90-2
  over apron 86
  sand wedge 102
  up two-tier green 130
  on to sloping green 95-7
  over bunker 88
  practice drills **119-22**
  sand wedge 101-3
  shank 345-6
  short
    over fringe 102
    over hazard 87
  thinned 364
  topping 350
  up two-tier green **129-32**
  uphill 96-7
chopping 350, 362
cigarette butts 186
clean strike drill 211, 287
close-ups
  divots **315-19**
  splash bunker shot **187-92**
club selection
  awkward lie 304
  bunker play 243
  chip 120-2
  deliberate hook 264
  drive 237-8
  sloping lie 286
clubface
  closed 344, 353-4
  open 334-6, 355
  square 57
clubhead
  heel, and shank 345
  hooded 324
  peripherally weighted 272, 276
  speed 51, 61, 215, 221
clubs 29
  anti-shank 346
  length 21, 48
  mini 46
  short game 108
competitiveness 121-2
concentration 36
confidence 35-6, 62, 136, 237
consistency, swing 21, 25, 39
control 39, 43
  approach shots 113
  grip 138
Couples, Fred 222
courtesy 385
Crenshaw, Ben
  putting **140-1**, 153
cross-handed grip 139, 159, 161, 165
cupped position 48
cut shot, from bunker 203-6
cut-up shot

Picture Credits

Photographs: Allsport 12, (Dave Cannon) 2-3, 6, 8, 10, 11, 27(r), 37, 38, 83, 84, 100(b), 140, 166, 198, 210(r), 214, 236, 241, 245, 248, 268(b), 320(t), 331, 332, 346(b), 367, (Steven Dunn) 246, (Scott Halleran) 345, (Mike Hewitt) 277, (Steven Munday) 1, 104(bl), 133, 213, 278, (Gary Newkirk) 4-5, 9, (Vandystadt) 34(t); Charles Briscoe-Knight 155(l), 206; Colorsport 274(bl); Peter Dazeley 106(br), 132, 196(bl), 234, 250(b), 254; Golf Picture Library 128, 161, 165, 264, 314(b), 320(b), 324(b), 330(b); Good Shot 194(l), 220(l); Keith Hailey 112(b); Brian Morgan Photography 194(r), 244(b); Mark Newcombe 238; Phil Sheldon Photo Library 127, 137(b), 149, 153, 162-164, 222, 239-240, 242, 256, 265(r), 275-6, 326(br), (Jan Traylen) 126(b); Sporting Pictures UK Ltd 193; Bob Thomas Sports Photography 26(l); Yours in Sport 26(r), 35, 139, 143, 150 151, 202, 260(r), 265(l).

All other photographs: Eaglemoss Publications/Phil Sheldon.

Illustrations: Mike Clark, Kevin Jones, Chris Perfect/Egg design.